HOUSES AND SOCIETY IN POMPEII AND HERCULANEUM

ANDREW WALLACE-HADRILL

HOUSES AND SOCIETY IN POMPEII AND HERCULANEUM

PRINCETON UNIVERSITY PRESS, PRINCETON, NEW JERSEY

Library of Congress Cataloging-in-Publication Data
Wallace-Hadrill, Andrew.
Houses and society in Pompeii and Herculaneum / Andrew Wallace-Hadrill.
p.   cm.
Includes bibliographical references (p.   ) and index.
ISBN 0-691-06987-5
1. Pompeii (Extinct city)—Social life and customs.
2. Herculaneum (Extinct city)—Social life and customs.   3. Material
culture—Italy—Pompeii (Extinct city)   4. Material culture—Italy—
Herculaneum (Extinct city)   5. Architecture, Domestic—Italy—
Pompeii (Extinct city)   6. Architecture, Domestic—Italy—
Herculaneum (Extinct city)   7. Pompeii (Extinct city)—Buildings,
structures, etc.   8. Herculaneum (Extinct city)—Buildings,
structures, etc.   I. Title.
DG70.P7W33   1994
307.3'3616'09377—dc20   93-17828

This book has been composed in Monotype Centaur

10

ISBN-13: 978-0-691-02909-2

ISBN-10: 0-691-02909-1

To my family

CONTENTS

LIST OF PLATES

LIST OF FIGURES AND TABLES

FIGURES

TABLES

PREFACE

THE ROMAN house, as Eleanor Winsor Leach has well reminded us, played a definitive role not only in the Roman's daily life but in his and her mindset.[1] According to the recommendations of the teachers of oratory, the house should serve as a storehouse of memories. So familiar and intimate a knowledge was the pattern of rooms that the individual points of a speech could be systematically deposited around it in safe storage boxes of the memory. Centuries later, the Italian missionary Matteo Ricci was to sell this classical system of mnemonics to the Chinese. But what the rhetoricians systematized and turned into an art was already an intrinsic feature of the house. In its shapes and patterns, volumes and sequences, ornament and decoration, it stored away and encoded the conscious and unconscious memories of whole rhythms of social life. To the contemporary users of the house, such memories were self-evident and self-explanatory. To us they are opaque, veiled by the gap between Roman experience and our own. The purpose of this book is to make some tentative steps toward unlocking the memories of the social language of the Roman house.

It is not a book I had planned to write. The subject grew on me, seducing me from other projects and constantly surprising me by its unexpected potential. In 1982 I started a study of the cultural transformation of Roman society in the late Republic and early Empire. Wishing to incorporate discussion of transformations of material culture, I visited Campania in 1982, shunning Pompeii which I regarded as overworked. But I was drawn back. Eloquent though the villas of Campania might be about the changing lifestyles of the powerful, I came to see that Pompeii and Herculaneum might offer evidence of a more impressive transformation, of the cultural idioms by which not only an elite but a whole society defined itself.

I formulated a project to investigate the social diffusion of the "luxury" material culture of the elite in Pompeii. The literature on the archaeology of the site proved to be overwhelmingly art-historical in the questions it posed, and selective in the houses on which it focused. At an early stage I decided to take a sample of houses by block, to look systematically at every house in the blocks selected, and to set up a database to analyze comparable features. Between 1983 and 1986 I returned to Campania annually, normally for periods of a fortnight, sometimes accompanied by a band of students whose curiosity constantly revived my own; and on the last occasion, in 1986, for a couple of months, thanks to the generosity of the British Academy and the British School at Rome, which financed me, and of my colleagues at Leicester, Duncan Cloud and Rhoda Lee, who by taking on my teaching for a month liberated me.

As I pursued this project, one diversion led to another. Before I could write the essay planned, I found that other preliminary essays were necessary. In the first I attempted to formulate what I thought the language of the Roman house was, and how we could set about reading it. That led to "The social structure of the Roman house," a paper written in the library of the British School at Rome, which provided easy access to a rich collection of books and to the ideas of other scholars (I reiterate my thanks to Keith Hopkins and Susan Walker).[2] A second preliminary was to engage directly the ideas of Amedeo Maiuri. I became aware that his massive presence lay behind the excavation, publication, and interpretation of the majority of the houses at which I was looking, to the extent that he had set the unconscious agenda for further interpretation. It was necessary to tackle some of his presuppositions head on, and my thoughts on this were aired in "Elites and trade in the Roman town," which I gave at a conference in Leicester in 1987 on city and country in the ancient world.[3]

I had also to grapple with the problems of how to relate the houses to the human households that populated them. Beryl Rawson's invitation to contribute to her second Canberra conference on the Roman family in 1988 provided the spur, though I was doubtful of finding "the family" at all. In the end, having to focus on the problems of how habitation related to the disposition of domestic space taught me to see much to which I had been blind.[4] An important bonus was the chance to meet and discuss questions with the impressive band of Australian scholars working on Pompeii: Frank Sear and Melinda Armitt at Adelaide, and Jean-Paul Descoeudres and Pim Allison at Sydney. Their scepticism and questioning proved a stimulus, and subsequent opportunities to read the work of Melinda Armitt and Pim Allison taught me more.

Finally, I was able to return to the project on the social diffusion of luxury from which I had started. Completed in 1989, its publication suffered unexpected delays; this, however, provided me with further opportunity to reformulate some of my ideas, particularly taking into account perceptive observations by Nicholas Purcell, and an inspiring exchange of ideas with Paul Zanker.[5]

Around the catalyst of an initially tangential study, a cluster of closely related papers with an interweaving set of arguments about the Roman house had grown. During a visit to Princeton over the spring semester of 1990, the enthusiasm of Joanna Hitchcock of the Princeton University Press persuaded me that these four papers could be drawn together as a book. It would doubtless have been better if radically recast, but I did not wish to prolong the diversion from my initial study of Roman cultural transformation. I therefore decided to reissue the existing papers in revised, updated, and adapted form, and to supplement them with descriptive material: more ample figures and illustrations, and brief lists of the features of the houses studied.

Part I of this book is essentially "The social structure of the Roman house"; because it has become known in its original form, I did not want to alter it substantially. I wish that when I wrote it I had been aware that the use of decoration and furnishings to differentiate the rooms of a house, for which I was arguing, was virtually described by Varro in his *De Lingua Latina*; I have since incorporated his evidence into the end of Chapter 1. The other three papers needed more surgery, as there was a certain amount of overlap, particularly in the description of the database. Three papers have become four chapters in Part II, the first setting up and describing the project of analysis of sample blocks of houses in Pompeii and Herculaneum, the second looking at questions of population (substantially derived from "Houses and households"), the third examining the relationship of commercial activity and the world of work to reception and social activity (based on "Elites and trade" with some additional material), and the fourth looking at the social diffusion of decoration (the core of "The social spread of Roman luxury").

I have added an epilogue (Chapter 8) to pull the threads together, and an appendix and numerous illustrations to give greater visibility to the material on which I base my conclusions. It is my experience that published images, which too frequently reproduce the same details of the same walls in the same houses, fail to convey the impact on the visitor to the houses of Pompeii and Herculaneum. Rather than further recycle professional photographs, I offer my own, in full awareness of their technical shortcomings, in the hope of capturing impressions seen through my own eyes. They are therefore to be viewed as part of my interpretation, not as decoration. Much is lost in moving from color to black and white, and I am grateful to the Press for permitting at least some color plates.

Throughout the text I have made small revisions, and where the book differs from the papers, it represents my most recent view. What I have not attempted is any basic rethinking in the light of more recent publications. When I started work in this area, it seemed to me much neglected in terms of fresh approaches. But there is a great revival of interest, particularly in the United States, and several works that have much in common with my approach have appeared recently. I draw attention to the collection of essays edited by Elaine K. Gazda, *Roman Art in the Private Sphere. New Perspectives on the Architecture and Decor of the Domus, Villa, and Insula* (Michigan 1991), and to the elegantly produced study of John R. Clarke, *The Houses of Roman Italy, 100 B.C.–A.D. 250. Ritual, Space, and Decoration* (Berkeley 1991). Both of these mesh with much of what I have to say, but I have not attempted at this late stage to introduce cross-references.

Nor have I attempted to pursue a variety of fresh lines of thought suggested by friends and colleagues. Natalie Kampen and Mary Boatwright, as readers for the Press, made a series of fruitful suggestions, for instance on the pursuit of gender issues, in addition to numerous valuable comments on detail. But to follow all these new lines of inquiry would lead to a different book. What I offer is anything but the final word. It is, rather, a progress report on some explorations in what I believe to be a rich area that has still much to yield.

I HAVE incurred more debts that I can fully acknowledge. Financial support, successively from Magdalene College, Cambridge, the Universities of Leicester and Reading, and the British Academy and the British School at Rome, made the fieldwork possible. I am obliged, for numerous *permessi* and for cheerful cooperation, to the authorities at the Soprintendenza at Pompeii: Dr. Giuseppina Cerulli Irelli and Dr. Baldassare Conticello as Superintendents, Dr. Stefano De Caro and Dr. Antonio Varone as Directors of excavations at Pompeii, Dr. Tomasina Budetta and Dr. Ernesto de Carolis as Directors at Herculaneum. Roger Ling has repeatedly given me the benefit of expert guidance in a field in which, as I remain too conscious, I have no more than amateur status. I am indebted to Janet DeLaine and David Sim for their kindness and skill in redrawing many of the figures, and to Joanne Berry for assistance with indexing. I am obliged also to the staff of Princeton University Press, especially to the patience of Lauren Osborne as editor, and to the thoroughness of my copy editor, Carolyn Fox, who taught me much about my own ethnicity by the excision of Briticisms from my English.

There are also more personal debts. One is to the friends in Italy who helped turn an academic project into a pleasure; particularly to Hugo Bowles, who so often provided me with a base in Rome; and to the many *custodi* who helped me by unlocking doors, particularly Mattia Buondonno, whose friendship has made Pompeii a home from home. The other debt is to my family, who have lived with me, during the years in which this work was done, in four houses in England and two apartments abroad. Together we have shared many thoughts about domestic environments. The dedication marks my debt.

NOTE ON FORM OF REFERENCES TO HOUSES

WHERE possible, all houses in Pompeii and Herculaneum are identified by the current system of numeration, and not just by the conventional (but variable) house names. In the case of Pompeii, each house is identified by Region, Insula, and door number: thus I 10.4 is Region I, insula 10, door 4, the Casa del Menandro. Herculaneum is not divided into regions, and numeration is by insula and door number: thus H IV.2 is Herculaneum insula IV, door 2, the Casa dell'Atrio a mosaico. I have given house names in Italian (and not as "the House of the Menander," "the House of the Mosaic Atrium") in order to emphasize that these are merely labels attached for convenience by the local excavators. In particular, they cannot be taken as dependable indications of the names of the ancient owners. The door numeration system is likewise a modern one: there was no such postal numeration in antiquity (see Ling 1990).

PART I

THE SOCIAL STRUCTURE OF THE ROMAN HOUSE

CHAPTER I

□

READING THE ROMAN HOUSE

She occupied, his hostess, in the Rue de Bellechase, the first floor of an old house to which our visitors had access from an old clean court. The court was large and open, full of revelations, for our friend, of the habit of privacy, the peace of intervals, the dignity of distances and approaches; the house, to his restless sense, was in the high homely style of an elder day. . . . He seemed at the very outset to see her in the midst of possessions not vulgarly numerous, but hereditary, cherished, charming . . .

Henry James, *The Ambassadors*

In the protracted dialogue about value that is embedded in consumption, goods in their assemblage present a set of meanings, more or less coherent, more or less intentional. They are read by those who know the code and scan them for information. The great novelists have never doubted just how far removed this function of creating meanings is from the uses of goods for welfare and display.

Mary Douglas and Baron Isherwood, *The World of Goods*

THE VISITOR to Trimalchio's house was confronted by a succession of signs, a mute but eloquent code that pointed past the fabric and subordinate personnel of the *domus* to the *dominus*, the master of the house himself, creating an impression that not only reflected on the standing of Trimalchio but conspired to enhance it. The green-and-red-clad porter, shelling peas in the entrance into a silver bowl; the golden birdcage suspended above the threshold; the startling watchdog painted by the porter's cell, followed by a biographical frieze representing the master's rise to fortune; the shrine displaying silver *lares* (protective spirits of the hearth), a marble Venus, and a golden box, the Homeric and gladiatorial pictures too multifarious to take in at once: all these were a prelude to the approach to the *triclinium*, where ultimately, after much further ado, the great man would greet his visitors.

Petronius's description is not easy to reconcile in all particulars with the archaeological evidence of Roman houses of the period,[1] but it does serve to make explicit Roman awareness of the social function of domestic architecture and decoration. That is to say, the modern visitor to Pompeii or Herculaneum who on entering a house senses that he can discern the personality of the owner[2] is experiencing something that the ancient visitor both did and was meant to experience, though indeed we are impeded by the absence of many of the crucial signs (there is no *ostiarius* to admit us at the door) and above all by uncertainty as to how to read the signs that do survive, coded in a language foreign to ourselves. The aim of the following chapters is to offer some suggestions on how this language should be interpreted.

HOUSES AND STATUS

That the quality and decoration of a Roman's house was closely linked with his social standing emerges again and again in the literature of the late Republic and early Empire.[3] From a moralistic point of view, in a characteristic Roman tradition that stretches from the elder Cato through Varro and Cornelius Nepos to the elder Pliny and beyond,[4] expenditure on housing was *luxuria*, a social malaise that involved the squandering of patrimonial substance on worthless and ruinous show. *Aedificatio* (the construction of residential buildings) was regularly represented as a vice, and its avoidance was applauded, whether by Cato warning the estate owner to defer building, or by Nepos praising Atticus as "minime aedificator," or by the younger Pliny contrasting Trajan with the palace-building Domitian.[5] Expenditure on decoration was equally reprehensible: Cato boasted of his lack of stuccowork; Varro sniped at the mode, linked with the name of Lucullus, for dining in picture galleries; and Pliny the Elder commented on the folly of committing expensive works of art to walls that could not be rescued from a fire.[6]

But luxuria was not a senseless waste; it was a social necessity in a highly competitive society, and we do not have to look very far to find voices admitting as much. Cicero in the *de officiis* (1.138–39) is candid and realistic. A man of rank (a *princeps*) needs housing to fit his social standing (*dignitas*). A house may even play an active part in enhancing his standing, as did that of Cn. Octavius on the Palatine, which was thought to have brought its builder, a *novus homo*, votes in the consular elections (*suffragata domino*). There are practical considerations as well. A house that must offer much hospitality and admit a crowd of every rank demands a certain amplitude. On the other hand, to overreach is counterproductive; an overlarge house merely draws attention to its empty spaces and lack of visitors. By itself a house cannot win an election: Scaurus, who reduced Octavius's Palatine house to a mere wing of his own, failed to maintain his inherited dignitas. Cicero in fact sees a close reciprocal relationship between the architectural entity of the domus and the social activity that goes on within it. Hospitality and the large-scale admission of visitors not only justify but necessitate opulent building; conversely, opulent building both makes possible and encourages an ample flow of visitors. And since a Roman's social standing depends partly on the volume of the social activity focused on his home, he is bound to bring aedificatio to the aid of his standing. These ideas were to be warmly endorsed by Vitruvius (below).

While admitting the social pressures, Cicero stresses the need for moderation. The immoderation of Lucullus's magnificent villas he condemns as a bad example, however widely imitated.[7] But in repeating his attack on Lucullus elsewhere, Cicero reveals that even in his case there were social pressures.[8] Cicero is discussing the proposition that the senatorial order should be a model for the other orders. Lucullus had replied to criticisms of his luxurious villa at Tusculum by defending his right to live up to the standards of his two neighbors, one an *eques* (member of the equestrian order), the other a *libertinus* (freedman). Cicero objects that Lucullus should not have provided them with the model of luxurious building in the first place, but Cicero's own position here is scarcely coherent. He sees the function of role model for the lower orders as implicit in the distinction of senatorial rank—a process that, as we shall see, archaeological evidence amply documents[9]—but he refuses to acknowledge that the process of imitation involves an ineluctable chain-reaction, leading to a sort of inflation as the lower ranks build to mimic their superiors and their superiors find themselves bound to keep one step ahead. This explains why the finest house of 78 B.C., that of Lepidus, consul of that year, no longer rated among the first hundred in distinction a generation later.[10] Precisely the same chain-reaction underlies the escalation of early imperial luxury described by Tacitus: the noble families of the epoch were ruined by their competition in extravagance (*studio magnificentiae*), which was itself fueled by the search for social status; for "reputation and following hung on a man's opulence, housing and trappings."[11]

The close nexus between housing and social standing is only comprehensible in view of the peculiar nature of Roman public life.[12] In a way and to an extent that was unknown in the eastern Mediterranean world, the home was a locus of public life. A public figure went home not so much to shield himself from the public gaze as to present himself to it in the best light. Two passages may illustrate Roman sensibilities on this point. One records an exchange between Livius Drusus, *tribunus plebis* in 91 B.C., and the architect in charge of building his house on the slope of the Palatine overlooking the forum. When the architect promised to make it "completely private and free from being overlooked by anyone," Livius replied, "No, you should apply your skills to arranging my house so that whatever I do should be visible to everybody" (Velleius Paterculus 2.14.3). And if Livius was here playing the *popularis*, his successor to the property, Cicero, felt no different: "My house stands in full view of virtually the whole city"—or did so until in 58 B.C. Clodius consecrated it as a shrine to Libertas (*de domo* 100). Except when closed as a symbol of mourning, the doors of noble houses stood open to all, a feature that allowed the entrance of ransacking Gauls in 390 B.C., and of Livius's own assassin in 91 B.C.[13]

Social pressures applied to rural as well as urban residences. The city was the focus of political activity, and it was there that the need applied to build to accommodate a large *clientela*, to which Cicero, Vitruvius and Tacitus all refer. But the social life of the city was in many ways transported to the countryside in the wake of the peregrinating rich. Varro credits "our ancestors" for their simple life in the country away from the "urban gymnasia" of the Greeks; but urbanity was the hallmark of the villas of the rich in his day.[14] Columella sensibly points out that neither the estate owner nor, significantly, his wife would be tempted to leave their urban residence for the country unless their quarters were up to urban standards.[15] But the villa was also a focus of hospitality, sometimes on a grand scale. Cicero, in his Cumanum, could find his morning receptions so packed as to seem a *pusilla Roma*, a Rome in miniature.[16] A hint of the potential strain of hospitality emerges from Columella's advice to build one's villa away from the main road, for the constant entertainment of passing travelers is a drain on resources (1.5.7). Since the upper classes traveled with very considerable entourages,[17] it is credible that even the occasional entertainment of a passing friend might be a grandiose affair.

If the exigencies of social life drove the Romans to build and decorate their houses as they did, it should follow that the remains of Roman houses are valuable documents of that social life. But what do they document and how are we to read them? At one level, they vividly document what Thorstein Veblen termed "conspicuous consumption."[18] The richness of the remains of Roman housing that continue to emerge, especially in Italy but also in the provinces, and the contrast with the general poverty of most pre-imperial Greek domestic architecture,[19] bears testimony to the scale on which Romans pumped their resources into their homes, to their *impendium furor*. The wealth of conquest was channeled into competitive ostentation—the ruling class sunk their patrimonies into ever more extravagant mansions in order to enhance their status and convert financial muscle into social muscle—and their social inferiors, rich equestrians or freedmen, sought to borrow their prestige by imitating their behavior. Consequently, the extent of any house and the opulence of its decor provide an index of the wealth and status of its inhabitants.

This conclusion is banal, and stops far short of what even the texts cited above can point to. We are hampered here by the poverty of the concept of conspicuous consumption and its limited ability to account for the patterns of consumer behavior. Desire to hold or improve one's place in the pecking order may explain the expenditure of wealth as such and helps account for the homogeneity and diffusion of waves of fashion, but it does not account for fashions taking the patterns they do. Cicero's objection is relevant: Ostentation in itself is ineffective and wins no consulships. What pays is ostentation carefully contoured to patterns of social life, and making maximum impact at the point of maximum effectiveness. The consumer through his expenditures transmits signals in a language of social communication. Like any language, it has its own grammar and rules, and signals improperly transmitted are ineffective, or even ludicrous, like a language abused by a foreigner. Petronius's description of Trimalchio's ostentation depends on an understanding that it is laughable to Petronius's heroes and presumably to the reader. Silver cooking pots and golden bird cages were not perhaps the way to impress a cultivated Roman; Trimalchio blunderingly parodies the language of Roman luxury rather than communicating in it.

If this is right, we cannot hope to interpret the social significance of any particular domestic structure unless we first establish the rules of the underlying grammar. In order to achieve such an understanding, two preliminary changes in approach are required.

First we must relate literary texts to archaeological remains in a more fruitful way. The structures and artifacts we disinter spoke to the Roman user in ways that are not fully self-explanatory; they made specific impressions, evoked moods, activated, even subconsciously, associations. Every guidance from contemporary texts as to how the Roman user responded needs to be brought to bear. However, the sources, notably Vitruvius, have instead been ransacked for labels, as if to designate an area *triclinium* or *oecus* or *diaeta* were to explain it.

Our central concern should be with the interpretation of social space, and literary sources can help us here because they document social life. Connections need to be made between the archaeological and literary evidence not only at the obvious level of finding explicit descriptions of specific objects or architectural forms but at the more difficult level of exposing the rhythms of social life that underlie and are implicit in the physical remains. It is true that we imagine ourselves hampered by a contrast in social milieus.

Literature (so it is commonly assumed) describes the life of the elite, whereas the archaeological remains penetrate to the lower levels of society. But this is precisely where archaeology offers such precious evidence to the social historian. It is only through making the attempt to relate the two categories of evidence that we can begin to discover how far the patterns of life we have come to think of as characteristic of the elite succeeded or failed to penetrate wider social circles. Without that, an understanding of the social basis of Roman cultural forms is impossible.

Second, if we are to use archaeology to illuminate society, it is vital to make the unit of study the social unit. The Vesuvian remains provide endless material for a variety of specialists, in domestic architecture, sculpture, mosaics, stuccoes, and mural decoration. The constant danger is that the house, the social unit, merely acts as a repository for items of evidence.[20] The objects studied are divorced, whether physically, as in the museum collections of the previous century, or conceptually, as in the publications of this century, from their social context. The study of wall decoration takes pride of place (as from the richness of the evidence it must) and here this tendency has been particularly pronounced. The field has been and still is marked by an obsession with questions of minute chronology. The persistent aim of scholarship is to arrange the evidence in a neat series reflecting an organic internal growth.[21] That there were chronological developments is indisputable, and it is arguable (as we shall see below) that the broad changes in fashion have significance for social history. But the thesis that the internal developments are so coherent and monolinear that every painted wall could be dated to within a decade relies on highly dubious assumptions too often unsupported by external controls.[22] Moreover, this is, from the point of view of the social historian, a sterile approach that succeeds in deflecting study from the nondiachronic dimensions of decorative practice.

THIS STATE of affairs has been made possible by an accident of scholarship. Of the four classic "styles" of Pompeian (and associated) decoration, only the first three have been studied in detail. We now have massive studies of each of these styles, each in minute detail, with nothing to correspond on the fourth.[23] This last style had been in vogue for probably over a generation at the time of the eruption of Vesuvius; consequently, it is not only overwhelmingly the commonest, but its social diffusion is vastly better documented than is that of any of the other styles. One may suspect that the neatness of the series constructed for the second and third styles is only made possible by the paucity of evidence involved. What is certain is that the fourth style will not lend itself to a similar treatment, and that classification will have to be based on more than the chronological dimension.[24]

Recent publications much concerned with the fourth style have moved cautiously toward modification of the traditional approach; for example, the study by the German team under Strocka[25] of the Casa del Principe di Napoli at Pompeii. Here is a house decorated wholly in the fourth style, probably before A.D. 62. This study succeeds in demolishing the view propounded by Schefold that variations in quality are attributable to differences in date. The house presents us with a coherent decorative program, and the palpable variations in quality result from the function of decoration itself: to differentiate and articulate social space, to set up contrasts and hierarchies that will make an impression on the user.[26]

This insight is developed in more general terms in Barbet's recent synthesis on Roman mural decoration.[27] That decoration serves a social function is a theme that recurs throughout her book; she is able to illustrate, not only for the fourth but for all styles, how contrasts in decoration serve to differentiate space, and how internal hierarchies of motifs and patterns consistently applied within individual houses can be detected.[28] My aim is to develop this insight further, not so much in questions of detail but in order to expose the underlying structures of the Roman house.

AXES OF DIFFERENTIATION

Anthropology can help the historian to see the social significance of the way various societies shape domestic space.[29] If the need to differentiate is universal, there is variety in the lines or axes along which differentiation is sought. It will help to point to two such axes that had little or no importance for the Roman.

One is that of gender.[30] In the Greek house the most important single contrast is that between male and female space (cf. Fig. 1.1); in the Roman it is virtually undetectable, and we should be surprised if it were otherwise in view of the literary evidence. Cornelius Nepos sees it as one of the salient contrasts between Greek and Roman society that the Romans do not segregate their womenfolk and that the *matrona* "versatur in medio," that is, moves about in the middle of male life in terms of both physical space and social occasion.[31] The same contrast is implicit in Vitruvius's description of the Greek as

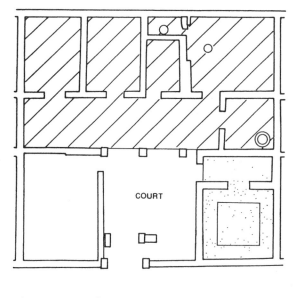

COURT

0 _____ 5m

Figure 1.1 Plan, house A vii 4, Olynthos (after Robinson and Graham). The house falls into two equal sections. The first and most accessible section includes the andron and its anteroom (dotted), set aside for men, to the east of the court. The farther half (shaded) is the women's quarter for family use, with kitchen and service rooms to the east, living rooms to the west.

opposed to the Roman house; he sees gender differentiation as fundamental only to the former.[32] Latin linguistic usage further bears out these direct statements. Though clothing or parts of the body are distinguished as *muliebris*, the only spaces so characterized are public baths, where mixed bathing was offensive to Roman sentiment. *Gynaecea* or women's quarters are not referred to except in special circumstances. In a memorable passage in Plautus's *Mostellaria*, the slave Tranio tricks his master's neighbor Simo into showing them his house on the pretense that his master plans to build a gynaeceum and has heard an architect praising Simo's as an excellent model. The master, Theopropides, is apologetic about looking around inside the house: "But the ladies . . ." Such embarrassment would be out of place in a visitor to a Roman house, and Plautus has conscientiously preserved the Athenian setting of the Greek original, down to the price in Attic minae for the building.[33] Of course, individual rooms in houses would have been used in appropriate circumstances by women, and there must have been gender distinctions to observe; but to identify whole areas as set apart for exclusive female use is arbitrary and unjustified.[34]

The second absent axis is that of age. In the modern Western house (and this is a Victorian heritage) it is normal to find space set apart for children—the nursery, the playroom, the children's bedroom, even bathroom, and similarly the play area in the garden (Fig. 1.2). No trace of such a contrast is apparent in the Roman material, and

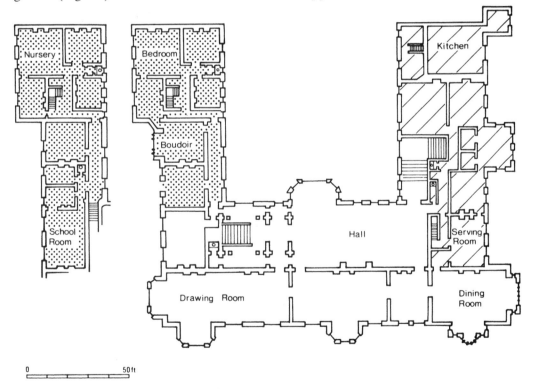

Figure 1.2 Plan, Thorsby Hall, Nottinghamshire (1864–75) (after Girouard). The main body contains public reception rooms. Service quarters (shaded) are in one wing, family rooms (dotted) in the other. Children's rooms are on the upper floor of the family wing.

again it would be surprising if one were insofar as the emergence of the child as a separate social personality only appears to have developed in the modern period.[35] Standard discussions of the Roman house give inadequate attention to the question of where children slept and played, and any attempt to distinguish neatly between "family" rooms and "slave" rooms ignores the likelihood that young children at least slept with servile nurses and pedagogues.[36] When poets give us rare glimpses of children at play, it is not in some playroom but in the columned atrium.[37]

Gender and age distinctions were of course perfectly familiar to the Romans. A standard description of a mixed crowd would be "sexus, aetas, ordo omnis"—"every sex, age, and rank."[38] When it came to shaping social space, the first two distinctions seem to have counted for nothing. The last, that of social rank, was central.

ROMAN domestic architecture is obsessively concerned with distinctions of social rank, and the distinctions involved are not merely between one house and another (as passages cited earlier might seem to imply) but within the social space of the house. This is the point of a familiar yet rather confused passage of Vitruvius. It is worth setting in context. Vitruvius prefaces his book on domestic architecture with some interesting considerations on the social relationship between architect and patron. He is anxious to emphasize the value of the architect's *doctrina* (education)—and warns patrons against the risks of amateur architecture)—but contrasts himself with those architects who have used their doctrina to achieve wealth and notoriety; this they do by advertising their profession (*rogant et ambiunt*). Conventional wisdom dictates that the architect is invited and does not invite custom; a true gentleman is embarrassed to ask (*ingenuus color movetur pudore*). An architect is entrusted with the expenditure of a family's capital (*patrimonium*); thus our ancestors selected architects on the grounds of birth, respectable upbringing, and a sense of social tact (*ingenuo pudori*).

By means of this preface, Vitruvius distances himself from those Greek-trained architects of servile origin who were common in his day. He establishes his own social credentials as an *ingenuus* (freeborn citizen) and insists that the kind of private patron likely to employ an architect, the paterfamilias with a substantial patrimonium, is or should be prepared to entrust his affairs only to an honest and honorable man. Thus it is when it comes to private commissions (as opposed to the public ones discussed in earlier books) that the architect feels the need to avoid being put in the position of a social inferior. He is asked to do a *beneficium* (favor) because of his learning, and does not ask for the beneficium of money. The patron will have to approach him (*ambire*), not the other way around.

This acute (and very Roman) social sensibility also informs Vitruvius's chapter on the social proprieties of domestic architecture (6.5). There are two overlapping themes. The first (1) is that the architect must distinguish within the house between the private (*propria loca patribus familiarum*) and the public (*communia cum extraneis*).[39] He explains the social background to this distinction: certain areas, notably bedrooms, dining rooms, and baths, are only open to *invited* visitors; others, notably vestibules, halls, and peristyles, are open to the public (*communia*). At this point the second theme is introduced, for not all the architect's clients have equal need of this differentiation of public and private. The common man (*communi fortuna*) has no need of grandiose *vestibula* (vestibules), *tablina* (record rooms), and atria, as he does his duty to others by paying calls (*ambiundo*) and does not receive calls of his own (recall Vitruvius's insistence that an architect should receive requests for business patronage).

We are now offered a brief conspectus of the social spectrum (2). The common man is negatively defined by his lack of need for public reception areas. The rustic is defined by a need for purely utilitarian spaces for storage, and in this there is an implicit social contrast between the utilitarian and the decorative (*ad elegantiae decorem*). Intervening categories are formed by financiers (*faeneratores* and *publicani*), who are deemed to require a degree of comfort and elegance, and by lawyers and advocates,[40] who require greater space and elegance for large receptions. Those in the highest class are the holders of public office, and it is these individuals (we now return to the initial theme) who require tall, regal vestibules, atria and peristyles on the grandest scale, and groves and walks to suit their rank (*ad decorem maiestatis*). Such high-ranking officials add libraries, picture galleries, and basilicas, all essentially public-building forms, to be built virtually on the scale of a public building, because of the public nature of much of the business done there (*publica consilia et privata iudicia*).

Need for elegance (elegantiae decorem, speciosiora, elegantiora, ad decorem maiestatis) is explicitly linked to position in the social hierarchy, which is dictated by the number of visitors one receives; it is because they are involved in public life and "offer services to the citizens" that members of the upper class require their grand surroundings. What remains less clear is how the differentiation within the house is meant to work. Although the public spaces where the masses press uninvited give the grand houses their grandeur, these houses are also somehow inferior precisely because they are thronged with the common man, and not the invited guest.

This ambiguity is not the product of any Vitruvian confusion; it is built into the structure of the Roman upper-class house itself. We are confronted with two contrasts that are not in fact identical: between the public and the private, and between the grand and the humble. The grand derives its grandeur from its position in public life; at the same time what is private and exclusive ranks above the common. The situation is best clarified by distinguishing and counterposing the two as separate axes. Graphically it can be represented as a quadrant.

It is possible to move in either direction along either of the two axes at the same time. An area may be public and grand (the magistrate's atrium) or private and grand (his triclinium or cubiculum). It may be private and humble (the slave's bedroom, the farmer's storeroom) or even—a class Vitruvius does not exemplify—public and humble (a shop, a public lavatory, or a service corridor).

This system of spatial differentiation is the direct product of Roman social relations. On the most obvious level, it is connected, as Vitruvius indicates, with the social system of *clientela*.[41] As has long been seen, the vestibulum-atrium-alae-tablinum complex lends itself to the *salutatio*, the traditional ritual of morning greeting; and archaeologists have not been slow to point out benches outside the doors for the convenience of waiting *clientes*.[42] But what is at issue here is more than a specific social ritual; it is the vital interface between public and private in Roman life. In sharp contrast to the Greek house, the Roman house was a constant focus of public life. It was where a public figure not only received his dependents and friends (the two categories flow into one another) but conducted business of all sorts. His house was a powerhouse; it was where the network of social contacts that provided the underpinning for his activities outside the house was generated and activated. Consequently, the dominant concern in articulating domestic space was to provide a suitable context for the differentiation of public activities from those of more private nature, and for the activities for persons from the full social spectrum: from members of a public figure's peer group and his circle, through lesser *amici* (friends), to humbler dependents, tradesmen, and slaves.

Postindustrial society has become accustomed to a divorce between home and place of work. Status is generated at work not home, so the home becomes endowed with a "privacy" alien to the Roman. It is significant that comparable patterns can be found in other societies where public and private life similarly interpenetrate. The nobility of the French ancien régime offers a particularly striking parallel.[43] Private houses were, according to the prescriptions of the *Encyclopédie*, hierarchically classified and labeled: Only a prince of royal blood inhabited a *palais*; the nobility had their *hôtels*; the third estate lived in *maisons*. Each of these had its proper architectural form. The public element of a palais seems obvious enough to us; that of the hôtel is no less important. The ideal building (Fig. 1.3) was hierarchically disposed. One passed first the *basses courts*, where low-status service activities took place—stables on one side, kitchens on the other, with servants' quarters around them—then moved on to the seignorial quarters, where separate and symmetrical private suites were provided for the lord and lady, whose social lives were virtually independent. Beyond these lay the central block and showpiece of the house, dedicated to the reception of visitors. Within this block was a further contrast, between the *appartement de parade*—consisting of the main hall (*salon*), reception rooms, gallery, and the "state" bedroom, where public business was done, generally in the morning—and the *appartement de société*—including the dining room, where more intimate entertainment took place, especially in the afternoon and evening. Like the Romans, the French nobility lacked our disjunction between home and office, place of habitation and place of work. Not only among the nobility but among the third estate, whether distinguished financiers and lawyers or tradesmen and shopkeepers, the house was also the place of work. A man's power base was his clientèle, the number of people who paid court to him, and the home was the locus of paying court. And as in Rome, this led to the lavishing of enormous resources on private building, often on a sufficient scale to cripple the builder financially. The underlying impulse was not to display wealth but symbolically to affirm status.

So dominant are the axes of public and private, grand and humble, that without them there can be no form. For the *Encyclopédie*, it is only the palais and hôtels that have perceptible architectural form; the maison is, so to speak, formless, though in fact the upper echelons of the third estate went far in imitating the forms of the nobility. This is equally true in the Roman house, both that of Vitruvius's description and that of the archaeological remains. The noble house is where Vitruvius starts in attempting to give an account of form; the houses of the humble he can only describe in negative terms, citing their lack of public space and their absence of need for elegance of decor; and the houses of the financiers and lawyers he describes in relative terms, as more endowed with

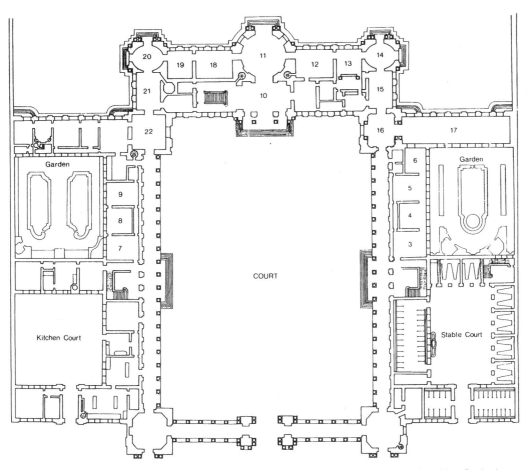

Figure 1.3 Plan, Hôtel of a noble (after Diderot, *Encyclopédie*). Service areas and stables flank the entrance. The private suite of the lord to the right (3–6, antichambre/cabinet/chambre à coucher/ arrière cabinet) corresponds symmetrically to the lady's suite to the left (7–9). The main reception rooms on the axis of the entrance (10–11, entrance hall and salon) lead on the right to the appartement de parade for morning business, including public reception suite (12–14) with state bedroom (13); and on the left to the appartement de société for afternoon entertainment, including reception and dining suite (20–22, petit salon/salle de compagnie/salle à manger).

the characteristics of the noble house. This chimes with the archaeological evidence, where the humbler housing is characterized by the relative lack of predictable and analyzable form,[44] and the intermediate levels by their imitation of the forms of the upper class.[45] This phenomenon is not simply one of mimicry ("aping one's betters"); the sheer insecurity of the freedman or the novus homo in the social structure drove him to affirm and legitimate his social standing by drawing on the cultural language of the dominant class.[46] Since this language is designed to express the axes of differentiation central to the upper class, it is ineffective to express any other type of differentiation. There is not one language for the rich and one for the poor, but a common language in which the rich are eloquent and the poor dumb.

GIVEN a society with such preoccupations, the social historian will want to know how the architect and decorator enabled the house owner to articulate his social space along these lines of contrast. Once we learn to recognize and read the language of differentiation, we will be in a better position to comment on its social diffusion. The suggestions I offer below will focus primarily on wall decoration, the best-documented category of evidence. It should however be borne in mind that many elements combined to endow a given area with its character—shape and size, orientation, illumination, ceiling and floor as well as wall decoration, not to speak of the (now largely invisible) furnishings.

The importance of the last comes out in Varro's *De Lingua Latina*, in which he pursues the analogy between linguistic usage and the usages of daily life: clothes, houses, furniture, and the like (*LL* 9.2off.). Just as there are two basic principles underlying the formation of language—analogy, the rational principle by which similar corresponds to similar, and anomaly, the irrational principle of custom by which arbitrary differences set things apart—so we may find both analogy and anomaly in daily life. In the house, as in language, there are some situations where you would expect similarity, some where you require difference. Were someone to set a triclinium with three dissimilar couches, we would correct them by analogy (*LL* 9.9). Yet different rooms would be distinguished by the use of different furniture: by use of couches with or without *fulchra* (decorative ends); by couches of triclinium (dining room) or *cubiculum* (bedroom) type; by ivory couches rather than *grabati* (pallets) (*LL* 8.32). Varro suggests that the principles of similarity and contrast work hand in hand. It is like setting out silverware on your *abacus* (sideboard): some pieces you arrange to form matching pairs, some to contrast (*LL* 9.46). Or again with couches in dining rooms: on the one hand you distinguish your triclinia using ivory-inlaid couches here, tortoiseshell there; on the other, you create matching sets by ensuring the couches in one setting are matched in height and material and shape, and using the same fabric for cushions, napkins, and so on (*LL* 9.47).

So much of what Varro takes for granted is lost to us. The visitor to a Roman dining room should know instinctively the implicit codings in ivory and tortoiseshell, refinements in fulchra, varieties of cushions or napkins. But if such detail is beyond recovery, the principle need not be. Every feature contributed to a process of differentiation, flagging contrasts of function and status. And just as Varro can treat the structures of language as analogous to houses and furniture, so we can reverse his analogy and treat houses and their decoration as a language, with its implicit structures and grammatical rules, its balance of arbitrary difference and rational similarity. The aim of the next two chapters is to tease out something of this underlying grammar.

In attempting this, I shall deploy the archaeological evidence of Pompeii and Herculaneum. It has long been traditional to use Pompeii and Vitruvius to illuminate one another; since the early nineteenth century the standard conception of "the Roman house" has been derived from this conjunction.[47] Yet there is an important methodological objection to be faced: the world of the metropolitan Roman elite to whom we owe our literary sources might be ill-matched with that of a second-rate Italian town of local landowners and traders. Indeed, it is quite normal for the basic structures of Pompeian houses, particularly the larger and more traditionally arranged, to date back to the period conventionally termed "Samnite," when Pompeii was an independent town, not "Roman" except in the distant sense of alliance and military cooperation. Until Sulla's capture of the town in the Social War, and its refoundation as a Roman colony, the Italic dialect we call Oscan was the language of public life; and metrological studies have shown that the Oscan foot, fractionally shorter than its Roman counterpart, was the measure on which houses like the Casa del Labirinto were laid out.[48]

The objection raises a valid point of principle: we are not dealing with a single monolithic "Roman world" but one differentiated through time, across region, across social divides. Yet the ease with which the evidence of Vitruvius and Pompeii have been persuaded to mesh indicates that there are significant intersections. It is above all at a particular period, in the last century B.C. and the first A.D., in a particular area, primarily central Italy, that this sort of overlap gives rise to the possibility of generalizations about "the Roman house." We can point to the intense contacts between the Roman elite and the Bay of Naples that date from the beginning of the second century.[49] It is not merely that Campania reflects metropolitan taste but that this area played a central role in the revolution of material culture that marks the period. The villas of the Roman elite provided conscious models, close at hand, for the houses of Pompeian shopkeepers, let alone those of the heavily Rome-focused local elite.[50]

At the same time, the literary sources are far from being metropolitan to the exclusion of Italian towns. Many of the Roman elite, most notably the literary authors, including Cicero and Vitruvius, had immediate origins in Italian towns. Vitruvius by no means aims at a metropolitan audience; when he contrasts, as he does often, "our" way of doing things with the Greek way, he is thinking not just of a Roman but of an Italian way. Quite specifically, in his discussion of domestic architecture he opposes the Greek custom to the *Italica consuetudo*. This is a tribute to the degree of perceived cultural unification achieved by the reign of Augustus, which only becomes more marked in the following century, as Italian towns seek to reproduce an authentic stamp of "Roman" character, and in their turn provide the model for Romanization in the provinces.[51]

Finally, the archaeological evidence of domestic architecture we have from the capital, fragmentary though it is in comparison to that of the monumental architecture of public buildings, is adequate to confirm the close relationship between Rome and Campania. This is most clearly the case with wall decoration; the Roman evidence meshes fully with the schemes of stylistic development based on Pompeii.[52] Certainly if the evidence from Rome were more ample, it would be easier to draw contrasts between metropolitan and provincial styles. The mere fact that decoration in Herculaneum has its own distinctive character confirms that one should predict local variations. But even if it is a local variant, Pompeian wall painting is a variant of something recognizably "Roman." It is a great frustration that the remains of republican houses on the Palatine, such as the Casa dei Grifi, the Casa di Livia, and now the so-called Casa di Augusto, are still insufficient to indicate how a truly aristocratic Roman house differed from Pompeian models.[53] The new excavations by Carandini of the aristocratic houses at the foot of the Palatine promise to transform this situation. Preliminary examination indicates that precisely the sort of atrium houses with shops in their frontages that are so familiar from Pompeii were also characteristic of the metropolitan elite.[54]

It makes good sense that the evidence of literary sources for the late Republic and early Empire should converge closely with the archaeological evidence for central Italy. But it would be quite mistaken to leap from this to the assumption of some sort of homogeneous "Romanness" that characterizes the Roman house at all times and in all regions. Already as we move to Apuleius's *Metamorphoses*, set in the eastern empire of the second century A.D., the picture is changing; the domestic settings of this novel fit better with the somewhat later remains of north African towns than with Pompeii.[55] Far from positing such a cultural homogeneity, the following studies seek to expose the fragility of the concept of Romanness, to underline the importance of the dynamics of change in the process of self-definition, and to explore how the domestic environment could be used, by people of very different status, to construct a stable sense of Romanness in the face of historical and social change.

CHAPTER 2

THE LANGUAGE OF PUBLIC
AND PRIVATE

BY WHAT MEANS was it possible to mark off and distinguish the public from the private in a Roman house? Though archaeologists (who know their Vitruvius) are well aware of the public dimension of the Roman upper-class house, approaches have been based on a conception of the public/private antithesis in terms of a black/white polarity. It is suggested, for instance, that the excavated areas of the so-called Casa di Augusto on the Palatine represent the private quarter, and that there was a corresponding public quarter.[1] But we are dealing rather with a spectrum that ranges from the completely public to the completely private, and with an architectural and decorative language that seeks to establish relativities along the spectrum. One space is more or less open or intimate in relation to the spaces around it, and contrasts of disposition, shape, and decoration establish such relativities. The pattern of Roman social life admitted numerous and subtle grades of relative privacy, in which, it must be apparent, greater privacy represented not a descent but an ascent in privilege, an advance toward intimacy with the paterfamilias. There is a hierarchy of social occasions from the promiscuous morning salutation to the sought-after afternoon *cena*. The triclinium will be private relative to the main circulation and open reception areas; yet the cubiculum is private relative to the triclinium, and this is a place not only for rest ("bedroom") but for the reception of intimate friends and the conducting of confidential business—and even for emperors conducting their notorious trials *intra cubiculum*.[2]

The distinction between public and private will lie partly in scale. As Vitruvius indicates, the "regal" feel of the noble house lies in the amplitude of the proportions of its public spaces, and the volume (height is important as well as area) of the largest reception room in a house is a possible index of the standing of the house as a whole.

Scale alone is a crude indicator, and the art of the architect and decorator lies in refining the contrasts. The most important technique, I would suggest, is that of allusion. It is by borrowing the language of actual public spaces in the domestic context that architect and decorator can evoke in the visitor the feel of something more than a private house. The use of allusion is so widespread that no more than illustration can be offered. In it lies the key to a central aspect of the process of "Hellenization": forms evolved in Greece for the enhancement of public space are translated by the Romans into the domestic context.[3]

A nice illustration of how this technique of allusion works in terms of architectural form is offered by the Casa dell'Atrio a mosaico at Herculaneum, one of the two main show houses of the present excavations (Figs. 2.1–2). The ample atrium is decorated with the striking mosaic that gives this house its name; beyond it, in place of the conventional tablinum, is a large structure of unusual architectural form. A series of pillars on either side divide it in the pattern of nave and two aisles, and above the pillars rises a second story with clerestory windows, reminiscent of classic basilica form. The excavator, Maiuri, rightly relates this to Vitruvius's prescription for the construction of an "Egyptian oecus"; but when it comes to analyzing the function of the space, Maiuri fails to follow up the allusion implicit in the architectural form, and drawing attention to the proximity of the kitchen, identifies it as the family dining room, distinct indeed from the dining room for the reception of guests, which enjoyed a sea view.[4] Scale alone makes this identification ludicrous, and it is notable that, for all his interest in social life, Maiuri thinks in terms of social institutions that better fit contemporary than ancient society. Vitruvius makes the architectural allusion explicit: the form of the Egyptian as opposed to the Corinthian oecus is that of the basilica (*basilicarum ea similitudo*). It evokes, in fact, a public building; and given its position on the axis of the atrium in place of the traditional tablinum, it must be seen as a public reception area for the conduct of quasi-public

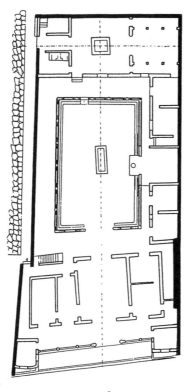

0   10m

Figure 2.1 Plan, Casa dell'Atrio a mosaico, Herculaneum. The vista from the fauces culminates in the tablinum/ oecus Aegyptius. The garden opens at a right angle to this vista, with a long suite of reception rooms linked by a corridor overlooking the garden.

business. As Vitruvius comments two chapters later, it is precisely because of their public function that noble houses need basilicas that draw on the magnificence of public buildings, "basilicas non dissimili modo quam publicorum operum magnificentia comparatas."

This observation may help us to identify comparable areas in other houses that deliberately evoke a public setting.[5] Both the Casa dei Cervi (H IV.4; see Fig. 2.3 and Pl. 1), neighbor and very much rival to the Herculaneum house in question, and the Casa del Menandro (I 10.4, Fig. 2.4), one of the most extensive and opulent houses in Pompeii, have a room of exceptional dimensions marked externally by a triangular pediment, enhanced in the first case by rich mosaic decoration.[6] The *fastigium*, as reference to the Roman literary usage as well as archaeological remains indicates, was characteristic of public buildings, particularly the temple, the palace, and the basilica;[7] it was because the house of Julius Caesar was latterly amalgamated with the Regia that it had the extraordinary distinction of a fastigium, and when Calpurnia dreamed of its collapse, it portended Caesar's fall.[8] This use of the associations of an architectural feature makes explicit that the room serves a quasi-public function (which its size makes possible). In each case Maiuri identifies the room as a triclinium; and though one cannot rule out the possibility that such rooms could be used for dining, they certainly vastly exceed the dimensions

Figure 2.2 Casa dell'Atrio a mosaico, Herculaneum, view of oecus Aegyptius from atrium.
The basilica-like construction permits a room of exceptional dimensions;
the clerestory lighting enhances the sense of spacious elegance.

necessary for the characteristic Roman couch arrangement. The resort to labeling (as tri-clinium) merely obscures what architecture indicates about the room, that it aspires to the regal, even divine, scale of a public building.[9]

Another architectural feature with public associations is the column. So widespread is the use of columns in Roman domestic architecture that we take it for granted as simply another method of construction. But the employment of the column was the hallmark of Greek public and sacred architecture, and we should ask whether associations with public buildings did not adhere, at least at times, in their employment by the Romans.[10] For the elder Pliny the column was a sign of Roman extravagance, and he explicitly links this to the appropriateness of marble columns in public buildings. Crassus, the censor of 92 B.C., had already six columns of Hymettan marble in his atrium, earlier imported as decoration for a temporary public stage, "at a time," comments Pliny, "when there were still none on any public building—so recent is opulence!"[11] Even if Pliny's emphasis is here on the material, the way the Roman compared public and private building is clear.

Peristyles offer the context in which the column is most frequently found, and it is easy (as was once normal) to assume that we have here simply a derivative of the Greek courtyard house.[12] Yet even our term *peristyle* (*peristyl-ium/ -os/ -um*) derives from Greek *public* architecture.[13] In the case of the more ambitious examples of the peristyle, like that

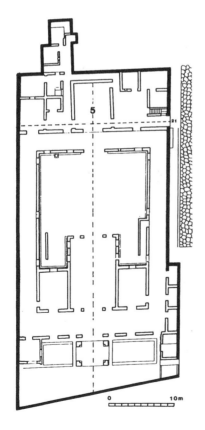

Figure 2.3 Plan, Casa dei Cervi, Herculaneum (after Maiuri). Note two sightlines: That from the entrance (at no. 21) leads past the nonimpluviate atrium across the main suite of reception rooms (service rooms are behind to the right of this sightline). Intersecting this is the sightline from the main reception room (5) through the garden. This view was flanked by statuary. The pediment is over the intersection of the two sightlines.

Figure 2.4 Casa del Menandro, Pompeii, view of peristyle, looking toward the
largest reception room, marked by its wide opening on the peristyle, the double spacing of the
columns, the high ceiling, and the pediment above a window for extra illumination.

of the Casa del Fauno, scale and associations reach far beyond a Greek domestic court.[14]
Long rows of columns suggest the public portico, the stoa, and when disposed in rectan-
gular form point to that hallmark of a Hellenistic city, the gymnasium. Occasionally we
find signs that make the allusion explicit. Cicero, fitting out his Tusculan villa in the 60s
B.C., was anxious to collect statues and Herms suitable for his "palaestra and gymnasium"; he was emphatic that they must be, in the Greek term, *gymnasiodê*.[15]

The repeated use of decorative marble pieces in the peristyles of houses in Herculaneum and Pompeii, frequently coupled with a central *piscina*, a swimming pool of however
diminutive proportions, suggests that it was the world of the public palaestra or gymnasium these peristyles sought to evoke.[16] There is no reason to associate these features, nor
the characteristic and charming garden settings in which they are placed,[17] with the Greek
domestic court. The Romans were conscious, in the cases of marble statues and panel
paintings, that they were privatizing a feature of Greek public life. It was the fault of
Lucullus, Cicero claimed, that one could see the villas of freedmen "packed with statues
and paintings, some of them public property, some even sacred and cult objects."[18]
Though the reproduction trade of the early Empire made the actual spoliation of shrines
superfluous,[19] the public and religious associations of both works of art and their architectural context surely still constituted an essential element in their attraction.

Atria and peristyles form the normal context for columns, both being, on Vitruvius'

Figure 2.5 Casa delle Nozze d'Argento, Pompeii, view of *oecus Corinthius*.
Four columns support a vaulted canopy, extending the illusionist effect
of the second-style wall decoration.

account, public areas. Columns within a room are rare and therefore worthy of comment. One striking form employed particularly in the late Republic in some of the most ambitious houses of that period is the "Corinthian oecus." As well as urban examples at Pompeii—the Case del Labirinto, di Meleagro, and delle Nozze d'Argento (Fig. 2.5)— Settefinestre has recently produced an example in the context of an aristocratic villa.[20] Here columns on three sides support a sort of canopy in the form of a vault in the center of the room. We should not be lulled by Vitruvius's discussion of "Corinthian" and "Cyzicene" oeci into taking this for an "ordinary" Greek domestic architectural form. The closest parallels lie in the fabulous accounts of festal tents and ships constructed by Ptolemy II and other Hellenistic kings for public receptions and festivals on a massive scale,[21] and what matters about the columns here, as is clear in the loving description of Callixeinos, is not their structural function but their ability to transport the diners into a world of luxury and monumentality, complete in Callixeinos's example with gymnasia and temples.[22]

Columns, whether in an atrium or a colonnade or within a room, have the effect of marking out space as prestigious; we will see shortly how decoration can serve to extend this effect. Other techniques for framing or emphasizing internal space also evolved, of which the most characteristically Roman is the use of curved walls and ceilings. A particularly striking example is the apsidal-ended room. The apse with its semicupola serves to frame the visual centerpiece of certain types of public room, notably the basin (*labrum*) recess of the caldarium in public baths, the cult-image recess in certain temples, and the tribunal of a basilica. The same feature appears in certain grand imperial reception rooms from the early Empire onward (the so-called Auditorium Maecenatis, the Aula Isiaca, the auditorium of Domitian's palace), and in rare instances in grand reception rooms in private houses (the Casa dei Capitelli Colorati at Pompeii [VII 4.51] and the Casa dello Scheletro at Herculaneum [H III.3; Figs. 2.6–7], and in the second century the Casa della Fortuna Annonaria at Ostia [V.2]). Here again we see the profane drawing on the sacred, the private on the public, but with an allusion that is surely deliberate.[23]

THE illustrations I have chosen of architectural forms with public associations are often ones found in houses that, though grand, do not represent the top of the scale of luxury. We are learning to recognize how the most opulent villas and urban *horti* (gardens) of the Roman aristocracy absorbed the forms of palatial and sacred buildings into their structures. But in a sense we are less surprised (though doubtless impressed) to learn that Lucullus's horti imitated a sacred precinct like that of Praeneste, with its complex of temple, theater, and portico.[24] We expect buildings on such a scale to outrun the vocabulary of the domestic, it is therefore the more important to recognize how socially pervasive was this employment of the language of the public. Trimalchio too could boast of his house: "It used to be a hut: now it is a temple."[25] Nowhere is this more clear than in Roman mural decoration.

The language of public and private is essential to the Roman approach to wall decoration, and one of the most obvious signs is the importance, at all periods, of architectural form, particularly the column. That Roman wall decoration is imitative, in some sense "illusionist," is almost inevitable; what is significant is its choice of what to imitate. One option open to the wall decorator is the imitation of fabrics; this is the origin of our own dominant style of wall decoration, with its characteristic diagonally repeating designs, and it was an option of which the Romans were well aware. Fabrics must have often been suspended over Roman walls and across openings (*aulaea* were a standard part of the apparatus of luxury and were certainly widespread in the Hellenistic East), though naturally the archaeologist finds few traces of them and therefore underrates their importance.[26] On occasion one finds painted plaster walls that create the effect of this fabric or "wallpaper" style—a charming golden-yellow room that gives its name to the Casa degli Amorini Dorati (VI 16.7; Pl. 2), a white-ground wall with floral designs set in diamonds in the Villa di Arianna at Stabia (Fig. 2.8), and now from Settefinestre a bedroom with red-ground walls with birds set in delicate floral squares. A rarity in Italy, the style is considerably more common in provinces like Britain.[27] The interesting point about this attractive (to our own taste) style is its rarity; other options were preferred, and this preference is indicative.

The conventional account, going back to Mau, which despite repeated questioning has in its broad outlines stood the test of time, divides the mural decoration of the late Republic and early Empire into four chronological phases. The main criterion for

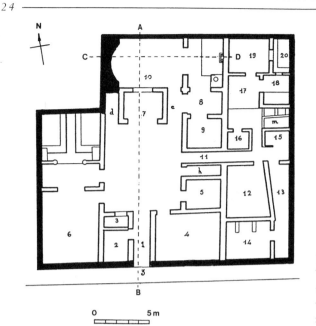

Figure 2.6 Plan, Casa dello Scheletro, Herculaneum.
The main reception room (10) lies on the intersection of
the sightline from entrance through tablinum (A–B) and
that from its own apsidal end to a mosaic-decorated
nymphaeum in a small court/lightwell (C–D).

Figure 2.7 Casa dello Scheletro, Herculaneum, view of apsed room (10) from entrance.
The window to the left opens on the tablinum. The decoration of the apse marks its center with an
architectural vista opening up a further apse. The floor is of marble opus sectile.

Figure 2.8 Villa di Arianna, Stabia. Room decorated in wallpaper style, marked by strong diagonals and repeating patterns. This may well have suggested woven hangings.

distinguishing these phases or "styles" is their use of architectural illusion. The first style creates an illusion, if no more than two-dimensional, of marble panels; the second extends illusion into the third dimension, setting up architectural vistas framed by columns; the third recedes from illusion, reducing the foreground of columns to "unrealistic" decorative motifs that simply frame panels; and the fourth partially returns to illusion, by employing elaborate, even fantastic, architectural vistas as the framework to panels. This account is reasonable enough as a description of the relationship between the painter's art and contemporary Roman (or Greek) architectural realities. The process starts with what is virtually a painted plaster reproduction of actual wall-cladding and ends with a decorative fantasy that takes its elements from reality but in no sense tries to reproduce it. Where the account is less adequate is in analyzing the impact of the decoration on the user. Was it really the intent of the decorator at some periods to try to deceive those who looked at his walls, and if so, why should this intent be abandoned later?

From the point of view of the social function of decoration, what matters are not the visual games played, but the associations evoked, by the decoration: its power not of *illusion*, but of *allusion*.[28] With whatever degree of realism, the decorators were concerned throughout with evoking (or not evoking) a world of buildings outside the domestic context within which they operate. It is the world of public rather than private buildings to which allusion is primarily made—the persistent variation on the theme of the column, perennial symbol of power, already points in that direction. Even the marble incrustations of the first style evoke public buildings; true, this was a decorative fashion already evolved in Greece,[29] but it is not a world of rich Greek houses, even palaces, to

Figure 2.9 Pompeii Basilica. The stucco on the wall is formed into panels characteristic of the first style. These were presumably painted ("marbled").

Figure 2.10 Casa Sannitica, Herculaneum, view of atrium from fauces. First-style decoration is preserved in the fauces and in the stucco colonnade above. The rest of the atrium (heavily damaged) has been redecorated in the fourth style.

which reference is made, when those houses were themselves imitating temples, basilicas, and gymnasia.

The basilica at Pompeii, itself still decorated in A.D. 79 in first-style incrustation (Fig. 2.9), offers a convenient illustration of the public world with which houses like the Casa del Fauno or the Casa Sannitica at Herculaneum (Fig. 2.10) were placing themselves on a par. In fact, the first style continued in use for public buildings and tombs long after it went out of vogue in domestic decoration; and the way it was carefully preserved and renewed in the atria and public spaces of some houses in which these public spaces were particularly dominant—the Case del Fauno and di Sallustio at Pompeii, and the Casa Sannitica at Herculaneum—indicates that the potency of this style to evoke the public survived into the Empire.[30]

The language of allusion becomes enormously more sophisticated in the second style. Here scholarship has pointed to two main alternative candidates for the "origin" of the style: contemporary stage scenery and painting,[31] and actual contemporary architecture,

Figure 2.11 Oplontis villa (Torre Annunziata), room 23. The second-style
decoration with its heavy use of architectural perspectives suggests a scaenae frons.
Note also the presence of masks.

whether of the Hellenistic palace or the Roman luxury villa itself.[32] But it is not a case
of the one or the other, or even simply both; for the stage and the palace are only a
fragment of the rich world of public architecture evoked. The allusions to stage painting
are unmistakable and on occasion explicit, as in the room of the masks in the Palatine
Casa di Augusto, where the explicit forms of the three-door stage scene are underlined
by the eye-catching series of masks, and the similar room in the villa at Oplontis (Fig.
2.11).[33] The link with scenography is a double one: it involves both scenographic trompe-
l'oeil techniques of creating three-dimensional space and also allusion to the appearance
of the stage (as in the room of the masks). The analogy between the scenographer and
the wall decorator is instructive; both create a backdrop against which action is to take
place and transport the actors into a world suitable for their action. And as on the stage,
particularly the tragic stage, it is above all to a world of luxury, grandeur, and public life
that the decorated wall transports us, to the palaces of kings and the temples of the gods.

Fittschen[34] makes good use of descriptions of the pleasure barges of the Hellenistic
kings in order to point out the links with the world of palaces, which archaeology has
been unable to recover in sufficient detail. But it would be wrong to think in terms of
palaces alone, for again it is the whole world of public architecture that is involved. Even
the palaces were themselves drawing on the language of public and sacred architecture.

In Lucan's description of Cleopatra's palace, which Fittschen cites, the building "recalls a temple such as is scarcely built in a decadent age."[35] The description stresses the use of marble incrustations, and the links with Rome are drawn by speaking of "the luxury not yet transported to Roman society" (11).[36]

Temples are a regular feature in second-style vistas; on occasion, the deity itself is half seen behind the temple door.[37] Other structures too are recognizable. Sequences like the Odyssey frieze from the Esquiline or the Macedonian frieze from Boscoreale,[38] where a series of scenes is glimpsed as if between pillars, explicitly evoke decorated colonnades going back to the Stoa Poikile of Athens,[39] which had numerous descendants in the public porticoes of Rome.[40] Gymnasia, as we have seen, are a likely source of inspiration, especially for the decoration of peristyles and colonnades; the caryatids and atlantes or telamones of the cryptoporticus in the Casa del Criptoportico evoke a standard feature of public architecture, and in the baths of the Casa del Menandro they neatly parallel the use of stone telamones in the forum baths of this same town.[41] Finally, we should remember that the stage itself, though at one level acting as a mirror to evoke a world of grandeur outside itself, also constituted one of the most ambitious forms of public architecture in the Greco-Roman city. It was on the *scaenae frons* that the aristocrats of the late Republic lavished some of their most extravagant displays, and that helps to explain its recurrent evocation in mural decoration.[42]

It may seem surprising how often the richest architectural vistas "are met in small rooms, in *cubicula* and *oeci*, rooms of private life and private entertainment."[43] In a small alcoved bedroom like that at Oplontis, the effect may seem overwhelming. But in the rare cases where we can compare the decorative scheme of a house as a whole, and see the decoration of one room in relation to others, we find that the second style allows a subtle system of differentiation. So with the Fannius Synistor villa at Boscoreale (Fig. 2.12): the area of the peristyle and its associated spaces, as an area of public circulation, are fairly simply decorated as if with marble panels hung with garlands; the largest reception room displays the famous large-figure frieze ("megalographia") in an impressive portico-style columnar framework, marking it as the most imposing public reception room of the complex; the smaller, balancing reception room has a portico-style columnar framework but lacks figures, while its linked cubiculum is privileged by a rich series of fantastical architectural vistas that seem reminiscent of stage settings.[44]

Analysis of the second-style decoration of the Casa del Labirinto at Pompeii (VI 11.8–10) has confirmed that similar contrasts result from a deliberate hierarchy and not from different periods of decoration or different workshops. Here the hierarchy rises from the plain enclosed paneling of corridors and subordinate rooms, through paneling enhanced by columnar elaboration in some reception rooms, to the walls that open up into trompe-l'oeil perspectives in the finest reception rooms, reaching a climax in the oecus Corinthius where columns extend architecturally the perspective effects of the painting into the body of the room.[45] The greater the depth suggested by the perspective effects, the higher the prestige of the room. Thus the second style opens up possibilities not available to the first of marking an area as both intimate and privileged. By concen-

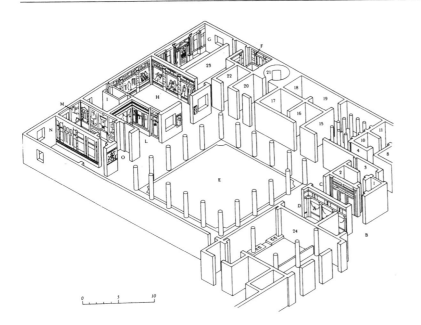

Figure 2.12 Isometric reconstruction of the villa of Fannius Synistor, Boscoreale (after Anderson). Different degrees of elaboration of the second-style decoration privilege the suite of rooms to the north of the peristyle.

trating the language of public architecture within a confined space, a feeling of rich luxury is generated, as if all the power and grandeur of the public figure who slept there had been focused on a single spot.

The third style, with its rejection of architectural vistas, marks a conscious change of taste, and one condemned by Vitruvius as an abandonment of the proprieties.[46] To our own taste, the third style may seem more suitable for domestic circumstances: pompous architecture is replaced by the elegant decorative frameworks that set off panel paintings with mythological subjects, faintly reminiscent of the sort of paintings that might adorn our own walls (Pl. 3). It is almost as if the chilly public idiom of the republican aristocracy had been domesticated. Given the dating of this shift, which an accumulation of evidence seems to tie to c. 30 B.C.,[47] it is tempting to associate a fundamental shift in fashion with shifts in ideology that are consequent on political changes.[48] The progressive elimination by Augustus during the twenties and teens B.C. of the traditional aristocratic rituals of public status advertisement (the triumph, the erection of public buildings, advertisement of family themes on the coinage, etc.)[49] might offer a context for the emergence of a new self-image among the aristocracy. The proper backdrop for the public figure is no longer highly public, indeed regal and verging on the sacred; instead a more intimate and private luxury is in place. Whereas the first style is the art of public places, such as Vitruvian regal atria and tablina, the third style, so one might argue, is the art of private places, private dinner parties for chosen amici. The shift in emphasis would correspond to a shift in the locus of political power: no longer won out in the open, in forum and senate, power is generated through informal contacts, at drinking parties, in the corridors and bedrooms of the palace. The dominant image of the aristocrat is no longer the republican *patronus*, surrounded by a crush of clients, but rather the imperial courtier or *amicus principis*, adept in his social contacts and mediating the web of imperial patronage.[50]

But even if there is something in this contrast, the decoration of the early Empire remains alarmingly undomesticated by our standards. The picture galleries typical of this style were no retreat from the public sphere. *Pinacothecae* were public buildings, often associated with gymnasia and porticoes; and the new fashion for decorating rooms to look like pinacothecae, which reached Rome at the very end of the Republic, was seen by contemporaries as a deliberate privatization of the public.[51] Just as the proper context for a Greek statue was a public building or temple, so it was for a Greek painting; Pliny sees a decline in the painter's art under the Empire because of the impossibility of "noble" art in the domestic context.[52]

Lucullus made a name for his private pinacothecae. Just as his private gardens imitated sacred architecture, so his picture galleries must have been a conscious domestication of a public style. Bearing in mind the impact made by the portico Pompey attached to his theater, with its outstanding collection of works of art, we may see Lucullus as consciously competing in the private domain with his old rival's efforts in the public. The feeling that Greek masterpieces ought to be public persisted: Agrippa was to propose transferring all such works in private hands to public collections. Perhaps he had in mind not only the looting of shrines but the political value a Lucullus could derive from the private display of masterpieces.[53] Vitruvius too is aware of the associations of the pinacotheca: it is suitable for a noble's house because, like a basilica, it is something public (6.5.2). And finally it is worth considering the standard setting of the third-style mythological paintings. Framed in columns sustaining a pediment like a little shrine or *aedicula*, the way they appear on domestic walls must mimic their appearance in public settings, whether in temples or the collections in porticoes. If it is rather late in the day that this new taste in domestic decoration emerges, that is surely because, as Pliny asserts, the Romans were slow to come to appreciate paintings in public; only with Caesar's dictatorship, he claims, did this art achieve full recognition.[54]

Other factors too are at work in the emergence of the new decorative styles of the early Empire. There are new artistic influences: the conquest of Egypt plausibly produced an influx of craftsmen from Alexandria to Rome, and the taste for Egyptianizing motifs in third-style decoration is marked—sphinxes, Isiac symbols, and Nilotic scenes become widespread in this period.[55] But to demonstrate an "origin" for an artistic phenomenon is not adequate to account for its social function. The Romans constantly borrowed new cultural goods from the eastern Mediterranean as new areas opened up to them, but they turned them to their own social ends. Perhaps if we knew more about the luxurious society of Alexandria and the Canopus, it would be easier to understand why Roman borrowing took the form it did.[56]

To understand the real social contrast implicit in the change of approach to wall decoration between Republic and Empire, it is better to focus on the fourth style, in many respects scarcely distinguishable from the third (which represents a fairly brief transitional period) and certainly much better documented in its social diffusion.

What is immediately striking about the fourth style from the perspective of social function is its range and flexibility. Just as the vocabulary of the second style is richer than the "marble incrustations" of the first and allows it to differentiate space more subtly, so the fourth style represents a further vast leap ahead in potential for differentiation. It is precisely this range of expressivity that makes it so difficult—indeed pointless—to characterize in terms of "illusionism." Decoration of this period comprehends everything from a white wall divided into panels by simple red lines to the most breathtaking confections of architecture receding into infinity. It is this range which allows the establishment of contrasts, both subtle and crude, between different spaces in a house, locating them simultaneously on the axes of public/ private and grand/humble.

Rather than attempt to categorize the varieties of decoration into artificial types,[57] it is helpful to think in terms of spectra that generate hierarchies. Three are of particular importance: color, motif, and framework. That colors fall into some sort of rank order is already apparent in the comments of Vitruvius and Pliny.[58] Pigment was valued in proportion to its availability and expense; the richest pigments, like red cinnabar, could be excluded from the decorator's contract and charged directly to the customer.[59] Variations in richness of color were consequently useful for establishing hierarchies of space. Plain white ground was obviously most economical, and is the commonest both in secondary rooms in richer houses and in less opulent houses overall (Pls. 4–6). Yellow ocher and red represent the norm for the background of the better rooms of houses both in the Campanian cities and in the later decorations of Ostia (Pl. 7). Blue pigment (already a source of profit to Cicero's friend Vestorius) is something of a rarity, applied only to the choicest rooms (e.g., in the Casa dell'Atrio a mosaico, Pl. 8);[60] and black is normally found in rooms of especial scale and grandeur (e.g., in the Casa dei Cervi, Plate 1).[61] In addition to the background color, one needs to take into account the richness of the palette applied in the walls as a whole; rich polychromies lend distinctive prestige.[62]

The second hierarchy is that of motifs. Mythological paintings are the hallmark of the third and fourth styles, at least as illustrated in the standard books (see Plates 3–6, 8). We have seen how the extraordinary prestige attached to mythological paintings of this sort is linked to the public associations that adhere to them. But such panel paintings form only the summit of a hierarchy of motifs that occupy the central field of the panels created by the framework. We find panel paintings on a small scale with less ambitious subjects than the great mythological scenes—landscapes (Fig. 2.13) and still lifes (Fig. 2.14), for example, or the vignettes and human faces often set in circular frames. Below these rank motifs not privileged by being set off from the background by a frame of their own: floating figures of gods, nymphs, and cupids, below them a variety of animals and birds, especially panthers, griffins (Fig. 2.15), and swans, and finally very simple objects, often of a quasi-religious character, vases, thyrsoi, thunderbolts, and the like. The hierarchy implicit in these motifs is one embedded in Greco-Roman culture: heroic and divine scenes enjoy prestige in the same way as heroic poetry and tragedy do compared to the "humble" genres of lyric or epigram.

But the most revealing hierarchy from the present point of view is that of frameworks. The hallmark of imperial (i.e., third- and fourth-style) decoration is that the architectural

Figure 2.13 Casa degli Amanti, Pompeii,
roundel with landscape. Such roundels mark the
center of the red panels of the decorative scheme
of the atrium.

Figure 2.15 Casa del Fabbro, Pompeii,
room 4, griffin motif
(see Fig. 2.16 for context).

Figure 2.14 Casa del Principe di Napoli, Pompeii, panel with birds and fruit.
This decorates a portico (Fig. 3.17) leading to a more ambitiously
decorated triclinium (Pl. 5).

Figure 2.16 Casa del Fabbro, Pompeii, room 4. One of a series of small cubicula along the side of the atrium (see Fig. 3.24), the left-hand wall incorporates a recess for a bed. The decorative scheme is simple but elegant, with panels demarcated by plain borders, and golden motifs (griffins and cupids) floating in the centers.

Figure 2.17 Shop/house I 7.18, axial vista. Although both architecture and decoration are crude, a calculated effect of axial "framing" is achieved. The large shop-opening frames a back opening; through this is seen across the courtyard the opening of the main reception room, which in turn frames the architectural *aedicula* of the decorative scheme. At the center of this is a very simple panel painting.

details, which previously had formed the focus of the decoration, are used only as a frame. This framework gives structure to the decorated wall, and it provides the context for the panel paintings which now occupy the focal point. But in framing central spaces and structuring walls, these architectural details also frame the social space of the room. A vivid illustration of the way in which painted architecture forms a continuity with built architecture in framing social space is offered by a group of small houses in which the symmetrical vista from the front door passes through several doorways to culminate in the architectural "frame" painted on the end wall of the main reception room of the house, like the modest shop (I 1.18) near the Casa del Menandro (Fig. 2.17). It is, then, the owner and his social activity that are framed by the decoration.[63] A similar point emerges from those triclinia in which three architecturally framed panel paintings

Figure 2.18 Casa del Fabbro, Pompeii, room 2. The first of a string of cubicula to the right of the entrance. The decoration is very basic: white-ground with red stripes to mark panels.

Figure 2.19 Casa del Forno, Pompeii. A cubiculum in the private quarters of a bakery (see Fig. 4.4), looking southward through a portico over the garden. The decoration is marked off by simple decorative borders forming panels; at their centers are motifs of panthers, etc.

Figure 2.20 Casa del Forno, Pompeii, detail of decoration of portico outside cubiculum (Fig. 2.19). The background is red; golden candelabra mark the division of the wall into panels, which are set off with decorative borders—floral designs to the left, a characteristic example of "embroidery border" (*bordo al tappeto*) to the right.

precisely surround the three couches of the triclinium at the upper end of the room. Here the paintings are scarcely visible to the diners themselves, who lie with backs to the walls; but the social activity of the convivium is magnificently framed from the viewpoint of an observer at the bottom end of the room.[64]

Thanks to their associations with public structures, columnar structures had a privileged status among other means to create such frames. The simplest and most humble walls, in rooms Strocka has termed "Nebenzimmer,"[65] may be virtually unstructured; either they have plain white plaster, or the vestigial structure of red dado and red vertical bands in the corners (Fig. 2.18). The next level of structuring lies in the creation of panels, most simply by plain bands, more elaborately by decorative borders (Fig. 2.19); the degree of elaboration here is crucial. Above this level, further elements are introduced to separate and articulate the panels; the candelabra and floral fantasies introduced with the third style, and condemned by Vitruvius as degenerations from the column, in fact generally serve as a hierarchically inferior method of articulation (Fig. 2.20). Columns survive through the third style into the fourth, particularly in the form of a shrine capped by a pediment that marks off the central zone of the wall (Fig. 2.21). The characteristic development of the fourth style lies in architectural structures that serve the function of the

Figure 2.21 Casa dell'Efebo, Pompeii, room 9, view to northeast. The bed recess suggests this was a cubiculum. The central panels in this white-ground decorative scheme are set off by aediculae formed by columns and architraves. The vignettes at the center of these panels are of divine "attributes" (to the left, the weapons of Mars, to the right, the eagle and thunderbolt of Jupiter).

column in dividing the wall into panels but are treated with such elaboration that they form panels in themselves. These may be groups of columns, or symmetrical aediculae (shrines), or receding vistas (Pls. 1, 5). It is thus at the top and bottom end of the scale that the fourth style distinguishes itself most clearly from its predecessors.[66]

It is the flexibility of these overlapping but distinct hierarchies that allows the systems of decoration that evolved with the early Empire to differentiate social space so finely. The three hierarchies need not coincide: one may find a white-ground room with elaborate architectural framework and mythological paintings (e.g., in the Casa dell'Efebo, Pl. 4),[67] or a rich black room quite without panel paintings or motifs (e.g., in the Casa dei Cervi, Plate 1).[68] Hence the range is further extended, and it is possible to differentiate simultaneously along the axes of public/private and grand/humble.[69] From the point of view of the ancient consumer, that is to say the inhabitant or visitor to the house upon whom the walls made their impression, decoration allowed a social orientation of two types: first, it helped to steer them within a house, guiding them round the internal hierarchies of social space (if a distinguished guest, toward the triclinium; if a slave, down the dark corridors to the service areas); and second, it offered social orientation by contrasting one house with another, indicating the level of resources and social aspirations of the household.

In retrospect, the development of decorative styles from the late Republic to the early Empire is not simply a matter of aesthetics, of changing tastes and changing attitudes to illusionism. Throughout a code has been developing—constantly drawing on public life—aimed at refining the hierarchical contrasts between the different social spaces of the house. If this code seems to move away from the direct "copying" of reality (aided by scenographic technique) into a realm of fantasy and artistic elaboration, this is because it is developing as a symbolic language. When their function is symbolic, columns and architectural frames no longer need remain realistic.

The other significant development that has emerged is the progressively greater and more subtle differentiation that decoration allows. Implicit in this is a growth in the social range of the consumers it serves and in the subtlety of differentiation available in their society. Throughout, the aristocracy of the capital act as trend setters, mimicked by those below them. The styles of the late Republic are patently generated by and for the Roman aristocracy, and express eloquently their public self-image.[70] It would be wrong to contrast the styles of the Empire as bourgeois, for they too reflect the taste of the imperial aristocracy. But they are well suited to also serve a much broader social spectrum, and the second part of this book will attempt to trace this process in the Vesuvian cities. As in other areas, notably the use of career inscriptions, a hierarchical language formulated under the Republic comes under the Empire to serve a much larger and more subtly differentiated population.[71]

CHAPTER 3

□

THE ARTICULATION OF
THE HOUSE

ONCE WE LEARN to read the social coding of architectural form and decoration, we should be able to come closer to understanding how the social space of the Roman house was articulated. What is at issue here is not so much identification of the physical function of an area (for eating, sleeping, cooking, washing, defecating, etc.), on which traditional room-labeling procedures focus. Rather we need to see how form and decoration guide the social flow of activity round the house, raising or dropping social barriers in the way of the actors concerned.

Three main groups made use of a Roman house: the owner's family, servants, and friends. The two axes of differentiation proposed earlier, of public/private and grand/humble, serve to distinguish these categories. The public/private axis distinguishes between the outsiders and the insiders; both slaves and family are insiders, though in social rank (grand/humble) they differ greatly. Friends are outsiders, if to varying degrees (a Roman called his closest friends his *familiares*), while their variation in social rank is reflected in the linguistic distinction of *amici* and *clientes*. Architecture and decoration served to channel the flow of these categories around the house, simultaneously distinguishing outsiders from intimates and grand from humble. The richer, more powerful, and more ambitious for social recognition the owner, the wider the social range of those

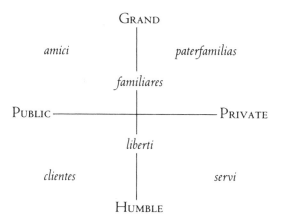

he would need to distinguish, having simultaneously more grand friends and humble slaves than would a mid-range houseowner.

One dominant imperative in a slave-owning society was to contrast adequately the servile and seignorial areas of the house.[1] It should be borne in mind that this is not simply a distinction of areas in which slaves were absent or present. Slaves were omnipresent in the rich household: *cubicularii*, *pedisequi*, and *ancillae* in the master's and mistress's bedroom—and presumably on call day and night, sleeping on mattresses at the bedroom door or in an antechamber; servers, cooks, tasters, carvers, and entertainers in the dining room; nurses, *paedagogi*, tutors, even grammarians and philosophers, round the children; and secretaries, clerks, and *dispensatores* round the master at work. Slaves indeed were as important as architecture in ensuring the proper social flow around the house, presenting living barriers to access to the master, from the ostiarius at the door to the cubicularii and *nomenclatores* (name callers) guarding the more intimate areas (Trimalchio's visitors were brought up short in their attempt to enter the triclinium by a slave's reproof).[2] The servile areas were those of exclusively menial or low-status activity—cooking, washing, working, and the private living and sleeping quarters of the slaves. But even among slaves there were sharply felt social hierarchies, chains of command from the *praepositus* (head of section) down to the *vicarius* (substitute), from the head cook (whose skills commanded inflated prices) down to his servers and oven-stokers, and there were positions of influence and power like that of the dispensator who controlled access to funds or the *cellarius* who controlled access to food supplies. As Ulpian comments, "It makes a great difference what sort of a slave he is, reliable, an *ordinarius* or *dispensator* or a common one or an oddjobber or any old one."[3] And even this "great difference" we find expressed in decoration, though whether financed out of the master's pocket or the slave's own *peculium* we cannot tell.

It is only in the richest houses that the slave/master distinction could and needed to be fully expressed. An important architectural feature of the houses is the way in which service areas are marginalized, thrust out to the edge of the imposing and often studiedly symmetrical master's quarters. The Casa del Menandro at Pompeii (Figs. 3.1–2) so successfully marginalizes its extensive servile areas that they are only accessible down long narrow corridors. The Casa dei Vettii (Figs 3.3–4), of a comparable degree of opulence, similarly succeeds in separating the service area, though it is directly accessible from the atrium. Here a secondary courtyard, dominated by a painting of the lares (hearth spirits), leads to the kitchen and a series of dark, ill-decorated bedrooms and storerooms. However, it is in cases where the architecture does not or cannot fully succeed in marginalizing service areas that the role of decoration becomes especially important. A striking recent example is the villa at Torre Annunziata ("Oplontis"), where the extensive service quarters lie at the center of the excavated half of the villa. What patently sets them apart is their decoration, with crude diagonal black and white stripes (Figs. 3.5–6), in a style which elsewhere too is regularly associated with low-status areas such as corridors and lavatories.[4] A more subtle example of differentials in a relatively modest house is offered by the Casa degli Amanti at Pompeii (Figs. 3.7–8). Here the kitchen, lavatory, and

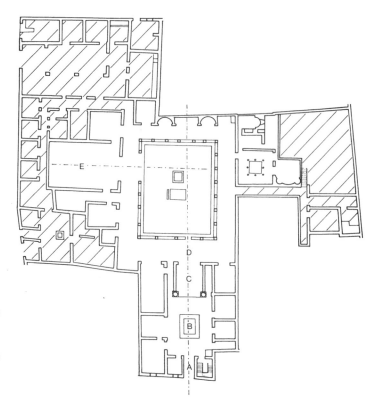

Figure 3.1 Plan, Casa del Menandro, Pompeii. A highly organized sightline runs from the entrance through tablinum and peristyle to the center of a symmetrical system of exedrae. A secondary sightline runs from the largest reception room through the fountain basin, placed off-center in the peristyle. Service areas (shaded) are only accessible down long corridors.

Figure 3.2 Casa del Menandro, Pompeii, corridor to service quarters. This is only reached via a dogleg in the far corner of the peristyle (see Fig. 3.1); the narrowness of the corridor further signals that this is not a reception area.

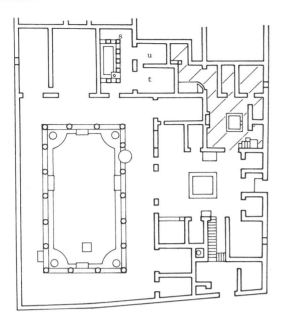

Figure 3.3 Plan, Casa dei Vettii, Pompeii. The service area (shaded) has its own atrium. Note also the separate suite s/t/u (see Fig. 3.25).

Figure 3.4 Casa dei Vettii, service court. A lararium to the left overlooks the impluvium. In the corner a door leads to the kitchen. The only decoration in this area of the (otherwise lavishly decorated) house is the pornographic decoration in the cubiculum beyond the kitchen.

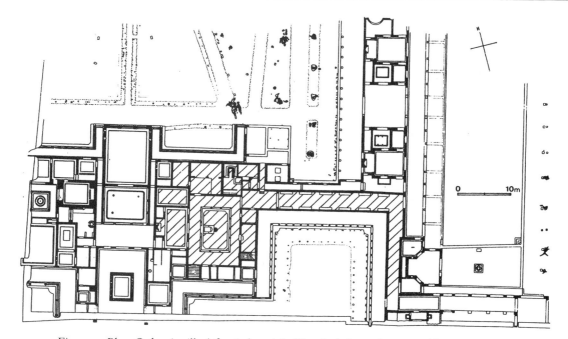

Figure 3.5 Plan, Oplontis villa (after Jashemski). The shaded area is presumably a service area, though it also seems to be used by visitors to the palaestra and swimming pool.

Figure 3.6 Oplontis villa, service-area peristyle. The crude zebra stripes extend through most of the shaded area on the plan and form a harsh contrast with the rich decoration elsewhere.

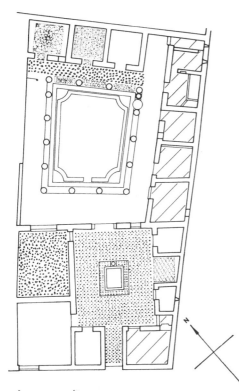

Figure 3.7 Plan, Casa degli Amanti, Pompeii (after Elia). Service areas (shaded) are to the right of the entrance, and the right-hand (north-facing) wing of the peristyle. Note that floor patterns mark the more elegant reception areas.

Figure 3.8 Casa degli Amanti, Pompeii, south wing of peristyle, viewed toward atrium, with service rooms to left. In the foreground is the well, close to the kitchen door.

associated service rooms occupy the south wing of the peristyle, the other wings of which contain the most prestigious rooms of the house. The decoration of the peristyle carefully differentiates the grand areas to the left as one enters, with their attractive white-ground paneling and duck motifs, from the crudely painted service wing to the right. The same contrast was, apparently, repeated on the upper floor.[5]

The aim of such marginalization, architectural and decorative, was to render the low-status areas "invisible" to the visitor. We may compare Pliny's descriptions of his own villas in which his minute account of "every corner" passes wholly over the service areas, except to remark the general position of rooms for slaves and freedmen in the Laurentine villa, and to comment (interestingly) that some of them were decent enough for putting up visitors.[6] This invisibility is also apparent in the modern publications, which rarely give more than passing notice to these relatively drab areas.

The contrast between the highly visible and the invisible areas is easy enough to read in the smarter houses. What is more elusive is the articulation of servile and free in more modest houses, where slaves might, for instance, be tucked away in now invisible upper stories. Nor is it easy in such houses to distinguish modestly but neatly decorated rooms which might equally (as Pliny envisages) be used for senior and trusted slaves and freedmen or for visitors. There is still much to be learned on this front.[7]

The Roman concern to differentiate slave and free is closely linked to the desire to articulate the house suitably for visitors. Here what is to a modern observer most striking about the richer houses is the low priority given to privacy. It is a misreading of Vitruvius if we take him to mean that there was a division between public rooms for the entertainment of visitors and private rooms for the family. This is to transport to antiquity the values of contemporary society, with its heavy emphasis on the privacy of the family unit. Vitruvius's contrast is not between public and private in our terms but between degrees of access to outsiders. Considering that the bedroom of the paterfamilias was a place for the reception of friends and the conducting of business, and remembering too the constant circulation of slaves, it must have been astonishingly difficult for an upper-class Roman to achieve real privacy. Nor did they apparently want to achieve privacy in several areas that we regard as intensely private, such as bathing and defecation, both regularly performed in public and communal establishments.[8] Indeed, the incompatibility of public life with privacy is something on which the Romans themselves commented. Augustus, we are told, when he wanted to conduct intimate business left his own house for that of a freedman, or for a refuge he called his "Syracuse." The archaeological evidence can and should be read in the light of such comments.[9]

One vivid sign of this lack of privacy is the visual transparency of the Roman house. The visitor standing in the fauces of the standard Vesuvian house is immediately presented with a vista that leads through the heart of the residence.[10] The emphatic importance of this vista is revealed by its elaborate symmetrical framing, by means of doorways and columns round the sides, and focal objects along the central axis—the impluvium basin, a marble table, and a statue or shrine at the end (Fig. 3.9). That this vista may not be geometrically symmetrical but only optically symmetrical—that is, symmetrical from the viewpoint of the observer in a given position—shows that the symmetry is not merely

Figure 3.9 Casa del Menandro, Pompeii, view of atrium toward fauces.

an architect's convenience but something designed to make an impression on the visitor.[11] This vista normally passes directly through the central point of the tablinum, and given its function as a morning reception area, one must visually reconstruct the owner sitting at the focus of the vista (or for that matter his wife, who "goes about in the middle of the house").[12] But the vista does not terminate with the tablinum: it passes through it, into the garden world of the peristyle or into an imaginary, painted garden,[13] and even past that to the mountain peaks of the real natural world (Fig. 3.10).[14] Beyond the visible owner lies (apparently) not the enclosed world of private space, nor indeed his neighbors crowding round, but the countryside and nature, even if suitably tamed. Comparison with Greek houses confirms the peculiarity of this phenomenon. There is no attempt at symmetrical framing of the vista from the entrance, whether in the fourth-century houses of Olynthos (Fig. 1.1), or in the grand peristyle houses and palaces of Hellenistic Pergamum (Fig. 3.11). The standard position for the andron, though close to the front door (and thus excluding the visiting male from the intimate and female-inhabited interior), is never opposite the entrance but rather to one side. Only in late Hellenistic Delos can anything similar be detected, when the andron is placed on the entrance axis and so on display to the world, and here we may infer Italian influence (Fig. 3.12).[15] The Greek house is concerned with creating a world of privacy, of excluding the inquisitive passerby; the Roman house invites him in and puts its occupants on conspicuous show.

Vitruvius's contrast is not between space for visitors and space for family but between space for uninvited and for invited visitors. Much closer in our terms is the contrast

Figure 3.10 Casa del Menandro, Pompeii, view from atrium toward peristyle.

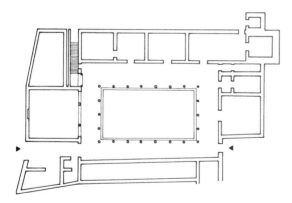

Figure 3.11 Plan, palace of Attalus, Pergamum. Although there is an axis across the peristyle, it is interrupted rather than framed by the positioning of the columns. Neither entrance leads to a significant vista.

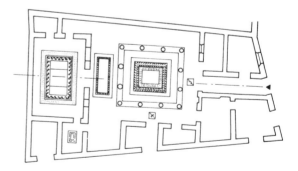

Figure 3.12 Plan, maison du Trident, Delos. Note the strong axial view from the main entrance, underlined by the positioning of mosaics.

between work and leisure. The Romans, as we have seen, lacked our distinctions of place of work (office, factory, etc.) from place of leisure (home). Business was regularly conducted at home, whether by an emperor receiving the reports of his secretaries and procurators, by a republican noble giving his legal advice, or by a merchant, craftsman, or shopkeeper operating from the *officina* (workshop) or *taberna* (shop) that were part of his house. To judge by the reports of daily routine, particularly those given by the younger Pliny, the *negotium*/*otium* (work/leisure) distinction of activity within the house corresponds broadly to a distinction of time, between morning and afternoon.[16]

The differentiation extends to space, and one can broadly distinguish the areas of public activity or business, which cluster round the main entrance—the atrium and tablinum and perhaps the cubicula and smaller rooms opening on the atrium—from the areas of private entertainment, which can only be reached by passing through further barriers—corridors and slaves posted at thresholds—and characteristically cluster round the peristyle. Of course one may find the best triclinium opening directly on the atrium, but where this does occur it suggests an inability to differentiate.[17] Thus the standard atrium-peristyle matrix of the Pompeian house, which is normally accounted for in terms of historical background (in the addition of the Hellenistic peristyle to the Italic atrium) has a structural significance in differentiating the accessible public areas of negotium from the less accessible private areas of hospitality.[18] Even in houses that lack a true peristyle (the majority) it is extremely common to find a secondary area differentiated from the front-door area and illuminated by an independent light-well (Fig. 3.13), and the frequency of this division points to the importance of the underlying social pattern.[19]

Decoration also helps to underline this differentiation. The decoration of atria is too varied to allow any useful generalizations (there is no single atrium style), but what is here relevant is the way in which contrasts are set up between the atrium and its associated areas and the peristyle (or peristyle substitute) and its surrounds.

An excellent and now readily accessible example in a house of relatively modest pretensions is offered by the Casa del Principe di Napoli at Pompeii (Figs. 3.14–17, Pl. 5).[20] In plan, the house falls neatly into two halves: rooms opening onto the atrium and rooms opening onto the porticoed garden. The decoration, which is all of a single phase, helps to set up a clear hierarchy. The appearance of the atrium is austere; the dominant impression—of the red bands that divide the white plaster into rectangles—is reminiscent of the masonry blocks of the first style, though below there are red panels with bird motifs. The atrium falls into two parts: the gloomy area to the right on entry, with no light source other than the impluvium, is where the service quarters are successfully marginalized: a porter's room (a) to the right of the entrance, without decoration, controlling stairs up to slaves' rooms above (Fig. 3.15), and opposite, the undecorated kitchen/lavatory (g) with a dark unplastered room beyond it (h) suitable for storage and perhaps slaves' eating space. The left-hand side of the atrium draws additional light from windows to the garden and is instantly more attractive (Fig. 3.16). Decoration supports this impression: the well-lit room corresponding broadly in position (and presumably function) to the traditional tablinum (e) is distinguished by elegant but simple

Figure 3.13 Casa del Mobilio Carbonizzato, Herculaneum. The axial view from the fauces, framed by the openings of the tablinum, is focused on the shrine on the end wall of the garden. The garden has no colonnade, but achieves a comparable effect to a peristyle.

Figure 3.14 Plan, Casa del Principe di Napoli, Pompeii (after Strocka). Service areas, to the right of the door, are shaded. Stairs up are located in the cella ostiaria (a) and kitchen (g). External stairs (p) lead to a separate apartment above. The main reception room (k), with its associated exedra (m), overlooks the garden (n), as does the tablinum (e) and the cubiculum at (f).

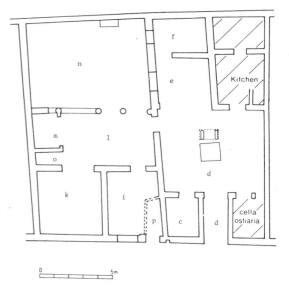

Figure 3.15 Casa del Principe di Napoli, Pompeii, view of atrium from tablinum toward entrance. In the far corner is a cella (a), with stairs to upper rooms.

Figure 3.16 Casa del Principe di Napoli, Pompeii, view of atrium from entrance. To the right is the kitchen, to the left the peristyle.

Figure 3.17 Casa del Principe di Napoli, Pompeii, portico. Small still-life panels are the focus of the decoration. The large entrance to the right is to room (i).

architectural articulation and simple still-life panels; beyond it a bedroom (f), also lit from the garden, has similar decoration. These two linked rooms, together with the atrium, might reasonably be assigned the function of "business" reception area.

The garden area establishes a clear contrast: an elegant portico leads (past a white-plastered room [i] of utilitarian function, Fig. 3.17) to the lavishly decorated triclinium (k) (i.e., major entertainment room) with its linked exedra or cubiculum (m) (i.e., private entertainment room), both distinguished by the rich fantasy architectural framework of the fourth style, with ambitious mythological paintings in the larger room, and figures of deities in the smaller (Pl. 5). Decoration and architecture cooperate to enhance the impression of luxury and privilege in the area most secluded from the front door and its general public traffic and the slaves' quarters. Private bedrooms for the family have been posited above the tablinum and kitchen,[21] but it is not clear that it is necessary or appropriate to imagine anyone other than children or slaves ascending the narrow wooden staircase that rises within the kitchen. The bedroom off the tablinum is surely the correct location for the private as well as the business life of the master.[22]

This house is valuable evidence because its decoration is all of a single style and period, and the contrasts set up by it must be assumed to be deliberate. Yet more often than not the decoration of surviving Roman houses is a hotchpotch of different styles and periods. It is easy to fall into the trap of supposing that we are looking at a house not of one moment (24 August A.D. 79) but of many successive moments, or of imagining all contrasts as accidental, due to chance redecoration. But for the living inhabitants of a house, the juxtaposition of old and new itself must have generated contrasts; and there are several cases in which we can see that the old was quite deliberately retained alongside the new.[23]

The Casa di Sallustio illustrates well how the retention of the old could create new effects. The first-style marble-incrustation decoration of its magnificent and spacious atrium area was carefully preserved over perhaps as long as two centuries, while alongside it the peristyle was richly and charmingly decorated in the "modern" taste of the early imperial period.[24] Why should we not accept that such contrasts could be both desired and effective? This is not to say that the contrasts always follow the same pattern; it is certainly possible to point to examples of houses where rich decoration concentrates on the atrium area, while areas beyond were left in a state of neglect.[25] But in all cases we ought to ask what the effects of such contrasts were, and how they related to the social life of the household.

The atrium-peristyle matrix was a heritage of the late Republic that left its character-istic stamp on the Vesuvian houses of A.D. 79. Yet there are slight but distinct signs of a shift in emphasis developing, which tends to a new pattern in the houses of the second century and is later exemplified at Ostia (e.g., the Casa della Fortuna Annonaria) and in the provinces. In the new pattern, the duality of atrium-peristyle is abandoned and is replaced by a single, columned court around which all reception rooms are grouped.[26] It is natural to ask whether this represents a new social pattern and abandonment of the contrast between public and private areas. Since the traditional atrium-alae-tablinum pattern in some sense embodies the patronus-cliens relationship of the republican nobil-ity, it might be tempting to see in the shift of emphasis from the atrium the abandonment of patronage and the withdrawal of the rich from public life.

This interpretation is not supported by our other evidence. The literary sources give no comfort to the idea of the abandonment of patronage under the early Empire; on the contrary, this is the period when patronal rituals are most abundantly attested.[27] And what archaeological evidence shows is not a retreat from public life but a continued penetration of public life into the house. In the republican house, the most important and striking vista, as we have seen, was that from the front door to the tablinum, and beyond it to the garden. From the start of the Empire there are signs that this image of self-presentation to the world outside lost in significance.[28] New vistas, within the peristyle, became more striking; the atrium vista dwindled in importance. So in the Casa dei Vettii (Fig. 3.3), the vista from the front door leads directly through to the peristyle; there is no tablinum in which the master can be found. More instructive is the Casa dei Cervi at Herculaneum (Fig. 3.18). Here, in contrast to the neighboring Casa dell'Atrio a mosaico, where the front door vista leads to the basilica-like structure discussed above, the atrium is dingy and unimposing. It has no axial center, only a glimpse through a door into a magnificent suite beyond. The whole visual drama of this house lies in the opposite axis that runs from the central black room with its fastigium through the peristyle to the sea view beyond, set in an architectural frame (Pl. 1). It is on this axis that the master of the house would present himself to the public.

What, then, we appear to be witnessing is the development of magnificent "audience rooms" that supplant the tablinum and focus on the peristyle rather than the atrium,

Figure 3.18 Casa dei Cervi, Herculaneum. The view from the entrance through the atrium
passes along a suite of rooms (see Fig. 2.3).

allowing for the eventual abandonment of the atrium as an architectural feature. This is
not a "bourgeois" pattern moving up from below; Domitian's new Palatine building
equally abandons the atrium. As did the shift in decorative styles brought in by the
Empire, this trend surely represents a shift away from the patterns of self-presentation
that typify the Republic—but rather than a stepping away from public life, it suggests
an attempt to impose greater control on the exposure of the master to the public. The
luxurious "private" life of the rich and powerful of the imperial period is precisely their
public facade, and access to it is a privilege carefully guarded.[29]

By the imperial period, a house which offered richly decorated reception in only the
atrium area was presumably operating under restraints of space and resources. One of the
most striking features of the richer surviving houses of A.D. 79 is the sheer proliferation
of space for entertainment. Trimalchio's boast of four *cenationes* (*Sat.* 77) is by no means
immodest to judge from the Campanian remains. The Vitruvian prescription of four
seasonally oriented dining rooms is not an adequate clue to this proliferation; for though
some degree of contrast in orientation is apparent and an approximate summer/winter
rhythm can be detected, houses like the Villa dei Misteri (Fig. 3.19) or that at Settefinestre
(Fig. 3.20), where disposition allowed orientation in four different directions, do not in
fact exploit this possiblity. Nor is it easy to explain multiplicity in terms of variation of

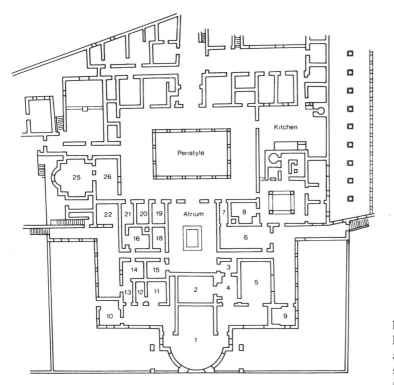

Figure 3.19 Plan, villa dei Misteri, Pompeii. Note double-alcove cubicula at 4, 8, and 16, and cubiculum/triclinium suites at 4/5, 8/6, and 11/12–14 (originally a single room).

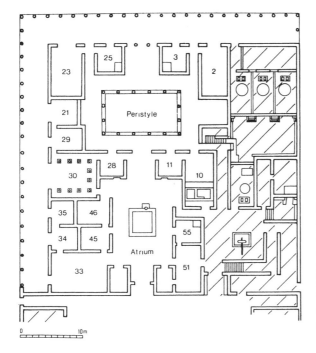

Figure 3.20 Plan, villa of Settefinestre, corpo padronale (after Carandini). Note double-alcove bedrooms at 3, 25, and 55; connected suites at 2/3, 23/25, 10/11, 51/55, 33/34/35/45/46; and the key suite at 28/30/29/21, with the oecus Corinthius (30) (see Fig. 2.9) at its heart. Service areas (wine and oil presses) are shaded. Slaves quarters are elsewhere.

function: to label some rooms *triclinia* and others *oeci* is at best to categorize their architectural form; inferences about social function are not possible.[30]

Rather the important factor seems to be the fact of multiplicity and choice itself. The Casa del Menandro (Fig. 3.1), outstanding at Pompeii in this as in other respects, has five major reception rooms of various size distributed around its peristyle. The largest of these, as we saw earlier, in its form and vast proportions points to a more public function than the normal private entertainment (Fig. 2.4); at the same time it is now clear that, situated at a point remote from the front door on a wing of the peristyle, it cannot have been a room of open public access. It does not stand alone but forms the climax of a suite of rooms running along the peristyle, linked to each other by connecting doors (Fig. 3.21). These lesser rooms have the proportions of a standard reception room and are carefully differentiated by color, red/black/yellow. Between the red and black rooms runs an intersecting corridor, leading to a smaller, more private room, presumably a cubiculum. To this suite, two further reception rooms on the north end of the peristyle, closer to the atrium, form a supplement (decoratively distinguished, the one as green, the other as red

Figure 3.21 Casa del Menandro, Pompeii, suite of interconnected rooms overlooking peristyle to left (see Fig. 3.1).

and yellow). It would be vain to attempt to attribute precise function to any of these rooms, not only because we lack the necessary evidence but also because there is no sign that Roman social life was so precisely and rigidly differentiated by social occasion as might be, say, a Victorian country house, with its drawing room, boudoir, parlor, study, smoking room, billiard room, and so forth.[31]

The essence of the Roman suite is that it provides an ample context for a crowded social life, allows guests to pass in astonishment from one fine room to another, and enables the master to hold court wherever the whim of the season or moment takes him. Cicero and Pompey, we are told, once tried to outwit Lucullus by inviting themselves to dinner that very evening and forbidding him to confer with the cooks about the menu. Lucullus, however, had the last laugh: he simply told his servant that he would dine that evening in "the Apollo," for each of his dining rooms had a fixed allowance for the dinner served there, and "the Apollo" was one of the most lavish.[32]

This otiose choice of which of a series of rooms to use for a particular function (dining) mirrors the upper-class pattern of multiplication of luxury villas up and down Italy, to be visited briefly according to the caprice of the moment. The social potency of such building derives from the manifest waste of space and money. The pattern of the Menander suite is easily paralleled in other very rich Vesuvian houses. One key suite in the Casa di Fabio Rufo (Fig. 3.22), built over the western city walls of Pompeii, has a lofty and richly decorated black room at its center (D), which is flanked by a red and a further black room (E, C).[33] The Casa dei Cervi at Herculaneum has a large black room leading to one (originally two) smaller but richly decorated reception room.[34] Its neighbor the Casa dell'Atrio a mosaico has an elegant suite overlooking the garden (Fig. 3.23,

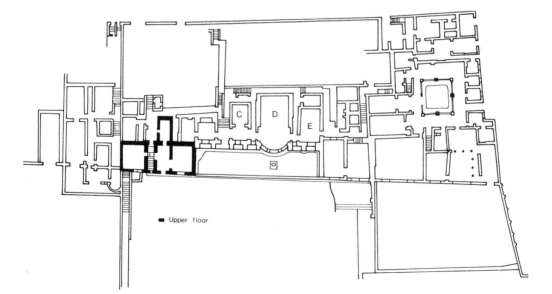

■ Upper floor

Figure 3.22 Plan, Casa di Fabio Rufo, Pompeii (after Barbet). The principal suite at C/D/E looks over a terrace and across the town wall toward the sea.

Figure 3.23 Casa dell'Atrio a mosaico, Herculaneum, view of suite of rooms facing west over garden (see Fig. 2.1).

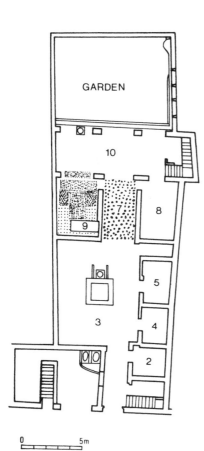

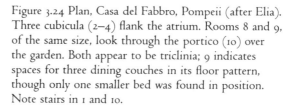

Figure 3.24 Plan, Casa del Fabbro, Pompeii (after Elia). Three cubicula (2–4) flank the atrium. Rooms 8 and 9, of the same size, look through the portico (10) over the garden. Both appear to be triclinia; 9 indicates spaces for three dining couches in its floor pattern, though only one smaller bed was found in position. Note stairs in 1 and 10.

Pl. 8). If such "waste of space" is not to be wondered at in the houses of the rich, its social potency comes across more clearly when it is mimicked in the houses of the humble. The very modest Casa del Fabbro (Fig. 3.24), next door to the Casa del Menandro, has two main reception rooms of almost the same size, equally fine decoration, and identical orientation toward the garden on either side of the passage from the entrance court.[35] No apparent functional contrast presents itself. It mattered to be able to say, "I have two cenationes."

For the same reason, it is virtually impossible to be specific in assigning the various bedrooms of the ground quarters to one or other member of the household. When Trimalchio boasts that his house has twenty bedrooms, he seemingly leaves those of his slaves, even apparently of his *hospites*, out of the count.[36] It is with evident surprise that Suetonius describes how Augustus used the same bedroom, in both summer and winter, for most of his life.[37] The younger Pliny seems to be closer to the upper-class norm in the casual way he describes the cubicula dotted around his villas: he has his favorites, but he makes clear that no single one is *the* master's bedroom.[38] The same deliberate wasteful consumption of space that affects the reception rooms surely applies to bedrooms, and it is rash to attempt to infer from the numbers of smartly decorated bedrooms in a particular house the size of the owner's family.[39]

What is worth observing is the way that the "master" bedrooms relate to other rooms in the house. There is a persistent pattern whereby a large reception room is juxtaposed to, and frequently by means of a connecting door physically linked to, a smaller room of suitable proportions for a bedroom. In the grandest houses, like the Casa del Labirinto, there may even be a cluster of such small rooms flanking a central reception room. That they served as bedrooms is confirmed by the typical presence of a bed niche, marked either architecturally or by contrasts in the decoration of walls and floor (though this has not deterred some from seeing in them women's dining rooms, segregated from men's dining rooms in accordance with an imaginary social ritual).[40] The coherence of such reception-room/bedroom units becomes especially clear where they are duplicated, notably in the pattern of fourfold repetition seen in the late republican structures of the Villa dei Papiri at Herculaneum, the Villa dei Misteri at Pompeii (Fig. 3.19), and the Sette-finestre villa (Fig. 3.20).[41] Here we find the further use of a bedroom alcove with vaulted ceiling, creating a notable hierarchy of intimacy that progresses from the reception room to the bedroom to the bed recess itself.

In such cases of duplication, a range of choice lies open to the master, though indeed the decoration of the rooms may privilege one set over the others, as was particularly the case with the "mysteries" suite in the Villa dei Misteri.[42] But we frequently find the same principle of linked reception/bedroom suites in much more modest houses where space allowed no duplication. The key rooms may interconnect, as do the black triclinium and the black cubiculum of the Casa del Frutteto; they may even be split by a corridor, as in the "private quarters" of the baker in the Casa del Forno (I 12.1) at Pompeii, or by a stairwell, as in the Casa del Sacerdos Amandus (I.7.7). In all these cases it is the close association of two rooms that distinguish themselves from the rest of the house by their decoration that points to the creation of a master suite.

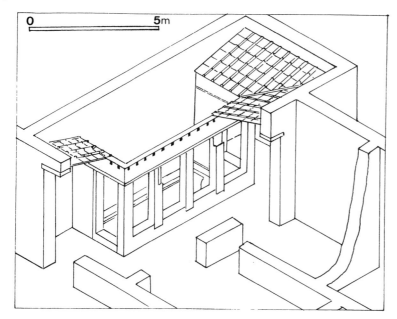

0   5m

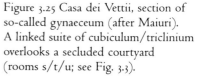

Figure 3.25 Casa dei Vettii, section of so-called gynaeceum (after Maiuri). A linked suite of cubiculum/triclinium overlooks a secluded courtyard (rooms s/t/u; see Fig. 3.3).

The recognition of such patterns has a certain value in helping to read the structure of individual houses. The peristyle of the Casa dei Vettii (Fig. 3.3), to take a familiar example, is surrounded by three reception rooms, one large (that of the cupids) and two medium in size. It has also a sort of annex alongside the largest reception room consisting of two interconnected rooms, the smaller clearly a cubiculum, approachable only through a miniature courtyard that illuminates them (Fig. 3.25). Traditionally this annex has been explained as a gynaeceum;[43] this, however, is only the product of the assumption that so secluded an area must be for women. That it is relatively secluded is clear—the visitor must pass many thresholds to reach it: from the front door, to the entrance to the peristyle, to the entrance to the cortile, to the entrance to the reception room, and thence (probably) to the cubiculum itself. But why assume that such seclusion was designed for the mistress as opposed to the master? There is no other cubicle on the peristyle, and the occurrence of the pair of interconnected rooms points to their importance. The arrangement is well designed to give a sense of increasing privilege in approaching the most intimate spot in the house.

But the real interest of this pattern lies in the implications for social life encapsulated within it. The triclinium is a place of reception, but so is the cubiculum, if on a more intimate scale (it is worth recalling that Tacitus sets his whole Dialogue on oratory in the cubiculum of the poet Maternus). The juxtaposition of the two rooms is the consequence of the desire to use the cubiculum for reception. Thus equipped, the Roman could carefully grade the degree of intimacy to which he admitted his amici—whether he received them promiscuously in the atrium, or entertained them in a large group in his grandest room, in a small group in his triclinium, or in ones and twos in his cubiculum.

Such a pattern would have been instantly comprehensible in seventeenth- or eighteenth-century England or France, where the *appartement* of *antechambre/chambre/cabinet*, or withdrawing room/chamber/closet, represented a hierarchy of intimacy, progressing from waiting room to reception room—for eating and sleeping as well as reception—to the inner sanctum of power. The similarities of layout are striking between the great republican villas and a house like Ragley Hall (Fig. 3.26). Again and again we need to strip away the assumptions that came with the industrial revolution concerning the use of the house. The boundaries between the public and the private have been transformed. For us the place of work is essentially separate from the home; social status is sought, confirmed, or lost, at work, not home, and if the home provides a context where success can be displayed, and the envy of the neighbors aroused, such display is idle, mere conspicuous consumption, since it is not in itself productive of success. The domestic world, though a place of entertainment, is one in which the family is cocooned from many of the pressures of social competition, rarely exposed to the inspection of either social superiors or inferiors. Being primarily the space of the family, priority is given in the home to the distinctions within the family, notably of parent and child. Further distinctions are primarily ones of function, and only secondarily of status: cooking, eating, relaxing, sleeping can no longer be easily arranged in a hierarchy.

The seventeenth-century house, like the Roman house, was one in which distinctions of rank and etiquette were dominant. The house did not merely reflect but generated status. Social success depended partly on the skill and understanding one displayed in playing a game of contact with others of widely varying social rank; on treating the distinguished with distinction and the obscure with sufficient distance. In a world oiled by patronage, social success could be heavily dependent on this domestic game. Conse-

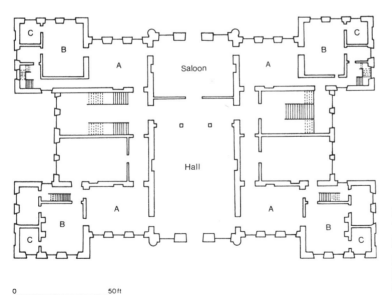

Figure 3.26 Plan, Ragley Hall, Warwickshire (c. 1678) (after Girouard). Four symmetrical suites open off the public area of hall/saloon, each with the progression antechamber (A)-chamber (B)-closet (C).

quently, the formal house of the period, like the grand Roman house, was arranged in terms of suites and apartments, with a succession of rooms differing more in hierarchic value than function. Here *privacy* takes on a different meaning: it involves separation from the vulgar crowd, but not from the battles of the social world outside.[44]

———

MY CONCERN has been to understand the social patterns that dictated the structure and decoration of the Roman house in the later Republic and early Empire. To do so, we must treat the house as a coherent structural whole, as a stage deliberately designed for the performance of social rituals, and not as a museum of artifacts. Realities in particular cases, the sceptic might object, are not so simple. It is the privilege of the spendthrift to conform his surroundings precisely to his needs and desired self-image. The majority, even of the rich, must live with compromise, houses designed by many hands, by a succession of architects half-following, half-steering the requirements of a succession of owners.[45] Many must have felt constrained by the inadequacies of what they had inherited, frustrated by their own inability to preserve it from decay and disintegration. Too often the house must have proved an insufficient shell for the life within it, unable to respond to the ever-moving life cycle of its inhabitants, the gradual or sudden rises and falls in prosperity or status.[46] On the other hand, even the most lavishly financed building may be poor evidence of the life of its inhabitants. The tallest atria may be empty and echoing; perhaps architecture expresses ideology or aspirations better than realities. But while all these points should be remembered in considering any individual house, what is here at issue is the recurrent pattern, the ideal type rather than the individual specimen.

The argument I put forward is that marked patterns distinguish the Roman house of the period from the houses of other societies (notably Greek) and other times, and that the dominant factor in determining these patterns is the interpenetration of the public and private life of the Roman ruling class. I have tried to illustrate how the basic structures are determined by the (to us) astonishingly public nature of domestic life, and how little weight contemporary Western preoccupations with privacy and family life carry. Implicit in the architectural forms and decoration of the Roman house is a language or social code that draws constantly on allusions to public and nondomestic forms.

A corollary of the argument is that the language of form and decoration even at a very modest social and economic level is dictated by the needs of the dominant social class. Particularly in the case of wall decoration, we see a development from the direct imitation of public structures by the republican nobility to the evolution of a complex and subtle language of allusion, socially widespread in its employment. This question of social diffusion deserves a fuller examination, to which I turn in the second part of this book.

But it is worth offering a preliminary reflection on the social significance of this phenomenon. It is possible, and among ancient historians even traditional, to view culture as something superficial that at best enriches the life of the elite, at worst merely serves as fuel for snobbery. If so, we may laugh at the Trimalchios of the Roman world as imitating the cultural language of the nobility for its snob value. But such an approach to culture seems to me both too cynical and too limited. Social anthropology points to a deeper reading of cultural languages, as serving to define the structures of integration within society, to articulate the social hierarchy, to include and exclude, communicate and excommunicate. Instead of laughing at Trimalchio's buffoonery, we might look at him as the insecure product of a highly mobile society fighting to establish his membership in that society. Because a Roman's house played a vital part in establishing his social position, we have, in the abundant houses that (more or less) survive, a particularly valuable document. For they not only constitute a reflection of other social realities now invisible but are in themselves one of the means by which the Romans constructed their social world.

PART II

SAMPLING POMPEII AND HERCULANEUM

HOUSES AND URBAN TEXTURE

IN A GENERAL sense, the evidence of Pompeii (not forgetting, as is easy, Herculaneum) has been endlessly exploited. One might argue that Pompeii has been only too dominant in setting our conceptions of the society of the early Empire: too urban and too Campanian. Hence, in part, the current attention to survey work that takes us out into the countryside.[1] But ancient civilization lies in a symbiosis of town and country, and it is premature to say that we understand Pompeii. It is at once the most studied and least understood of sites. Universally familiar, its excavation and scholarship prove a nightmare of omissions and disasters. Each generation discovers with horror the extent to which information has been ignored, neglected, destroyed, and (the most wanton damage of all) left unreported and unpublished. Enormous efforts are being made now to repair the damage, but the sheer size of the site continues to defeat.[2]

There are other obstacles in the boundaries of disciplinary specialization. Much excellent work has been done in the last generation by both classical archaeologists and social historians. Archaeological (and, more specifically, art historical) study has elaborated with great finesse the chronology of decorative fashions, while fighting shy of any systematic investigation of the implications for social history.[3] Simultaneously, social historians have revealed much about the political, social, and economic structures of the city through study of epigraphic documentation, without making more than incidental use of strictly archaeological material.[4] This is absurd, for the archaeological evidence is the best social document Pompeii has to offer.

All this means that there is still ample scope for using Vesuvian evidence to illuminate the social and cultural world of late Republic and early Empire. In particular, the archaeological evidence is susceptible to quantification—imperfect, without doubt, but at least to an extent that allows us to move beyond the impressionism that is bound to affect social history based purely on literary sources. In using the evidence of Pompeii and Herculaneum to achieve a more controlled analysis of Roman households, I do not underestimate and shall not conceal the methodological difficulties involved. Often the results of this investigation prove ambiguous and frustrating. Even so, there is enough to gain a far less anecdotal picture of the full spectrum of urban society, from little shops to magnificent mansions; enough to understand how households were populated, how space was used, and how the language of architecture and decoration was deployed in the construction of social standing.

VITAL STATISTICS

The first step should be toward some purely statistical calculations. It is true that Della Corte's *Case ed Abitanti di Pompei* expended considerable ingenuity in pinpointing the social standing of house owner after house owner; and for Herculaneum, Maiuri was prepared to characterize socially not only the final owners, but their predecessors as well. Much of this has passed into general circulation in guide books, the "Life at Pompeii" literature, and the oral tradition offered to visitors. But too little is reliable to be of use.[5] Della Corte's use of graffiti and dipinti (painted messages) conjured names of owners out of thin air; while Maiuri's use of house decoration to infer the status of the owner would in the present context lead to circularity. It is, we shall see, pure assumption that the builder of a handsome tablinum such as that in house V.ii at Herculaneum had been a "patrician," or that crude patching of earthquake damage in the same house indicates its descent into the vulgar hands of a member of the *ceto mercantile*.[6]

Doubtless there are broad limits within which one can speculate with reasonable confidence about the standing of the inhabitants of any particular house, on the basis of a general knowledge of the sites uncontrolled by statistics. Nobody would doubt that the owner of the Casa del Menandro, with its spacious peristyle, handsome decoration, luxurious private baths, spectacular silver service, and extensive service quarters, would have been of the highest standing in local terms, and arguably on the level of the senatorial elite at Rome itself; and the epigraphic evidence may point to the consular family of the Poppaei Sabini. Or, at the other end of the scale, there is no mistaking the relative modesty of the likely inhabitants of the two upper flats in the flimsily constructed Casa a Graticcio in Herculaneum, which sometimes does duty as the "typical" artisanal dwelling, though in fact neither flat is without decoration, charm, and a scatter of possessions improbable among the truly poor.

But this anecdotal method throws too much weight on subjective impression and uncontrolled conjecture. Some sort of statistical control is essential. Just how big is a big house, how small a small one? What is the distribution of the various sizes? What architectural and decorative features, and what level of possessions, indicate wealth or social standing? Can one distinguish wealth and rank—for instance, the wealthy freedman from the local magistrate? What is the relationship between residential and nonresidential (commercial, artisanal, horticultural, etc.) use of space, and what does the fact that part of a given house is used nonresidentially indicate about the social and economic position of the inhabitants? All these are questions to which Maiuri (and many others) presuppose a series of answers, but on which no explicit or systematic discussion has focused.

In offering now an experiment in supplying some preliminary answers, I do not delude myself that definitive figures are attainable. It is difficult to set up any statistical experiment without building in presuppositions in the form of the questions asked; there is a tendency to find precisely what you were originally looking for. The approach also threatens to reify the questionable categories from which the enquiry started: as we shall see, in counting "houses" not the least interesting point that emerges is how fluid the boundaries are and how slippery the category of "house" proves to be. At the same time, a statistical approach tends to stress factors that allow themselves to be reduced to numerical values; if the ground area of houses tends to feature largely in what follows, this is because it is a feature that lends itself to measurement. Above all, there is a need for caution in the interpretation of statistics. In drawing inferences from a given pattern of figures, it is necessary to be alert both to statistical significance and to significance in the layman's sense. Apparently contrasting (or similar) patterns of figures may be the product of the random scatter of chance; statistical science offers methods of calculating mathematically (via such factors as standard deviation and standard error) the probability of a given set of figures resulting from mere chance. In the interests of intelligibility, I have on the whole avoided any calculation requiring mathematical sophistication.[7] But even if one has established statistically significant patterns, it does not follow that inferences of any historical significance can be based on them. Rather than using statistical analysis to generate supposedly significant figures, I have thought it more fruitful to use them to test assumptions based on impressions and to throw up new questions.

Analysis of the whole of Pompeii is out of the question. In the first place, the labor would be immense, and its value would be undermined by the law of diminishing returns.[8] In the second place, neither state of publication nor state of preservation would permit it. Pompeii is the victim of more than two centuries of archaeological experiment, and it is no surprise that so much of the site now stands ruinous or obstructed by a fairy-tale thicket of impenetrable scrub. The state of publication of what has been disinterred (*excavated* is largely a misnomer) is equally lamentable: only in exceptional periods have even sketchy reports been made public, and omissions continue to include virtually all excavations since the Second World War. Small wonder that, in the face of obstacles of this magnitude, systematic study has been lacking.

Sampling offers a way around these problems, at least in part. So long as one can isolate a representative sample of a given population, it is superfluous to undertake the costly and usually (as in this case) impossible business of examining the whole population. But is it possible to take a truly representative sample of Pompeian houses? Most scholarly discussion of the site (and almost all discussion of wall-decoration) depends on taking a scattered selection of houses. Although at first sight this technique might seem to suggest random sampling, it is the opposite. Houses are chosen for their bearing on the matter being discussed, and because it is more often than not an aspect of fine decoration or architecture, the best known and most frequently discussed houses are inevitably a special set, only too likely to coincide with the better-off inhabitants. A "small" house seen from this perspective is likely to tend toward the average overall.[9]

By choosing a group of adjacent blocks (*insulae*)[10] it is in fact possible to get a remarkably good cross-section of the range of Pompeian houses. That this is so is a result of the strikingly mixed distribution of houses in Pompeii (see below). To achieve a representative cross section, I have chosen three different samples for comparison. The first is a group of seven adjacent blocks, comprising some seventy-eight houses, in Regio I (Fig. 4.1).[11] Excavated in the course of this century, mostly by Maiuri, they represent the best-preserved major section of the city. This is essential, for the houses which have suffered most neglect are those that are poorest in the material sense. Any gulf between rich and poor will be much exaggerated by the tendency to preserve and even improve the finest houses, while the plaster and masonry of the poorest is left to disintegrate. But while *relatively* well preserved, this group of blocks is very unevenly published and studied. The first publications of Insulae 6, 7, and 10 must count among the most thorough to date in Pompeii;[12] Insula 10 has the additional advantage of being the focus of the very complete British survey.[13] On the other hand, Insulae 8, 9, 11, and 12 were excavated in the early 1950s in a great hurry and remain without excavation reports, though individual houses have been examined by various scholars.[14]

As a control I have taken a group of eight blocks, comprising some 104 houses, in Regio VI (Fig. 4.2). Excavated in the course of the nineteenth (and very early twentieth) century, the preservation of this area is very uneven, and if it sometimes enjoys the reputation of having been the "smart" quarter, this is partly due to the virtual obliteration of all but the show houses. Again the publication is very uneven: the more westerly blocks predate the days of archaeological reporting, but the easterly blocks were reported, particularly by Sogliano and August Mau, one of the giants of Pompeian scholarship.[15]

As a second control I turned to the central group of four Insulae (fifty-two houses) in Herculaneum (Fig. 4.3). This has several attractions. By affording a glimpse of a different town it helps to reveal in what ways Pompeii itself may have been atypical, even if in two neighboring towns the differences are in any case not likely to have been

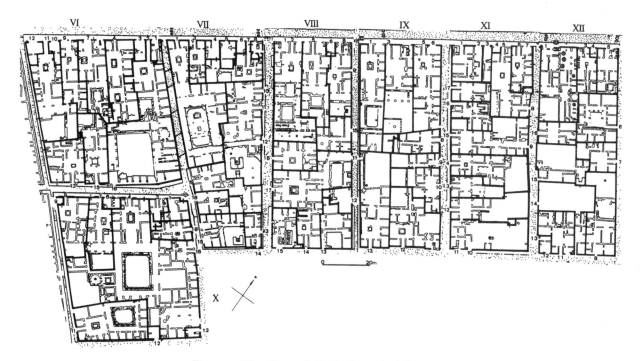

Figure 4.1 Plan, Pompeii, Regio I sample (after *CTP*).

marked. Its excavation, like that of Regio I in Pompeii, is relatively recent, and it is if anything rather better preserved. It has the particular advantage of preserving much of the upper floors, which also existed at Pompeii but have been largely lost. Finally, it is fully published in the lavish volume by Maiuri, though here, as elsewhere, he eschewed the humdrum details that are normal in archaeological reporting, including virtually any mention of the finds.[16]

In gathering data, I have made a detailed study of all the houses in the Regio I and Herculaneum samples, and a partial study in the (far less rewarding) Regio VI. However, in order to avoid distortions resulting from either bias or ignorance, I have only made use

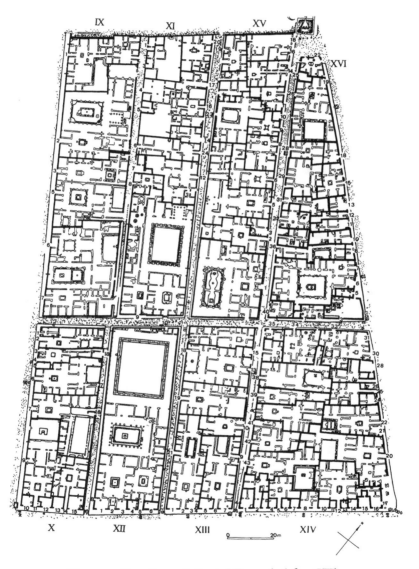

Figure 4.2 Plan, Pompeii, Regio VI sample (after *CTP*).

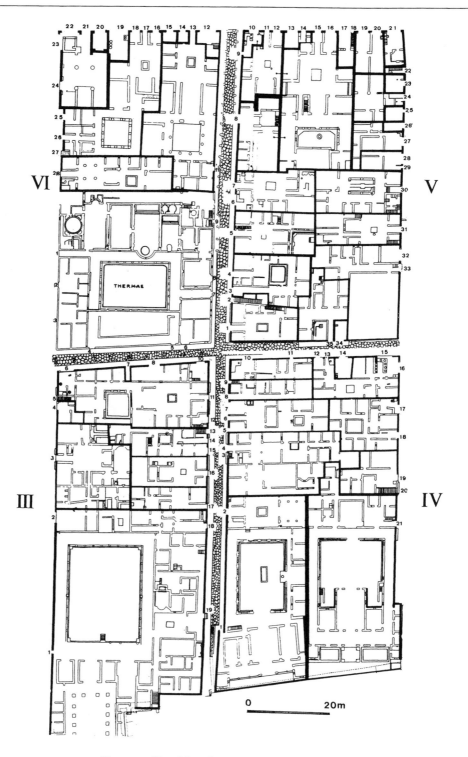

Figure 4.3 Plan, Herculaneum sample (after Maiuri).

of my data where confirmed by published sources. Three major recent works have been essential in supplying data. The first is Hans Eschebach's *Die städtebauliche Entwicklung Pompejis* (1970). As the first attempt to list systematically all excavated houses, and above all to give a detailed general plan, this has been of constant help to students of Pompeii for twenty years. However, as detailed inspection of Regio I soon revealed, it is highly unreliable in point of detail. Mapping errors even afflict houses published accurately in *Notizie degli Scavi*, but the sheer magnitude of the task bravely undertaken by Eschebach is adequate excuse. His work has been in part superseded by a much more ambitious and thorough project, the series of volumes of the *Corpus Topographicum Pompeianum*. Though much of this project suffers from the inclusion of inessential information, the new maps of volume 3, both the overall site plan and particularly the block-by-block plans at 1:500 scale, are admirable, and correct every error in Eschebach that I have observed.[17] While Eschebach and the *CTP* provide information in ground plans, decorative features are now comprehensively surveyed in the official catalogue to the photographic archive, *Pitture e Pavimenti di Pompei* by Bragantini, De Vos, and others.[18] This seemingly impenetrable list of decorative features, house by house, room by room, wall by wall, offers an excellent tool for statistical purposes. It satisfies one important requirement for statistics in its comprehensiveness, and offers a clear and accurate record of the period and degree of elaboration of all wall, ceiling, and floor decoration either surviving or once photographed. It would be of great value if the project were extended to Herculaneum.

Finally, the recent publication of a semiofficial inventory and computer-based analysis of Pompeii has a direct bearing on my own project. The two volumes of *Pompei. L'informatica al servizio di una città antica* (1988) constitute a major step toward rectifying neglect of basic statistics.[19] This offers a new official cartography of the site; unfortunately, the presentation is much inferior to that of the *CTP*, and where it differs in point of detail, suggests more hurried and less reliable surveying. In addition it offers a new directory identifying the houses region-by-region according to usage. Here too it is less than fully reliable, for the identifications of usage are conventional, not the result of new research; and while it performs a useful service in identifying the *principal* entrance of each complex that has several entrances and multiple usage, the subsequent analysis confuses the issue by treating each door as a separate unit. Its major drawback, however, as a contribution to statistical analysis of the site, is the complete absence of measurements. To treat every unit as equal, irrespective of size, is to invite misunderstanding, as the bar charts and pie charts analyzing usage of space soon reveal. Ambitious projects to establish at Pompeii a computer center with a database that rectifies these shortcomings are now in progress, and it is to be hoped that it will soon be possible to control and move beyond my own experimental and tentative calculations.

From a database covering some 234 houses in the three sample areas, a range of information can be assembled for each house.

    1. *Size.* How large is the house (ground area)? How many rooms does the ground floor comprise? How much of the ground area is built over, how much open?

2. *Function.* What proportion is residential? What proportion serves some economic function—commercial/artisanal, horticultural, or other?

3. *Architecture.* Does the house have an impluviate atrium? Does it have a colonnaded garden (peristyle), and if so of what size and with how many colonnades? How much space does it occupy?

4. *Decoration.* How many rooms have wall decoration, and in which of the four standard styles? How many have notable decorative features, especially mythological paintings and mosaic floors?

Most of these questions can be answered with a reasonable degree of reliability for the majority of the houses involved. Ideally, a fifth category should be added, covering the nature and richness of the finds (silver, carved marble or bronze, coins, utensils in bronze, glass, terracotta, and so on), but the states of publication and of scholarship make this aim frustratingly unattainable (see below).

In the following chapters, I shall look at each of these aspects in turn, exploring both the rationale for and limitations to these questions and examining the implications of the results that emerge.

SIZES AND DISTRIBUTION

In general terms, one may expect the size of a house to be a measure of the wealth and status and number of its inhabitants. For the Romans in particular, size is likely to be of significance; the *laxitas* of the spreading houses of the rich attracted persistent criticism from the moralizers of the period,[20] and we have Vitruvius (see above, Chap. 1) to remind us that public figures needed ample reception space and that the humble did not. House size constituted not merely an indirect reflection but an explicit statement of social rank; the municipal law of Tarentum actually required any decurion of the city to possess a house there with a roof of a minimum fifteen hundred tiles,[21] and one would anticipate similar expectations at Pompeii. The prevalence and scale of slave owning in the period is another vital factor; because slaves were at once a product and a symbol of wealth, the houses of the wealthy were likely to have been both larger and more populous.

The first step must be to measure the ground area of each house. No published figures are available, but the much improved cartography makes measurements adequate for the purpose possible, that is, normally to within about 10 percent either way. Various limitations on the value of this exercise are worth noting. The first is a difficulty in the definition of *house.* In the majority of cases the matter is unambiguous: it is a unit of habitation (which may also be used for nonresidential purposes) that is inaccessible from any other unit; one may only gain access via the public street. But there are other units, particularly small shops and large horticultural areas, that may well have been uninhabited. We cannot be sure. To exclude them would be arbitrary; we must therefore stretch the definition of house (*unit* would be a more neutral, if pedantic, term) to include these, but must remain conscious of the possibility that any unit with a predominantly nonresidential function may not have been inhabited. Similarly, there were almost certainly some houses which by A.D. 79 were uninhabited because abandoned. Only careful examination of the finds can establish abandonment with reliability, but inadequate publication of a large proportion of these houses makes the necessary information unavailable. Therefore, the possibility that any given unit may have been unoccupied in A.D. 79 must be borne in mind.[22]

In some cases it is clear where to draw the boundaries of a house. Many units are evidently formed either by combining previously separate units, or alternatively by splitting up a single unit. The most common case of the latter is where a shop has been opened up in what was a front room in a house; traces of this process are visible in blocked-off doors (one of the merits of the *CTP* map is that it marks such *ostia murata ab antiquis* systematically). In these cases it is obviously right to treat a shop, if inaccessible from the house, as a separate unit. In a statistical comparison, it is necessary to limit the enquiry to one point in time (in theory 24/25 August A.D. 79), though we are constantly reminded that Pompeii was an organic entity in a state of flux, each unit the product of changes in the past, and in turn liable to generate changes in the future.[23]

The hardest cases are those in which two houses are linked by an interconnnecting door, and yet potentially function as separate units. Here it has been necessary to exercise discretion. Thus I 12.1–2 is formed of two units of the same size; one is a bakery, complete with mills, mixing room, oven, and stables, while the other is a residential unit (Fig. 4.4). The interconnecting doors show that this functioned as a single unit, and it has been treated as such; but naturally the fact that half is a bakery will affect our expectations of signs of wealth in the residential quarter.

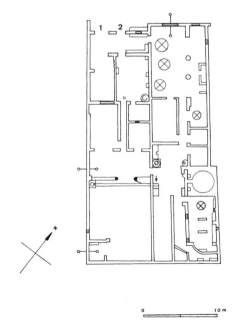

Figure 4.4 Plan, Casa del Forno (I 12.1), Pompeii (after *CTP*). The house is formed of two sections, originally separate. The right-hand section is taken up by the bakery, mills, stables, oven, and bread-making room. The left is the private quarters, with a triclinium and cubiculum overlooking a porticoed garden. The two sections link near the street and at the back.

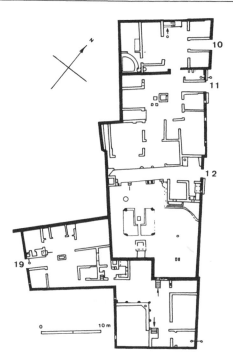

Figure 4.5 Plan, Casa dell'Efebo, Pompeii (after *CTP*). Though one complex, this divides into three distinct units of habitation, with main entrances at 10, 11, and 19.

On the other hand, the complex at I 7.10/11/12/19 (the Casa dell'Efebo), while formed from up to four previous units, falls distinctly into two halves, each with a separate main entrance (at 10 and 19), atrium, and garden (Fig. 4.5). Connected at the bottom of their respective gardens by a small door and a flight of steps, they ought in A.D. 79 to have formed a single unit of ownership. Yet it is hard to envisage their operation except as two separate units of habitation, and I have followed *CTP* and others in treating them as separate "houses." But in reality the division goes further. Entrances 10 and 11 are both apparently main doors, and inside the house between them were found traces of a heavy wooden partition with locks.[24] The whole house, then, is quite likely to have functioned as three separate units; but because features like wooden partitions do not appear on the ground plans, such subdivisions are obscured. In interpreting the statistics, it is necessary to allow for the possibility of multiple residence within units like this. At the very least, they serve to remind us that units of *habitation* or *usage* are not the same as units of *ownership*. Ownership is much harder (and usually impossible) to trace archaeologically; we must often deal with rented accommodation and the like.

The second limitation on the value of measuring ground area is that it ignores the vertical dimension. Herculaneum offers a vivid reminder of the frequency of upper floors, and though these do not generally survive in Pompeii, architectural traces, particularly stairs, show that the same was the case there. Measurement of the ground floor alone is not equivalent to total living space, though it may act as an indicator. For some purposes, this limitation is of great significance—for instance, in any calculation of population, it would be foolish to lay weight on the number of bedrooms *downstairs*. Again, the absence of decoration on the ground floor does not prove its absence from the house as a whole, and, as we shall see, it is by no means unlikely that undecorated shops had decorated living quarters above. But the limitation does not matter where one is comparing like with like. The ground area of a house dictates its maximum possible size, and a plot with a smaller ground area cannot sustain a larger house than a plot with a larger ground area, so long as the two are of the same constructional type. To compare the ground area of a Pompeian house to that of an Ostian multistory insula would be highly misleading, and for this reason I have deliberately omitted from the sample the Palaestra block at Herculaneum, the one case of a multistory brick and concrete block.[25] As with the problems of defining a "house," this limitation will have an important bearing on our *interpretation* of any statistics, but it does not mean that the data is less worth gathering and analyzing.

Uncertainty about what constitutes a house, and just what it is that we are counting and comparing, may seem to diminish the value of the exercise. But the very uncertainties are its most illuminating outcome. *House*, like *regio* or *insula*, or for that matter *family*, is a modern concept, derived from our assumptions about how life is or should be organized. The extent to which we discover that our concepts of house and family do not comfortably fit the Pompeian material is the measure of our progress in learning to reconceptualize the material, and instead of conforming it to our categories, allowing it to build its own. To these uncertainties the analysis will repeatedly return, and the reader should not be lulled by the apparent precision of the figures and charts offered into supposing that the aim of the argument is to generate "hard" statistics.

Let us, then, first consider the distribution of house sizes, measured on ground area alone. Anyone visiting the sites or even consulting the map must be struck by the extreme variation in sizes of units and the intricate jigsaw they form, an interlocking pattern of large and small units within virtually every block. That pattern surely reflects social contrasts between the now invisible inhabitants. One has only to compare the site plan of these Roman towns to those of Greek cities like fourth-century Olynthos (Fig. 4.6) or third-century Priene, with their regular blocks of equal house plots laid out in neat grid patterns, to realize how remarkable and interesting the Vesuvian evidence is. If the classical Greek evidence points to democratic societies with *oikoi* (households) of regular and predictable size,[26] Pompeii and Herculaneum surely suggest a society with very unequal distribution, whether of wealth or of family or household size.

Figure 4.7 (cf. Table 1) attempts to represent the range of plot sizes and their distribution by grouping them into successive bands of $100m^2$ up to $1,000m^2$, and larger bands thereafter. Not surprisingly, it emerges that the smaller size is also the more common, and if the group with the largest number of plots, that of houses under $100m^2$, is subdivided, those under $50m^2$ are commoner than those above. What is more impressive is the result of comparison of the three component samples (Fig. 4.8). They are remarkably consistent in the broadly similar distribution of different sizes within each sample. It is also striking how similar the average house size in each area is (all figures in square meters):

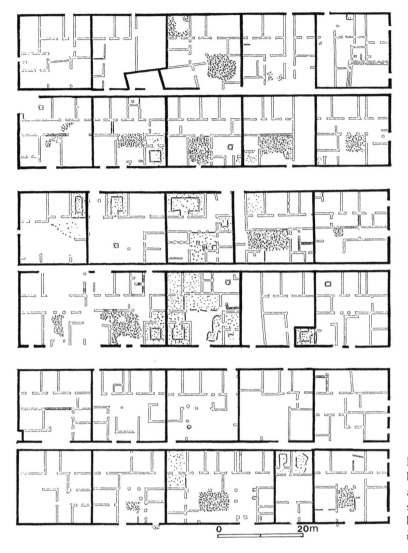

Figure 4.6 Plan, Olynthos, blocks of houses (after Robinson and Graham). Contrast the standard size of units within the blocks to the uneven sizes of those in the Pompeian plans.

Pompeii Reg. I	266	Herculaneum	241
Pompeii Reg. VI	289	Overall	271

These figures in turn may be compared with those given for the Greek "Typenhaus" or standard oikos unit:[27]

Priene	207	Miletos	259
Abdera	212	Olynthos	294
Kassope	226	Dura Europos	311
Piraeus	242		

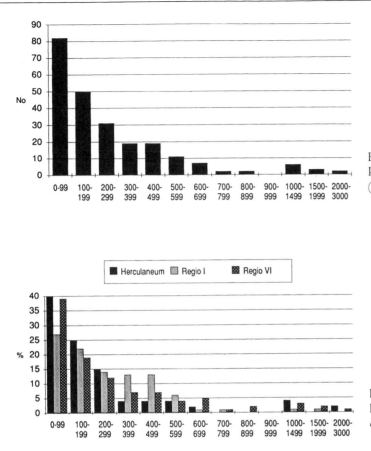

Figure 4.7 Distribution of houses in Pompeii and Herculaneum samples (total numbers).

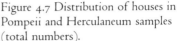

Figure 4.8 Distribution of houses: Pompeii and Herculaneum samples compared.

The vital difference lies in the fact that the Greek figures represent the sizes of "typical" house-plans repeated again and again within the same blocks, while the Vesuvian figures are mathematically derived averages from houses of a wide range of sizes.

In itself, this consistency in the three groups of houses suggests the potential value of the sampling method. It confirms that a sample of as few as fifty-two houses in adjacent blocks will give a reasonable cross section of house sizes at least, and that this cross-section is not likely to be radically different in different areas of the city, or even within two neighboring Campanian towns. It also suggests that our understanding of the distribution of house sizes in these towns would not improve greatly if we (say) doubled the size of the sample. Figure 4.9 compares the distribution of house sizes in the total sample of 234 houses with that of the Regio VI sample (104 houses); the close similarity of the patterns shows how little is changed by doubling the sample size.

This is far from suggesting some sort of total homogeneity, let alone an identical pattern in all Roman towns. Of course, there are marked variations in distribution from block to block and from area to area.[28] Thus it is notable that shops cluster along the

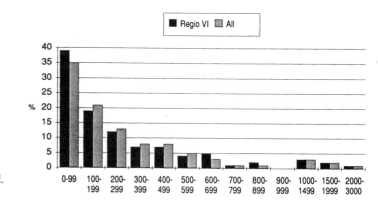

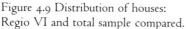

Figure 4.9 Distribution of houses:
Regio VI and total sample compared.

frontages of main streets. Since each of the three samples includes at least one major public thoroughfare, the smallest units, formed by shops, are well represented in each sample. But there are blocks in Pompeii, like VI 9, 11, and 15, that have few small units, and others, like VI 16 (on the intersection of two main roads), with disproportionately many. The largest houses too may tend to cluster locally. Herculaneum offers an unmistakable cluster of very grand houses along the seawall, doubtless attracted by the fine view of the bay, while in Regio VI of Pompeii there is something of a cluster of larger houses along the Via di Mercurio leading directly to the head of the forum. It is also possible to detect local groupings of commercial and horticultural plots in Regio I (below). But even these minor local variations are not enough to disrupt the underlying pattern of mixture of large and small. There is no hint of the sort of zoning that typifies the post-industrial city and which has attracted so much attention among urban geographers (Fig. 4.10).[29]

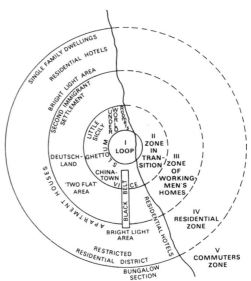

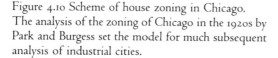

Figure 4.10 Scheme of house zoning in Chicago.
The analysis of the zoning of Chicago in the 1920s by Park and Burgess set the model for much subsequent analysis of industrial cities.

Other basic measurements may help refine the picture of the range of housing suggested by ground area alone. One traditional and convenient measure of house size is number of rooms. The value of this measure is obviously limited by our inability to quantify missing upper rooms, but so long as it is remembered that these figures are not equivalent to a total room count, they are of great assistance in comparing like with like. A "room" is as elusive to define as a "house." Standard plans carry room numerations, but many of the numbers refer to public circulation areas rather than rooms (e.g., fauces, atria, alae, passages, or peristyle gardens). I have excluded such areas from the count, as well as areas too small to rate as rooms (especially latrines and small cupboards/storerooms). Generally I take a room to be an enclosed area accessible through its own door, though even with this restriction there are often ambiguities, and my figures (Table 4.1) must be taken as approximate, establishing an order of magnitude.

Because a room count does not adequately reflect the importance of areas like peristyle gardens, I have added a further figure for the ground area of open space within the house, whether its use was utilitarian or recreational. It is a notable feature of the larger houses of both towns that they include a great deal more open space, not only absolutely but also proportionately, than do the smaller houses. It is also the case that larger houses have more large rooms; indeed, the largest room in a house as grand as the Casa del Menandro (I 10.4) by itself covers an area (c. 90m^2) equivalent to the total of as many as a third of the houses in the sample. One way of expressing the more lavish use of space in the larger houses is to divide the total ground area by the number of rooms. The resulting figures for density of rooms show a fairly consistent easing of ratios, from the cramped one room per 19m^2 in the smallest houses to the spacious one per 81m^2 in the largest.

TABLE 4.1
Averages for area, rooms, and open space (total sample)

Size sq.m	No. of houses	Avg. area sq.m	Avg. open area sq.m	Avg. rooms per house	Density (rooms:area)
10–99	82	38	0	2	1:19
100–199	50	145	2	6	1:25
200–299	31	240	22	9	1:27
300–399	19	337	73	9	1:38
400–499	19	435	87	12	1:36
500–599	11	527	85	13	1:41
600–699	7	665	103	17	1:39
700–799	2	775	134	18	1:43
800–899	2	825	165	21	1:39
900–999	0	—	—	—	—
1000–1499	6	1152	179	20	1:58
1500–1999	3	1677	215	32	1:52
2000–2999	2	2658	692	33	1:81

The disadvantage of presenting the data in this way, by equal bands, is that the largest houses are split into too many categories with too few members, while the smallest band contains too many houses and so conceals large contrasts. A more intelligible procedure is to quarter the whole sample according to size ranking, with the smallest houses in Quartile 1, the largest in Quartile 4 (Table 4.2; note that the quartiles are not exactly equal, since houses of the same area may bridge the exact quartile point).

Though by this approach we lose in terms of fine precision, it is of great benefit for statistical reliability to have a larger number in each group, and from this point onward the data will generally be presented in this form. The four groups represent substantial contrasts, as we shall see, in terms of function, architectural features, and wealth of decoration. Although we are dealing with a continuum from smallest to largest that allows many types of variation, in architectural plan, balance of usage, density of rooms to area, wealth and elaboration of decoration, and so on, it is helpful to characterize the quartiles according to the types of units they commonly represent. This is not typology in an archaeological sense but a guide to what, in the spectrum of possibilities, each quartile covers. Figure 4.11 illustrates one or two specimens from each quartile that exemplify (without defining) each type.

Type 1

Almost all units in the first quartile are shops or workshops. Obviously a number of these would be uninhabited, worked in during the day by people living in nearby houses. On the other hand, it was also a familiar pattern for the shopkeeper, like Trimalchio's fellow freedman Pompeius Diogenes, to live in a room above or behind the shop.[30] A careful study of Pompeian shops reckons that 40 percent had stairs to an upper room; hearths, latrines, and stoves may also point to habitation.[31] Of the first quartile in the sample, thirty-nine units (67 percent) are single rooms. Many of these are cramped and unlikely to have been inhabited, but in others there are traces of stairs to an upper room where the shopkeeper or assistant (*tabernarius, institor*) and a small family might have lived. Nineteen units (33 percent) have at least one back room as well as the shop front, and these offer adequate space (25–45m^2) for lodgings above. What is essential to bear in mind is that this type of unit is also commonly found incorporated into larger houses. If we prefer to imagine that the tabernae of the poor were materially poorer and physically more crowded, we should also allow for the tabernae that form part of other houses to be equally poor and crowded.

Type 2

Houses in the second quartile range from two to seven ground-floor rooms; thirty-seven houses (61 percent) include shops or workshops. A striking feature of most houses in this range is their lack of regular plan. The smallest are shops with back rooms, as in the first type. But most are large enough to allow for a central circulation space (possibly called the *medianum*) between front and back rooms (Fig. 4.11, Type 2a). In larger houses the central circulation space may serve as a core off which rooms open in various directions; the odd plots onto which some houses are squeezed militate against predictable

TABLE 4.2
Averages for area and rooms by quartile

Quartile	No. of houses	Area sq.m	Avg. area sq.m	Avg. open area sq.m	Avg. rooms per house	Density (rooms:area)
1	58	10–45	25	0	1.4	1:18
2	61	50–170	108	1	4.7	1:23
3	57	175–345	246	16	8.4	1:29
4	58	350–3000	714	104	16.4	1:45

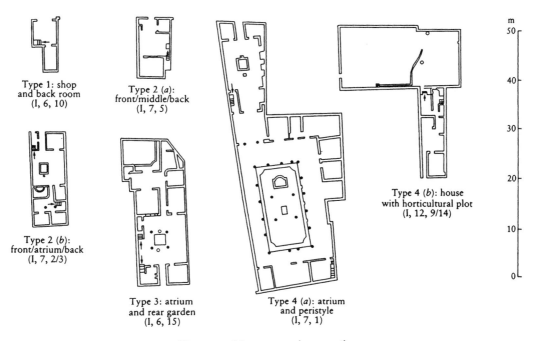

Type 1: shop
and back room
(I, 6, 10)

Type 2 (a):
front/middle/back
(I, 7, 5)

Type 2 (b):
front/atrium/back
(I, 7, 2/3)

Type 3: atrium
and rear garden
(I, 6, 15)

Type 4 (a): atrium
and peristyle
(I, 7, 1)

Type 4 (b): house
with horticultural plot
(I, 12, 9/14)

Figure 4.11 House types by quartile.

plans. Few in the bottom half of the range have detectable rainwater basins (*impluvia*), indicating roofs with central openings. This may be because they were not solidly constructed and were missed by archaeologists in a hurry, but many houses must have lacked an internal light source. In the upper half of the range impluvia become more common, together with a pattern of two rooms flanking the door, an atrium, two rooms on the far side, and a scatter of rooms beyond. Sixteen houses (26 percent) have an atrium, and three have both an atrium with impluvium and a little garden at the rear (Fig. 4.11, Type 2b). This category includes some very attractively decorated houses, which have been dignified with names and not mere numbers (e.g., I 7.3, Casa di Fabius Amandio). Stairs to upper rooms are normal in houses in this quartile.

Type 3

This quartile includes in its range the "average" size, and indeed the range of sizes standard for most Greek houses (see below). Many of these would be regarded as "typical" Pompeian houses. A substantial proportion (60 percent) include shops or workshops; in some cases these shops could easily be split off to form separate units, and some have already been divided in this way. Many (44 percent) have more than one entrance. Symmetrical planning becomes more normal; thirty-four (60 percent) have an atrium, and sixteen (28 percent) fall into the familiar pattern of atrium plus colonnaded garden (at this level the gardens can scarcely be dignified as peristyles). About a quarter are named houses visited by modern tourists. Four include a large area for horticulture or similar usage (stableyards). The number of ground-floor rooms ranges from five to thirteen, with eight as the average.

Type 4

The top quartile obviously includes the richest and most famous houses in the sample (Case dei Vettii, del Labirinto, di Paquio Proculo, del Menandro, dei Cervi, dell'Atrio a mosaico, etc.). Nearly half may be said to engage the regular attention of both tourists and art historians. The majority (44 houses, or 76 percent) have a traditional atrium; thirty-six (64 percent) have both atrium and colonnaded peristyle (Fig. 4.11, Type 4a); the very largest houses (over 1,000m^2) may have a second atrium (dei Vettii, del Menandro, del Labirinto) or a second peristyle (dell'Albergo). Despite large areas given over to ornamental gardens, the largest houses have considerable numbers of ground-floor rooms (20–36) and are evidently designed to accommodate a large slave household. On the other hand, eleven houses (19 percent) included large areas for horticulture (Fig. 4.11, Type 4b) and were neither richly decorated nor densely populated, with as few as four rooms. A notable feature of houses in this category is the large number of entrances they have: forty-five (78 percent) have more than one entrance, and twenty-two (38 percent) have three or more doors. A secondary entrance may simply be a back door, but often it reflects the fact that the house has been formed from an amalgamation of separate units. In several cases it becomes difficult, as we have seen, to decide whether to treat them as single units at all; invisible partitions remain a possibility. In terms of population, these large houses cover a wide range of possibilities, from uninhabited horticultural plots, through family houses with substantial servile establishments, to what we would regard as "multiple-occupancy" houses with more complex patterns of habitation, and finally to ostentatious show houses with slave numbers running into dozens and the owners potentially absent for much of the year.

ATRIA AND PERISTYLES

A familiar pattern of spatial organization rates as typical for the Roman house: an axial line runs the depth of the house from the door through fauces, atrium with impluvium in its center, and tablinum with wide opening on the atrium and often also a wide win-

Figure 4.12 Casa del Tramezzo di Legno, Herculaneum, axial view of "classically framed" impluviate atrium.

dow on the peristyle garden behind, with its four neatly symmetrical colonnades around (Fig. 4.12; see also Fig. 3.9). Atrium and peristyle thus form the essential matrix of this "traditional" house; they are the twin sources of light, and around them are organized the main reception rooms. Ideal rather than typical, this matrix is anything but universal. Partly this is a function of size: a house must be of a certain minimum size to enable construction of an impluviate atrium let alone of a peristyle. But, more significantly, it is a question of the social use of space. Vitruvius makes explicit the social considerations behind Roman architectural form: spacious public areas in a house are designed for the reception of the public, and he does not expect them to be needed in the houses of the humble. These architectural features simultaneously fulfill a practical function—letting in light, air, and water—and a symbolic one—giving dignitas to the home, in a society in which so much turns on social standing. We might anticipate that these features should provide a good index of the standing of the inhabitants; they are regularly so treated by archaeologists. A house that includes these features is often distinguished by modern scholars with the label *domus*, a practice also applied in discussions of Rome and Ostia, where in a later period the contrast between houses that possessed or lacked these architectural features became more marked.

But if this is right, just how exclusive is the atrium/peristyle house? And how far can it be distinguished on other counts, in terms of size, number of rooms, economic activity, decoration, and nature of finds? Identification of these houses presents few problems. The impluviate atrium is betrayed by the basin of the impluvium in the floor; because it needs to catch rainwater it must be a fairly substantial structure, and the excavators (who in any case tend to start from expectations about the house derived from Vitruvius) both find and record the impluvium. On the other hand, Vitruvius also includes in his classification the *displuviate atrium*, which sheds water outward instead of inward and so lacks an impluvium, and naturally this type does not show up on the ground plan. But the displuviate atrium failed to bring light into the heart of the house, and one may doubt whether it brought in social standing either. Most houses must have a central circulation space of some sort, even a shop of the front/middle/back room pattern, and these circulation spaces may have been called atria as well. Equally, there are houses for which the peristyle acts as only circulation space (e.g., the house in Herculaneum known after its Corinthian atrium, H V.30, Fig. 4.13), and these too may in fact have been called "atria." It makes sense to treat the impluviate atrium as the distinctive feature (and *atrium* will be used below to indicate this type), while remembering that its absence may be explained in a variety of ways.

More subtle is the question of defining the peristyle. The classic image is of a pleasure garden surrounded on four sides by colonnades. These stand out on any plan, and are of course a rarity—only 10 percent of the sample. But it would be unhelpful to restrict attention to these. Other, recognizably similar, peristyles only have colonnades on two or three sides; a blank garden wall on the other sides may well have engaged half-columns or even painted representations of columns to give the illusion of continuity (e.g., the Casa del Sacerdos Amandus, Pl. 3). Attention will then extend to the numerous gardens with a portico on a single side, typically that nearest the entrance and tablinum, which may frame the view from the atrium between a pair of columns and thereby give the impression of a full peristyle beyond (Fig. 4.14). And of course, porticoes are not always constructed with true columns; a couple of square piers, as in the Casa del Fabbro (Fig. 7.16), may achieve the same effect, of a sheltered walkway communicating between different areas of the house, open on one side to a garden. Finally, there are houses with open areas, whether gardens or not, that function as a light source and focus of a vista, but which lack porticoes; thus the charming nymphaeum with its fine mosaic of Neptune and Amphitrite in Herculaneum (V.7, Fig. 4.15) catches most of the "dignity" of a peristyle without including any colonnades, and the little Casa di Fabius Amandio uses a tiny backyard, its walls painted with shrubs, to give an impression equivalent to the grandest peristyle (Pl. 7).

On opposite page:

Figure 4.13 (*top, left*) Plan, Casa dell'Atrio Corinzio, Herculaneum (after Maiuri). The entrance leads directly into a peristyle, with an axial view to the main reception room. It is unlikely that this is what Vitruvius meant by a *Corinthian atrium*.

Figure 4.14 (*top, right*) Caupona di Sotericus (I 12.3), Pompeii, backyard. The tablinum looks over an open area with a two-sided portico, supported at the angle by a brick column. Scarcely a garden (the yard has a solid floor of *cocciopesto*, crushed pot), the back wall originally carried a garden painting.

Figure 4.15 (*below*) Casa di Nettuno e Anfitrite, Herculaneum, backyard. The eye-catching mosaics, visible from the entrance through the tablinum window, surround a nymphaeum with dining couches. Here a single element characteristic of luxurious gardens occupies the small yard space available, evoking the opulence of a large peristyle.

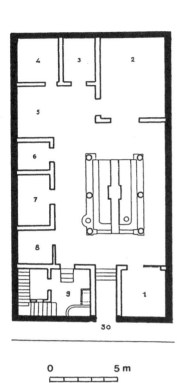

TABLE 4.3
Frequency of atria and peristyles

Feature	No. (%)	Avg. area sq.m	Avg. open area sq.m
Atrium	94 (41%)	480	62
Atrium, no garden	34 (15%)	224	0
Atrium and garden	60 (26%)	626	98
Garden	81 (35%)	552	87
Garden, no atrium	21 (9%)	341	56
Garden, no colonnade	7 (3%)	231	28
Garden, 1 colonnade	22 (9%)	340	63
Garden, 2 colonnades	21 (9%)	433	55
Garden, 3 colonnades	7 (3%)	408	58
Garden, 4 colonnades	20 (9%)	789	110
Garden, 8 colonnades	4 (2%)	1970	424

NOTE: *garden* here indicates open areas that appear to serve an ornamental function, as opposed to horticultural plots.

The very statement of these problems already throws a light on the nature of housing and society in the Vesuvian cities. We are not dealing with polarities, of one class of atrium/peristyle house in sharp contrast to a nonatrium/nonperistyle house, but with gradations, spreading like ripples through the different levels of housing. The figures from our samples bear testimony to this ripple effect.

The atrium is more common than the decorative garden (41 percent against 35 percent), and over one third of atriate houses lack gardens. These houses are, naturally, relatively smaller than those possessing gardens. The average size of the house tends to rise with the number of colonnades; houses that have a garden without colonnades are distinctly the smallest, while those with one, two, or three colonnades are larger, but not much different in size from each other. The leap between the average size of houses with one to three colonnades and those with a full four-sided peristyle is marked, and the average area enclosed within the colonnade almost doubles. There is another dramatic leap to the next level—those with more than four colonnades—a small handful of double-peristyled houses like the Casa del Fauno (which concentrate, in fact, in Regio VI among this sample).

The strong correlation between house size and occurrence of atria and peristyles comes out clearly in their distribution across the size quartiles (Fig. 4.16). The little shops and workshops that typify the first and much of the second quartile, and most of the small three-to-five room houses, do not have space for either an impluviate atrium or colonnaded garden. In fact, the smallest house in the sample with impluvium is 100m^2. The smallest with both atrium and garden, the Casa di Fabius Amandio (Pl. 7), is c. 125m^2. In the third quartile both atria and colonnades become more prevalent, atria in over half the cases, colonnades in slightly more than a third. Single colonnades are much more

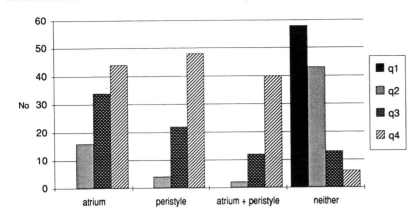

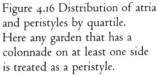

Figure 4.16 Distribution of atria and peristyles by quartile. Here any garden that has a colonnade on at least one side is treated as a peristyle.

common in this range than full peristyles. In the top quartile, by contrast, peristyles (79 percent) are even more frequent than atria (76 percent), and a full third of the units have at least one four-sided peristyle.

There is also a regional contrast to observe. Both atria and peristyles seem to be more common in Pompeii than Herculaneum. Only 29 percent of the Herculaneum sample have atria, as against 42 percent in Pompeii Regio I, and 45 percent in Regio VI. Partly this is attributable to the somewhat different balance of sizes in Herculaneum, which has a smaller proportion of the houses in the top quartiles and a greater proportion under 100m² in which atria are unknown (Fig. 4.8). But that changing architectural fashions are also involved is suggested by a group of handsome houses that lack impluviate atria (H V.30, c. Atrio Corinzio; III.3, c. dello Scheletro; IV.3/4, c. dell'Alcova; IV.21, c. dei Cervi). These include one of the most magnificent houses in Herculaneum, and it does seem to be the case that here we can already see the beginning of the shift away from the atrium matrix discussed above (Chap. 3).

FINDS

In any survey of the social and economic aspects of houses in Pompeii and Herculaneum, study of the finds should play a crucial, perhaps *the* crucial, part. The attempt here to gain a picture of household wealth and social standing relies almost entirely on structures and decoration. Yet these are imprecise (though not, I hope to show, worthless) measures. Finds have the potential of supplying precise and reliable answers to many of the questions I have asked, and compared with almost any other archaeological site, the finds of Pompeii and Herculaneum are extraordinarily rich. At the very least, finds should indicate whether any unit was actually inhabited—and that many were abandoned in the aftermath of the earthquake of A.D. 62 is highly likely. Finds also give vital clues as to the economic and social activities within the house, in the presence of equipment and structures indicating economic activity, as well as the apparatus and furniture of social life. To some extent, of course, this evidence is already incorporated into traditional identifications of shops, workshops, etc., used in the analysis below; though as I have stressed, it is only where activities leave behind unmistakable structural traces, such as shop fronts, counters, ovens, grinders, vats, and the like, that we can be sure that they have in fact been observed.

Finally, finds offer an ideal measure of wealth and standing. Structures and decoration both outlast their original creators; it is not infrequent that, as in the Casa del Criptoportico, modest inhabitants are found amid the ruins of erstwhile splendor.[32] Finds, particularly those of an intrinsic value, come and go with the current inhabitants and offer a far more sensitive measure of their wealth. The best pointer to the wealth and standing of the final inhabitants of the Casa del Menandro is not the exceptional size of the house, nor the fineness of its decoration, but the unparalleled silver service found in its cellars. The poverty of shop I 10.9 in the corner of the same block is seen not only in its minute size and lack of decoration but in the total absence of furniture and finds.[33] It would therefore be of great value to examine the distribution, between houses of different sizes and types, of artifacts that could be taken as status markers: marble and bronze statuary; marble tables and furniture; precious metal objects, whether coins or plate; jewelry of all sorts; and a variety of miscellaneous objects such as ivory combs, alabaster scent-bottles, or even Arretine pottery.

The reason I make virtually no use here of this vital evidence lies in the state of the scholarship. Excavation methods have been crude; nevertheless, copious evidence has been unearthed. Reporting has been patchy and inadequate; nevertheless, lists of finds are preserved in the excavation journals on site. Evidence is there, but its complexity and richness make it impossible to deploy until it has been afforded the same degree of serious study as has been lavished on the decoration. The difficulties can be exemplified briefly. House I 10.8 was traditionally identified as that of the weaver Successus.[34] The evidence lies in a graffito of no necessary relevance in the neighboring tavern I 10.2 and in the finds of the house, which include fifty-three loom weights in the atrium. The inadequacy of this evidence has been rightly emphasized by Jongman in his recent study of Pompeian economy and society.[35] The loom weights might indeed belong to a traditional domestic loom. But did they? To answer this question would require systematic study of loom weights and other traces of weaving in Pompeii. The situation is obviously different from that in fourth-century B.C. Olynthos, where almost every house had loom weights.[36] But the evidence in Pompeii has never been studied, so we have no idea to what extent weaving was the female domestic activity of Roman ideal, and to what extent a commercial undertaking.

The use of evidence from finds is much complicated by the manner in which it has been disrupted over the course of centuries. Herculaneum is riddled with the tunnels of eighteenth-century explorers; Maiuri, who understood something of the importance of finds, complains repeatedly of their destruction of the evidence.[37] Indeed, the tunnelers confused as well as removed the finds: an impressive collection of finds in one room is best explained as a cache left behind by previous looters.[38] But tunneling was not confined to the eighteenth century. The Insula of the Menander in Pompeii shows numerous traces of holes hacked through from room to room and house to house (Fig. 4.17). It is

Figure 4.17 Casa degli Amanti, Pompeii, sequence of holes, c. 18 inches above floor level, penetrating three consecutive walls along the east wing of the peristyle. Such "looters'" holes are frequent but normally filled in by modern restoration. They are likely to have been made before the rooms filled with lapilli, in the immediate aftermath of the eruption.

unclear whether these are the responsibility of looters in antiquity, or even of trapped inhabitants trying to make their way out. But the consequence is that much appears to be missing or displaced.[39]

Thus the elegant Casa degli Amanti (I 10.11) is almost devoid of finds, apart from humdrum hinges, lamps, and the odd bronze coin, while the smaller and in every other respect more modest Casa del Fabbro (I 10.7) is a veritable treasure house, with a variety of jewelry, silver coins (including a collection of republican *denarii*), perfume bottles, writing implements, balances and weights, measuring and surveying devices, as well as a set of joiner's tools from which the business of the inhabitant has been inferred.[40] Either the Casa degli Amanti has been thoroughly looted, or the inhabitants packed their bags well, whether during or before the eruption. Without systematic investigation of the presence and absence of finds, and of the patterns left behind by abandonment, bag packing, looting, and primitive excavation, we are simply not in a position to assess their significance. When such a study has been completed, it may be possible to give more sophisticated and reliable answers to some of the questions raised in this book.[41]

ACCURATE and well-researched studies of the finds could transform our understanding of these sites. But in the meantime there is still much that can be done with what has been published, whatever the inadequacies of the process. Such is the extraordinary richness of the Vesuvian sites that, like the chemical-rich Vesuvian soil, they can bear many crops a year, and even after poor husbandry, gleanings remain. In the chapters that follow, the information that the three sample areas produced, patchy and approximate though it often has proved, is brought to bear on a succession of issues.

The first issue is how we can make the leap from houses to inhabitants. That in broad terms we are dealing with a progression of wealth and status of inhabitants between these quartiles must be evident, though it will be equally clear that not every large house necessarily contained, or even belonged to, wealthy people, and that not every small shop belonged to, or was inhabited by, poor people. The distribution of house sizes will be a very different matter from the distribution of wealth within society, as indeed from the distribution of population. The bottom quartile of houses judged by size cannot conceivably have contained all the bottom quartile of the population. Nor is it likely that the poorest lived exclusively in the smaller houses; they may equally have lived in the largest houses, as slaves, dependents, tenants, and lodgers of the rich. The inferences we can draw about population and household structure are a complex issue, which I discuss in Chapter 5.

Chapter 6 is concerned with the usage of space and the balance between residence and work: the use of the house for reception of visitors, and its use for production and profit. Analysis that ignores this basic contrast would swiftly run into confusion. A large open area might serve to enhance considerably the standing of a house, if surrounded by gracious porticoes, planted with specimen trees and flowering shrubs, and decorated with statuary and plashing fountains. On the other hand, it might serve the purely practical function of a horticultural plot as a vineyard, for the commercial cultivation of flowers, or simply for raising vegetables for the table.[42] Equally, the rooms and other areas of the house might serve either for gracious living and reception or for practical purposes such as manufacture and processing, sale of goods, or storage. The usage of space has an obvious bearing on the analysis of luxury in housing, not least because the Romans themselves regarded utilitarian usage and luxury as alternatives.

Chapter 7 turns to decoration—specifically wall painting—the light it casts on the spread of luxury and its role in the construction of status and identity. Here the interest lies not so much in the inhabitants as in the houses themselves. The largest houses offered the greatest potential for status display, and if we were dealing with a society in which only a narrow elite deployed such status symbols, we would not expect many traces of these symbols outside the largest houses. In fact, as we shall see, the largest houses do indeed give the richest displays; yet ripples of luxury spread outward and downward to all but the smallest houses. The interest lies in tracing the progression of these ripples, both over different grades of house and over time.

CHAPTER 5

□

HOUSES AND HOUSEHOLDS

What do we mean by a big house? Something very different from the meaning we would give today to the same expression. A house today is said to be big in relation to the density of its population. A big house is always a house with few people in it. . . . In the seventeenth century, and also in the fifteenth and sixteenth centuries, a big house was always crowded, with more people in it than in little houses. . . .

In these big houses, neither palaces, nor yet mansions, we find the cultural setting of the concept of childhood and the family. . . . The big house fulfilled a public function. In that society . . . it was the only place where friends, clients, relatives and protégés could meet and talk. To the servants, clerics and clerks who lived there permanently, one must add the constant flow of visitors. . . .

It is easy to imagine the promiscuity which reigned in these rooms where nobody could be alone, which one had to cross to reach any of the communicating rooms, where several couples and several groups of boys or girls slept together (not to speak of the servants, of whom at least some must have slept beside their masters . . .) in which people forgathered to have their meals, to receive their friends or clients, and sometimes to give alms to beggars. One can understand why, whenever a census was taken, the houses of notabilities were always more crowded than the little one-room or two-room apartments of ordinary folk. One has to regard these families, for all that they were giving birth to the modern concept of the family, not as refuges from the invasion of the world but as centres of a populous society, the focal points of a crowded social life.

Ariès, *Centuries of Childhood*

THE RECONSTRUCTION of past families in the late medieval and early modern periods has been made possible by an abundance of documentary material, both precise and extensive. Only by careful statistical analysis of such documents, pioneered by the Cambridge Group for the History of Population and Social Structure,[1] has it been possible to break from Le Play's simplistic hypothesis of a general historical development from the extended to the nuclear family.[2] The quality of documentation varies considerably, but, at their best, census records may cast a bright shaft of light on a local society at a particular moment in time. Such is the Florentine Catasto of 1427 from which David Herlihy has reconstructed Tuscan families in such vivid detail,[3] or the 1523 survey of Coventry from which Charles Phythian-Adams drew his picture of the desolation of a late-medieval English town.[4]

The ancient historian is unlikely (outside Egypt, I add cautiously) to hit upon documentation of this quality; yet without statistical study we have the greatest difficulty in rising above the level of the anecdotal, and consequently in constructing hypotheses any more convincing than Le Play's. We have too little evidence to say just how typical or atypical of what social groups at what period in what areas was the multinuclear family attested in the case of the Aelii Tuberones. Saller and Shaw have made exemplary use of statistical analysis of funerary commemorations.[5] But valuable though this study is, it can only build up the balance of probability against the widespread occurrence of the extended family, and can give no accurate picture of its distribution.

One source of evidence available to us in abundance (indeed, much more so than for the modernist) is the archaeological; it has not been exploited in this context. Whatever the difficulties in using it (and they are legion), there is a strong prima facie case for predicting that archaeological evidence should have a direct bearing on the question of the family. *Family* is a concept of elusive definition, and indeed we may doubt that the modern concept finds an exact match in either the early modern world,[6] or the medieval,[7] or the Roman.[8] Nevertheless, the object of investigation both of census takers and of modern researchers is normally defined in *physical* terms: those who live "under the same roof," "all those who stay and sleep together in one and the same residence and who survive together on the same bread and wine" (Tuscan village scribe, quoted in Herlihy and Klapisch-Zuber 1985). Taxman and historian focus on the household in its house (though what the house holds may prove, in Laslett's terminology, a "houseful" rather than a "household," that is, a group unconnected in family terms except by coresidence): the symbol of its unity is the place of common food-preparation, the *fuoco*, just as the lares above the hearth symbolize the unity of the Roman household.

The sample of houses from Pompeii and Herculaneum here under examination is no substitute for the sort of archival material offered by medieval census returns, but it does at least allow us to gain a precise picture of the sort of physical context in which our reconstructions of Roman "families" or "households" need to be set. The aim of this chapter is to look at two separate aspects of the problem: first by an attempt to reconstruct the distribution of households of different sizes in the urban fabric and to consider its implications, and second by asking about the composition of the "houseful" represented by the living unit.

HOUSEHOLDS AND FAMILIES

The prevalence of "extended" families in Europe in the past may have been shown up as a myth, except indeed across a northwest/southeast divide.[9] It is notable too with what consistency average household size, even within communities where multinuclear households were a standard pattern, proves to have been as low as four to five. Thus Laslett's average of 4.73 persons for a hundred English parishes between 1574 and 1821[10] compares to an average of 4.42 in Tuscany in 1427.[11] Nevertheless, what such averages conceal is the importance of the "big house," which Ariès (cited above) so powerfully evokes. In sharp contrast to contemporary circumstances (which do much to form our image of the family), households in the past varied sharply in size. There is a close correlation between wealth and size of household; whether because they produce more children, because they favor extended households, or because they have more servants, the wealthy live in above-average-sized families. Thus the population of a Kent village in 1676 may range

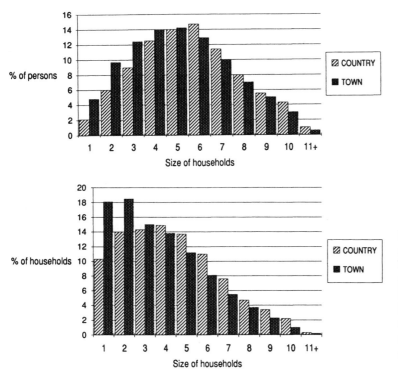

Figure 5.1 Tuscan households in 1427 (after Herlihy and Klapisch-Zuber). Contrast the distribution of population with the distribution of household sizes. Although households of one, two, or three persons are common, particularly in the town, they account for a relatively small proportion of the population.

from the family of the lord of the manor, including 6 children and 15 servants, through substantial yeomen with 8 to 10 persons per household, to laborers and poor without servants and only 1.2 and 0.9 children per family, respectively.[12]

A further point must be emphasized. In a society that favors the big house, small households of one, two, or three persons may be common enough, yet even so may contain only a small part of the total population. Herlihy and Klapisch-Zuber calculate separately the distribution of household sizes in Tuscany as a percentage of the total of households and as a percentage of the total of persons. The Florentine Catasto shows the smallest households, of one or two, to be the commonest, at least in the towns (Fig. 5.1b). But, for obvious mathematical reasons, this is very far from saying that the majority (even the majority of the poor) lived in small households. In fact (Fig. 5.1a), they account for a mere 14 percent of the population; more people lived in households of 5 than any other size, and over half the population lived in houses of 5 or more, and this despite an *average* household of 4.42.

The Tuscan evidence offers a graphic illustration of the demographic importance of variation in density of population between households. In one crucial respect, however, it is positively unhelpful to the historian of classical Italy. The census deliberately excluded servants from a *famiglia*, preferring to register them with their own families of

TABLE 5.1

Household size in Coventry, 1523; Sizes and composition of households by categories of goods

Categories	No. of households	% of all households	Mean sizes of households	% of households with servants	Mean sizes of servants groups	% of households with children	Mean sizes of "sibling" groups
1. Nil assessments	268	20.6	2.8	17.2	1.3	42.9	1.8
2. £0–2	218	16.7	3.9	45.4	1.5	61.5	2.06
3. £3–5	120	9.2	4.8	73.3	2.1	66.7	2.0
4. £6–10	72	5.5	5.4	86.1	2.4	70.8	2.0
5. £11–16	32	2.5	5.7	87.5	2.6	71.9	2.2
6. £20–49	65	5.0	6.6	92.3	3.4	67.7	2.3
7. £50–99	25	1.9	7.3	100.0	4.0	76.0	1.95
8. £100+	14	1.1	11.8	100.0	7.6	78.6	2.8
9. Rest of city	488	37.5	2.6	18.4	1.8	37.5	1.7

birth, and correspondingly included children within the *famiglia* even when resident abroad.[13] That deliberate choice reflects the Tuscan conception of *famiglia*. Although the basic definition is by residence ("those sharing the same bread and wine"), absent children are seen as exceptions to be discounted. Presumably the perceived norm of the large household was one with an extended family rather than one with numerous servants. Doubtless the large household, particularly in the town, also had more servants.

For an example in which servants, not extended family, are the vital factor in building larger families, it is better to turn to sixteenth-century Coventry. Here too there is a strong correlation between wealth and size of household.[14] Whether measured by rental categories or by assessments of total value of goods in the household (Table 5.1), the wealthier houses are consistently more populous, both in servants and children. But though the wealthiest houses are more likely to have children (78.6 percent) and more of them (2.8) than the poorest (42.9 percent, with average 1.8), the contrast in servants is much more marked: 100 percent of the richest with 7.6 servants each, as against 17.2 percent of the poorest with 1.3 servants each. These figures represent a city in a period of steep demographic and economic decline. The average household size was a mere 3.7; in periods of prosperity an English town would have had a far larger proportion of prosperous and densely populated households.

A century apart, Tuscany and Coventry produce similar patterns of household densities by different routes. Though servants were familiar enough in Italy, and extended families quite possible in England, there is a clear cultural contrast. Italian visitors to England remarked with surprise on the way the children were sent out to live and serve (and of course learn) in other households. Service and extension of the family operated to some extent as alternative strategies for increasing labor and hence wealth.

These patterns have an obvious bearing on antiquity. About sizes of family groupings in our sense, whether the average number of children or the frequency of nonnuclear families, we have quite inadequate evidence. But the abundant evidence for a massive presence of slaves in Italy in the first centuries B.C. and A.D. makes it clear enough that, in a society in which production was based on the household, there must have been a similar correlation between wealth and size of household. That the wealthy Roman had a vast slave household, with as many as four hundred slaves under a single roof, we know. But can we learn a little more about the distribution across society of different sizes of familia, slave and free?

The archaeological evidence should permit at least a few first steps. What can the distribution of houses of different sizes tell us about the distribution of their inhabitants? Attention must be drawn at once to the extraordinarily precarious nature of attempts to reconstruct the population of Pompeii and to the assumptions such attempts have incorporated. Discussion has always focused on the problem of the total population of the city. Current estimates vary from 6,400 to 6,700 to the still repeated figure of 20,000.[15] Various indicators have been deployed, from the (manifestly irrelevant) seating capacity of the amphitheater, to extrapolations based on the number of skeletons discovered (the figure of 2,000 is offered, but this proves to be either itself an extrapolation from the number excavated in one sample area, or a bold guess at the numbers currently stored in the repositories, lying as they do in jumbled heaps, dismembered, uncatalogued, and uncounted).

One method of arriving at an overall figure, which has been employed from Beloch to Russell, is to use an average figure of population per hectare derived from comparative statistics of the population of medieval cities. But this method incorporates assumptions that undermine the whole interest of the inquiry. Russell suggests an average of 100 to 120 persons per hectare, with a maximum of 200. The figures derive from his own earlier tables of populations of European cities in the thirteenth to sixteenth centuries.[16] But not only may we question the assumption that a medieval city can be a reliable model for the population density of a Roman city, we may ask whether a figure for the average population density of a medieval city is itself meaningful. Russell's tables show a wide range of variation, from 40 to 289 persons per hectare. It is surely in itself an interesting fact about medieval cities that their population densities could vary so widely.[17] By reducing the figures to an average, we rule out inquiry into the circumstances that made one city more crowded than another, and the inferences we can draw from these variations.

The same issue has provoked considerable controversy among archaeologists concerned with prehistoric settlement. There is a tradition of attempts to extrapolate from comparative ethnographical evidence a cross-culturally valid figure for population density. Narroll offered $10m^2$ roofed space per person; Kolb refined this to $6.12m^2$ of inhabitable roofed space per person. But these attempts miss the force of Roland Fletcher's objection: perceptions of overcrowding, which underlie the expansion of inhabited space, are themselves the result of attitudes that vary widely from society to society.[18] Or, as Ian Hodder put it, hypotheses that assume constant density neglect the symbolic meanings of the use of space that are a vital feature of a society. Spatial organization is not simply a neutral reflection of social organization but is an independent variable complementary to social organization.[19]

All this has direct bearing on the question of Roman households. If it were true that population density in preindustrial cities could be treated as a constant, inquiry into the population of Pompeii would not be of great value; the supposed population figure would merely be another way of expressing the figure for the area of the city. But it is the variations of density, variations over time, between different societies, different areas, even different social categories within the same city at the same period, that are most interesting. We want to know how Pompeii differed from fourth-century Olynthos or fifteenth-century Florence and what that tells us, rather than generating apparent facts about Pompeii on the assumption that all were, on average, the same.

The alternative approach is to work from the bottom up. Instead of basing calculations on an assumed overall average, we could look in detail at the evidence of the houses themselves and see what they imply about the density and distribution of population within the city. In a sense, this has been the basis of traditional calculations from Fiorelli onward. Fiorelli himself took as a sample the portion of the city excavated to 1872, and dividing houses into categories on the basis of the number of their rooms, extrapolated a total of 12,000 for the total population.[20] All subsequent estimates have taken the form of modifications of Fiorelli's initial calculations. Nissen thought that Fiorelli had failed to allow adequately for the number of upper rooms not preserved archaeologically, and therefore doubled his calculation of 1,800 houses to 3,600 to include upper flats, so arriving at a population of 20,000.[21] Beloch, feeling that Nissen had gone too far, recalculated, still on the basis of the houses excavated before 1872, a population of 17,000 to 18,000, which he arbitrarily reduced to 15,000 because he felt that the (implied) average of 10 slaves per house was too high.[22] Eschebach further reduced the total to 8,000 in the light of the excavations of Jashemski, which had revealed that as much as a third of the city was only thinly inhabited, with substantial areas under cultivation.[23]

It is strange that for over a century, despite a massive extension of the available archaeological evidence, nobody has returned to the house as the basic unit of calculation. Moreover, obsession with the figure of the total population has distracted attention from the vital point implicit in Fiorelli's first calculations, that the houses come in a wide range of sizes, and that the variation in house size implies a variation in household size. Unlike Olynthos, where one might reasonably attempt to calculate an average family size, it is evident that Pompeian households will have ranged from single-person units to palace-like units with dozens of slaves.

Careful attention to the archaeological evidence now available ought to allow considerable refinement of Fiorelli's calculations. The evidence is better in significant respects. In Herculaneum in particular, but also to some extent in Regio I of Pompeii, it is possible to reconstruct upper stories in detail. There is also abundant evidence of beds, whether from bed niches in the masonry, or from the wooden frames themselves found in lower

Figure 5.2 Casa a Graticcio, Herculaneum, bed frame. The frame measures 1.10 by 2.12 meters. A child's bed was found in the same room, measuring 0.7 by 1.20 meters (see Fig. 5.15 for layout of house).

and upper floors at Herculaneum (Fig. 5.2). This evidence has its own difficulties of interpretation: How many sleepers should we allow per bed? How many beds were not slept in on a regular basis? How many slept elsewhere than in beds, for example, on mattresses on the floor? Nevertheless, they constitute good prima facie evidence of habitation, and, by extrapolating from those areas where the evidence is well preserved, it should be possible to build up a convincing overall picture.

Unfortunately, it is not possible to make such a detailed study without considerable further research. Investigation is beset by at least two substantial problems. The first is the wholly inadequate state of reporting of the archaeological finds. Without a record of precise distribution of artifacts, normal in modern archaeology, it is difficult to pronounce with any confidence on room use. It is frequently impossible to tell, for instance, where a room designated by the excavators as a cubiculum contained any evidence of sleeping. Only thorough study of the distribution pattern of artifacts can reveal what the telltale criteria of sleeping should be.[24]

The second major problem is that of change over time. Populations are not constant; neither are families, nor the usage of houses. Children are born and die, slaves are bought and sold or liberated, wives are married and divorced, husbands die and leave widows in possession, tenants come and go. A site like Pompeii does not reveal a population in a permanent state but freezes it in one moment of a process of constant change. As human life changes, so does the surrounding environment of houses; yet the rhythms of change are not necessarily the same, and buildings may lag behind, not always at a constant interval. A once-crowded house may lie empty, though leaving evidence of its previous crowding; likewise, a house once shaped for a small family-group may have become overcrowded, yet not reflect in its structures its new population. What the archaeological evidence attests beyond doubt, in the constant adaptation of properties, is the process of change itself: joining neighboring properties into one, splitting single units into new separate ones, opening and closing connecting doors, adapting spaces for radically different uses, and so on.[25]

This raises the question of the exact moment to which any global population figure for Pompeii would refer. Even the destruction of Pompeii was a process, lasting over time. The fact that an incalculable proportion of the population fled during this process means that the count of skeletons in Pompeii can never give more than a minimum figure for the population immediately preceding the eruption. But, on a longer time-scale, the destruction of Pompeii starts with the earthquake of A.D. 62. Comparative evidence makes it clear that the earthquake will have had a major impact on the population,[26] and archaeologists have frequently commented on the slowness of the process of reconstruction. Hence it becomes unclear whether proposed figures refer to the actual population in A.D. 79, or to an ideal for the early Empire, ignoring the effects of the earthquake. Again, it may be argued that, instead of trying to reconstruct an ultimately unprovable figure that implies a mythical constant population, it is precisely the variations over time we ought to be studying.

In view of these major difficulties, I do not intend to indulge any further the pursuit of chimerical absolute figures. Instead, it may be worth using the existing evidence, inadequate though it is, to explore what consequences the assumptions we make on the macro level about the total population of the city have on the micro level for the population of the household. Let us suppose, purely for the sake of hypothesis, that the figure of ten thousand, to which scholarly consensus seems now to tend, is more or less right for the total population within the walls of Pompeii before the eruption in A.D. 79. What implications follow for the size of individual households?

Fiorelli extrapolated a figure of eighteen hundred for the total of houses, including shops, in the city. Nissen wanted to double the figure to allow for independent upper flats (this, as will emerge, is a wild overestimate). But even Fiorelli's figure, after more than a century of active excavation, can now be seen as overoptimistic. Initially, indeed, the computer-analyzed material in the new *Pompei. L'informatica* volume seems to support a generous estimate of the number of units in Pompeii, recording in the excavated or partially excavated portions of the city some 818 residential habitations, 890 commercial premises, 207 workshops, 47 public buildings, 17 temples, 27 horticultural plots, and 263 miscellaneous or unidentifiable units (63ff.). These figures, however, though amassed and reduced to percentages as if each unit counted were a separate entity, prove to result from extensive double-counting (a flaw that renders the graphically presented material virtually worthless). The listings of individual units, which carefully distinguish the principal entry to a unit from subsidiary entries to other parts of an integral complex, reveal a different picture. The total given for units excavated to date is 1,435, and when 174 tombs or suburban villas outside the walls and 64 public buildings and temples within the walls are subtracted, 1,197 remains as the maximum for houses, shops, workshops, horticultural plots, and "other" miscellaneous usage. To extrapolate a figure for the whole site including unexcavated portions, we must exclude the numerous partially excavated blocks, often with only one frontage exposed. We are left with scarcely 1,000 units in 72 blocks. For the 40 or so unexcavated or partially excavated blocks we may add a maximum of 550 further units; but because the unexcavated areas lie largely on the outskirts of the town, which were evidently less densely built up than the center, and because we must allow for some proportion of horticultural plots and other miscellaneous nonhabitable units, it is not easy to imagine a total of habitable units in excess of 1,200 to 1,300.

This estimate would in turn suggest an average household size, if we want to imagine a population of 10,000 within the walls, of 7.7 to 8.3 (or, even allowing for a maximum of 1,500 units, of 6.7). If (but only if) each house represents a separate family, we are dealing with an average notably higher than the early-modern European one of 4 to 5. However, in a slave-owning society, this may be precisely the way in which a Roman town differed from medieval and early-modern conditions. How plausible that might be we cannot judge until we consider the distribution of the average figure among units of different sizes.

One of the most striking features of the housing of Pompeii and Herculaneum that emerged from the previous chapter is the diversity of shapes and sizes of houses within any given area of the towns. The interlocking jigsaw of large, medium, and small houses repeats itself constantly; and though there may be some areas with more large houses, and others, particularly those fronting on busy roads, with a higher proportion of small shops, in general the admixture is surprisingly even. Dividing houses on the basis of their ground areas into bands of 100m^2, it emerged that the pattern of distribution of different house sizes in the three sample areas was closely comparable (see Fig. 4.8).

Can we estimate the likely distribution of population across the different house sizes? We have seen that the guess of ten thousand for the total population of Pompeii implies an average of about seven to eight persons per house. An average house size (derived from the sample) of 271m^2 implies an average of 34–39m^2 per person. We could then estimate, on the assumption of an even distribution of ground area per person throughout the city, the distribution of population among the different house sizes (Fig. 5.3). Thus a house of 100m^2 will have had three inhabitants, one of 1,000m^2, thirty.

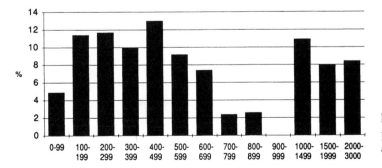

Figure 5.3 Hypothetical distribution of population across house sizes assuming a constant one person per 35m^2.

But there are grave objections, as we have already seen, to the assumption of a standard ratio of space per person. We would expect, at least in housing conditions similar to our own, the poorest households to have been the most crowded; yet, as Ariès makes clear, that too may be a false expectation based on modern Western conditions, and societies with crowded big houses are also conceivable. Ground area is misleading in several respects. First, it makes no allowance for upper floors; the evidence is good enough to show that these were significant in extent, though not good enough to let us calculate precise figures for the whole sample. Second, the larger the house, the greater the amount of open space it includes, whether for ornamental peristyles or horticulture and other nonresidential use. Individual rooms also tend to be larger, so the density of ground-floor rooms per house drops markedly as the area increases (see Table 4.1).

A rather more plausible way of estimating household size is to allow a suitable ratio of persons per room. This is a fairly traditional method.[27] An ethnoarchaeological study of western Iran, for instance, points to a one-to-one ratio.[28] It would be arbitrary to attempt to establish this ratio as a cross-cultural norm, for everything depends on housing types and living patterns, degrees of differentiation of space and ideas of privacy. A room-to-inhabitants ratio makes sense only insofar as it reflects our needs for private space. In modern Western conditions, a house in which the individual cannot achieve a private space may be perceived as crowded. Thus one of the standard uses of census figures is to identify areas in which houses are "overcrowded": a ratio of more than 1.5 people per room is regarded as an index of overcrowding. In Britain in 1951 average room densities of over 1.1 per room were not found outside the Glasgow area, while in the south the average was below 0.8 per room.[29]

The average number of ground-floor rooms per house for the whole Pompeii/Herculaneum sample is 7.5 (I have excluded from the count public-circulation spaces like vestibules and atria, together with spaces evidently not for living, such as storerooms and latrines). This figure coincides strikingly with the average of seven to eight persons per house implied by the hypothetical population of ten thousand. But far from giving us an overall ratio of one person per room, the implied ratio, when we take into account the upper floors, is of up to two rooms per person. Either we must infer that Pompeians lived in standards of privacy approximating to those of modern southern England, or that the estimate of ten thousand for the total population is very conservative. It was precisely this sort of consideration that led Nissen to posit a population of twice this size. On the other hand, the higher we raise the figure for the total population, the higher we raise the average number of inhabitants per house. It was unwillingness to envisage what he assumed must be a vast population of slaves that led Beloch to whittle down Nissen's estimate.

It is here that the dilemma of reconstructing Pompeii's population lies. If we consider the number of houses, we are pulled toward a low estimate; consider the number of rooms and we are pulled to high one. But rather than attempting to strike a balance between these conflicting considerations, the dilemma should make us think again about what a Pompeian household was. In England in 1951, when the average population density was under 1 per room, the average household had (taking into account regional variation) between 4.5 and 4.9 rooms.[30] The Pompeian household in terms of rooms alone is

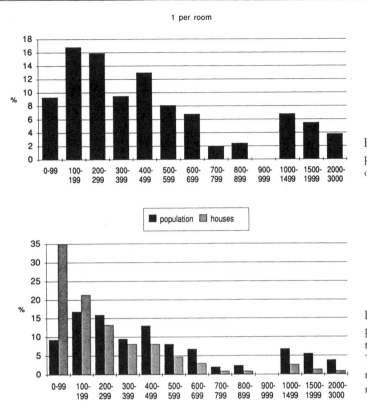

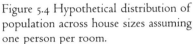

Figure 5.4 Hypothetical distribution of population across house sizes assuming one person per room.

Figure 5.5 Distribution of house sizes plotted against distribution of population assuming one person to room. Though the smallest houses are the most common, they cannot be the most populous.

substantially larger than what we are used to. It is this that makes Ariès's "big house," with its implicit contrast to modern conditions, so attractive as a model. We are dealing with houses that are physically larger, looser, and less discrete than the homes of the modern nuclear family, combining public and private, residential and nonresidential, in ways that are unfamiliar to us (a point already stressed in Part I).

It is interesting, then, to use room count as a provisional index of population and to see what pattern this implies. The results of assuming a flat-rate distribution of one person per ground-floor room across the 100m^2 size bands is shown in Figure 5.4. We may note how, just as in Herlihy's calculations for Tuscan households (Fig. 5.1), the distribution of persons contrasts with the distribution of households (Fig. 5.5). Though the smallest houses, those under 100m^2, may be commonest, their population will have been relatively small. On the two different calculations of population distribution attempted here, only 5 or 9 percent of the population inhabit the bottom 35 percent of houses. A greater proportion of the population will have lived in the next two bands, houses between 100m^2 and 300m^2, that is, houses closer to the average size of 271m^2, and also closer, as it happens, to the standard house sizes of Greek cities. The impression of the "big house" as the norm is thus reinforced.

It is, as we have seen, both cumbersome and unsatisfactory for statistical purposes to divide the sample of houses into so many bands. Division into quartiles allows a more convenient overview of the housing stock (Table 4.2). If we review the four categories or types distinguished above, we can form at least an impression of the plausibility of populating each quartile at a given rate. Type 1 consisted almost exclusively of shops and workshops, mostly with only one room and at best a small backroom. Many of these may well have been uninhabited. Yet the frequency of stairs to now-invisible upper rooms above the shop should discourage us from depopulating this quartile; and some of these upper rooms might have been quite crowded (say two to three per room). Even so, when these are balanced against tabernae without inhabitants, the average figure of 1.4 persons per house suggested by the ratio of one per room might not seem unduly pessimistic.

Type 2 houses range from two to seven rooms. The majority of these can quite plausibly be populated with family units, and it is not hard to imagine a group of four to five, corresponding to a ratio of one per ground-floor room, inhabiting the average house. Type 3 houses are substantially larger, ranging from five to thirteen ground-floor rooms, with eight as the average. Here we begin to encounter problems. Should we increase the family size proportionately? But since it is reasonable enough to imagine more slaves per household in these larger structures, at least the ratio need not be dismissed out of hand. In type 4 houses, with an average of sixteen and a maximum of thirty-six ground-floor rooms, and multiple entrances, the ratio begins to strain credulity. Doubtless there will have been houses in Pompeii with a dozen, or even several dozen, slaves, but to imagine this as a norm in as many as a quarter of the households of the town is not at all easy.

The larger the house, the more perilous becomes any attempt to estimate its population. Perhaps, if sticking to the hypothetical total population of ten thousand, one might prefer to crowd houses in the bottom quartiles slightly more (say 2.5 average in the first quartile, 6 in the second) and reduce the top quartile correspondingly (to 14). Those who feel that ten thousand is too high for the total will want to thin out numbers further in the upper quartiles and will thus reduce the differentials; those who feel it is too low will need to increase the averages all around and will inevitably increase the differentials (it is much easier to increase the average of the top quartile to 20 than that of the bottom quartile to 5).

But any attempt to attain precise figures is surely pointless. We can talk about the capacity of houses of different sizes, without ever knowing whether at any given point in time they were in fact occupied to the limits of capacity. The essential point about Pompeian housing is that it implies an *expectation* that households will vary enormously in size. The contrast with Greek houses is highly revealing, for it suggests radically different expectations about how people ought to and do live. A city like Olynthos that is set out in regular and equal plots is based on expectations that are fundamentally egalitarian: the citizen's *oikos* is expected to be of a certain standard size. In fact, there must have been considerable variations in the populations of individual houses at Olynthos too; some families at some stages naturally had more children or slaves or extended family or whatever than others. By contrast, the pattern of house plots at Pompeii, which evidently derives from the operation of the market rather than from central planning, incorporates the expectation of inequality. Whether in wealth and ostentation or in number of inhabitants or plot size, the range of variation is enormous and continuous.

The size of the average plot is ten times that of the smallest, while the largest are ten times the size of the average.

Thus, although we cannot say, based on our present evidence, that any given house actually did have at some given time a certain number of inhabitants, it is surely clear that some houses were constructed in the expectation of containing many more people than were others. The houses in the top half in terms of size contain three times as many ground-floor rooms as those in the bottom half; those in the top quartile contain eleven times as many as those in the bottom quartile. It is senseless on the basis of the expectations of contemporary Western societies to envisage a poor majority crowded into the smaller houses, while a rich minority rattle around in lonely splendor in the larger ones. It is here that the model of the big house offered by Ariès is helpful. By envisaging big houses as "the focal points of a crowded social life" we can begin to make sense of the physical evidence. Nor should the big house be seen as the exception, restricted to the upper elite. We are dealing not only with palaces and mansions but with a widespread phenomenon. From this perspective, the pursuit of "lower-class" and "middle-class" housing[31] is misleading, for the poor of Pompeii, as slaves and dependents, were surely to be found in the big houses too, and probably in greater numbers.

FAMILIES AND "HOUSEFULS"

Having come this far in our speculative repopulation of Pompeian houses, we need to ask what bearing it has on our understanding of the family. In Laslett's terminology, are we dealing with "households" or "housefuls"? That is to say, would all the inhabitants regard themselves as a single *familia*, or do houses hold composite groups of *familiae*? And are large *familiae* extended family groups, or nuclear families with large servile staffs?

There has been a strong tendency to treat the *domus* of the traditional Pompeian type as a family unit belonging to owner-occupiers, in contrast to the *insula* of the Ostian type, consisting of several separate units (*cenacula*) occupied by tenants (Figs. 5.6–7). This may well be accurate in broad terms, but the contrast requires modification. Legal sources have been illuminatingly employed to analyze the landlord/tenant relationships of the *insula*.[32] But it has been assumed that the Pompeian house represents a pattern of living that was already out of date by the early Empire,[33] and perhaps for this reason the relevance of the legal sources has been missed. In fact, provincial evidence undermines the thesis of a unilinear development from *domus* to *insula*; one may suspect that multistory brick and concrete blocks remained the exception away from the crowded metropolis. Most of what the lawyers have to say about the rental market applies with equal validity to the rather different *insulae* and houses of Pompeii and Herculaneum.

Perhaps the most valuable lesson to be learned from the legal sources is the potential complexity of relationships of ownership and habitation. In this analysis, I have followed convention in treating as a house or single unit any discrete physical unit that is inaccessible from any neighboring unit. Thus shops have been treated as independent units when they lack a connecting door to a house of which they may form a structural part.

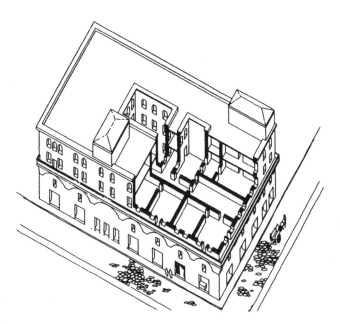

Figure 5.6 Plan, Ostian insula block.

Figure 5.7 Insula Orientalis, Herculaneum.
The facade to the left is the one multistory
insula of the Ostian type found in
Herculaneum and Pompeii.

But when we think about either legal ownership or habitation, the situation must be considerably more complex. On the one hand, shop and house, though unconnected, may form a single unit of *ownership*; on the other, shop and house, though connected, may at any given moment form separate units of *habitation*.[34]

On the whole we are probably right to assume that a single physical unit belonged to a single owner, yet even this may depend on circumstances. Papinian considers the problems of a house left to a legatee: The legacy would include an adjacent bathhouse (*balneae*) if access to the baths was from within the house, if they had been habitually used by the paterfamilias and his wife, if the income from them was entered in the same account as the other income from the house, and if house and baths had been bought with a single payment. Similarly, an adjacent garden (*hortus*) purchased after the house would become part of it if purchased as an entity and made accessible through the house. And again, an adjacent insula might be included in the property if both were bought with a single payment and the rents were entered in the accounts together. In all three cases, it is assumed that the heirs are trying to minimize the legacy by denying that profit-making adjuncts form part of what is bequeathed. Physical boundaries are relevant to the legal argument but are not by themselves conclusive; the account books matter as well.[35]

Moreover, it could happen that two people owned a single house in common, presumably on the understanding that each had use of a separate part of it. Paulus regards this as a difficult situation, since neither party could undertake any construction or alteration without the consent of the other; given the countless potential disputes, this usually leads to proceedings for division of the property.[36] According to Ulpian, you could sell part of a house, just as you could sell part of a farm; but if the master constructed a partition wall to divide what had been built as a single house, "as they often do" (*ut plerique faciunt*), then it became two houses.[37] Hence it was possible for two houses with a single roof to be left to two legatees, with consequent complications for rights over that roof.[38]

Ownership is complex, and therefore frequently beyond the reach of archaeological reconstruction; habitation is subject to further complications. Apart from the two obvious situations of owner-occupier (*dominus*) and tenant (*inquilinus*), there is also the common legal situation of the usufructuary, who is left the use or right of dwelling (*habitatio*) in a house, normally for life.[39] The first-century A.D. jurist, the younger Nerva, ruled that the usufructuary of a house was allowed to alter it by putting in windows and changing its decoration, frescoes, and statuary, but should not impose structural changes such as altering rooms, entrances, the atrium, or the layout of the garden. He could also rent the house out as a house, but he could not divide the house into lodgings (*cenacula*) or let off rooms as *meritoria* (rented property), for instance as a guest house (*deversorium*) or as a fullery. Nor could he establish a public path (*balineum*) or rent out a private bath suite in the private quarters ("in intima parte domus vel inter diaetas amoenas").[40] Nerva's careful distinctions between what was and was not permissible are incidentally revealing of what the owner, as opposed to the usufructuary, might do in the normal course of events.

Something of the variety of possible combinations of inhabitants of a house emerges from the discussion of who was entitled to cohabit with a usufructuary. Ulpian was clear that a husband left the use of a house by his wife was entitled to live there with his *familia*, that is, presumably, his children and slaves. There was some dispute as to whether freedmen too were allowed; Celsus and Tubero thought so. Labeo thought that lodgers (*inquilini*) were permissible, and added guests (*hospites*) and freedmen (*liberti*); Paulus added *clientes*. Proculus noted that *inquilinus* was not strictly the proper term if the usufructuary was living in the house himself. Suppose a man of modest status (*homo mediocris*) had use of a spacious house and only required a small portion for his own use; one could scarcely object if he took paying guests. And if he lacked slaves of his own, but used as laborers the slaves of another or free men, they too might live with him.[41] Or suppose a widow, left the right of habitation, remarried. Pomponius and Papinian agree that her new husband is entitled to live there with her, and Ulpian adds not only her children and freedmen but her parents as well.[42] The right of habitation left to a *filiusfamilias* or a slave extended to the paterfamilias under whose power he or she was, and this, according to Africanus, was true even if the usufructuary did not live in the house.[43]

The situation envisaged above, of the "mediocre" man living in the spacious house, must not have been uncommon, given the practice of leaving freedmen the right of habitatio in the master's old house.[44] A possible example is a certain Olympicus, who was left as a legacy the use of a house and store (*horreum*) for life, but not that of the adjoining garden and lodging (*cenaculum*). Scaevola was of the opinion that the heir had reasonable right of access to the garden and lodging through Olympicus's house, so long as the legatee was not inconvenienced.[45]

The value of these passages, cited as no more than samples from legal material stretching from the late Republic to the third century, is to remind us of the variety and complexity of the situations thrown up by real life. Lawyers, of course, are attracted to those difficult situations that will stretch their powers of distinction and definition; but the effect is to summon up a vivid picture of a range of possibilities we might otherwise ignore. Alongside the standard figure of the paterfamilias surrounded by his family and slaves, we are invited to imagine widows, freedmen, heirs, and legatees anxious to exploit urban property for the rich range of opportunities it offered: on the one hand opportunities for habitation, whether for gracious living with frescoes, statues, gardens, and private baths, or as lodging for a motley crowd of dependents, freedmen, employees, clients, and visitors; on the other hand, opportunities for profit, from lodgers, shops, fulleries, warehouses, and baths to let.

The Pompeian archaeological evidence seems to cohere with the picture that emerges from the legal sources. In two cases, well-known graffiti advertise the exploitation of the assets of substantial urban properties. At the insula Arriana Polliana of Gnaeus Alleius Nigidius Maius, property to let comprises shops with upper balcony-rooms, "equestrian" lodgings, and a house or houses (Fig. 5.8).[46] This is a large block dominated by a fine house, the Casa di Pansa (VI 6.1), surrounded by a penumbra of a dozen or so shops (2–7, 13–23), three small houses of Type 2 (central space off which rooms open; 7, 9, 10), and a number of external stairs to flats above (6, 8, 11, 18, 19).[47] Similarly the Praedia Iuliae Felicis (II 4) offer five-year leases on baths, shops, upper balcony-rooms, and lodgings.[48] The peristyle and nymphaeum attached to the baths are most elegantly deco-

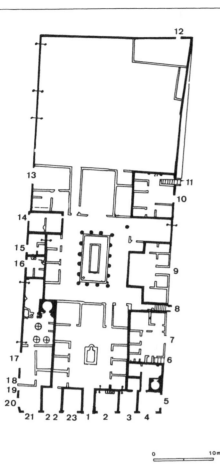

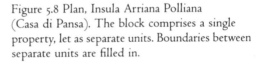

Figure 5.8 Plan, Insula Arriana Polliana
(Casa di Pansa). The block comprises a single
property, let as separate units. Boundaries between
separate units are filled in.

rated, and without the epigraphic evidence one would not suspect their commercial usage.

Owners of blocks as large and prestigious as these two might well put up conspicuous advertisements. Lesser houses may be presumed to have been engaged in similar transactions, even if less obviously. One indicator that these houses represent far more than single-family residential units is the frequency of multiple doors. Of the units in the sample, 98 (42 percent) have more than one door, 32 (14 percent) have 3 or more, 16 (7 percent) have 4 or more, 6 have 5 or more, and 1 has 6. Multiple doors are equally common in the Pompeii (42 percent) and Herculaneum samples (40 percent). They are, naturally, progressively more common as house size increases: 9 (16 percent) in the first quartile, 19 (31 percent) in the second, 25 (44 percent) in the third, and 45 (78 percent) in the fourth. Secondary doors reflect a variety of circumstances, some of which are compatible with single-family usage: grand houses like the Casa del Fauno may have two atria, the second perhaps for less formal use (the "trade entrance"); many have backdoors that open onto side streets. Secondary doors are often for commercial usage, leading into shops and workshops incorporated within the building. Occasionally, as we have seen, they reflect the amalgamation of separate units, which may in some cases have continued to function separately. In other cases, additional doors point to the letting of lodgings.

Can we estimate how common rented apartments were in Pompeii and Herculaneum? Della Corte found evidence of lodgers in his attempts to identify by name inhabitants of individual houses. Thus in the Casa dei Vettii (VI 15.1) he identifies P. Crusius Faustus as a lodger in the upper floor on the basis of a signet ring; a couple of doors down (VI 15.5, Casa di Pupius Rufus) he finds three lodgers: L. Sepunius Amphio, C. Stlaccius Epitynchianus, and Titinia Saturnina.[49] The unreliability of Della Corte's methods is now notorious;[50] moreover, this method would be worthless for statistical purposes, as it depends on the casual survival of evidence.

Subletting is obvious in the insulae of Ostia precisely because these units are constructed to facilitate the social pattern, with independent staircases from outside and common circulation areas allowing independent access to separate flats (see Fig. 5.7). Similarly at Pompeii and Herculaneum, the clearest evidence of lodgings is a separate set of stairs from the street leading to rooms above the ground floor. Because of the structure of houses of this type, built around the lightwells of impluvia, peristyles, or courtyards, houses rarely could have a continuous upper floor such as we are familiar with; instead there were a series of separate second stories, each accessible from its own set of stairs (see Fig. 5.10). The street frontage is the commonest location for a second story, and this could be made accessible either from immediately within the atrium or from outside; to change the access from inside to out was not a complicated building operation.

Cenaculum is the proper Latin term for such an upper room or lodging, and the usage goes back at least to the early second century B.C., where we find the Jupiter of Plautus's *Amphitruo* jestingly referring to his abode as "in superiore . . . cenaculo" ("in the attic upstairs"),[51] and Ennius coining the phrase "cenacula maxima caeli" ("the great attics of the heaven").[52] The ease with which an upper room could be made available for a lodger and accessible from the street or within can be seen in Livy's narrative of the Bacchanalian scandal of 187 B.C.: When Hispala Fecenia turns informer, the consul finds her safe lodgings in a cenaculum in his mother-in-law's house, and has the stairs to the street blocked off and replaced by internal stairs.[53] At the same time, we may note, Hispala Fecenia's lover Aebutius is moved in with a client of the consul.

One illustration of the architectural possibilities is the Casa del Principe di Napoli (VI 15.7/8) discussed above (Figs. 3.14–17). The German team that reexamined the house gave attention to the question of the number and status of its inhabitants.[54] The house has three sets of stairs: one immediately inside the atrium above the cell of the doorkeeper (ostiarius), which Strocka takes to be the access to (ill-lit) slave bedrooms for three to five slaves; another, from within the kitchen, leads to rooms looking over the garden, taken to be the private suite for a family of six to ten; the third leads from the street, and is taken to be a flat for a family of four. We have seen that there is a strong contrast between the dark, northern part of the house and the light, southern part overlooking the garden, which gives plausibility to the suggestion that the southern part was for the family. Yet what is to exclude the possibility that at one time or another slaves, or freedmen, or dependents, or even further lodgers lived there too? Or that usage changed over time?

Figure 5.9 Facade of Insula V, Herculaneum (Casa del Bicentenario). Visible in the frontage from left to right are the following: no. 18, narrow entrance to stairs to upper apartment; no. 17, wide entrance to shop; no. 16, wide shop opening; no. 15, narrow entrance to main house of block, Casa del Bicentenario, distinguished by its elevation; no. 14, narrow entrance to stairs to upper apartment; no. 13, wide shop opening. Holes for beams to carry upper *maeniana* (balconies) are visible.

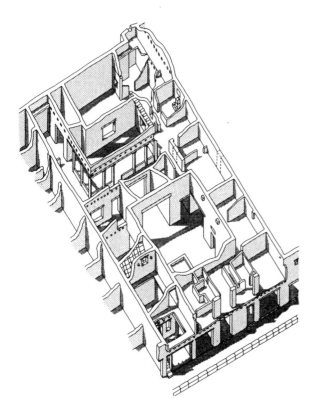

Figure 5.10 Reconstruction of Casa del Bicentenario with upper floor, Herculaneum (after Maiuri). The division of the apartments above the front is indistinct, but note that three separate stairs give access.

It would be rash to take external stairs as a measure of the total extent of lodgers in either town, for the lawyers make plain that houses continued under the Empire, long after the development of the tenement block, to provide shelter for tenants, inquilini, as well as for dependents of various types. Evidence of internal staircases is normal enough, but often there are no obvious criteria for determining whether these were in particular cases *intended* for the use of family, slaves, other dependents, or lodgers, let alone by whom they were *actually* used in A.D. 79. It is perilous to infer from architecture how a house actually was inhabited; architecture does not dictate usage but opens up a range of possibilities. One can only say that some of the appeal of owning a big house must have been its potential flexibility of use, whether for a large extended family, for an ostentatious slave household, for a workforce (slave and free), or for letting.

External staircases, then, offer evidence of the *minimum* extent of lodgings. In the samples for this study, 25 (just over 10 percent) of the houses have external staircases. They are fairly evenly distributed among all size quartiles except the first (4 in the first, 8 in the second, 6 in the third, 7 in the fourth quartile). There appears to be some contrast between Herculaneum, in which external stairs are relatively frequent (15 percent), and Pompeii (12.5 percent in Regio VI, 5 percent in Regio I). Herculaneum is closer than Pompeii to the Ostian pattern in other respects; only here do we find (in the Palaestra block) an example of multistoried brick and concrete construction. Perhaps, then, the contrast is real. Perhaps too we are witnessing a change over time, with a movement from a late-republican pattern of big-house living to an imperial pattern of multiple, small, independent units. To assess this possibility would require more extensive examination of the archaeological evidence elsewhere than Pompeii.

Because upper floors are better preserved at Herculaneum, it is also easier here to see how separate lodgings functioned. One interesting feature that emerges is the separate hearth or lararium. The hearth makes possible independent eating; lares symbolize separate worship and family unity. Like the independence of access, they reflect a desire to eat and be seen as a separate family unit, not an extension of the big house. So the flat above the front door of the Casa del Bicentenario (H V.14/15) (Fig. 5.11) has a characteristic lararium painting (lares and serpents), while the upstairs rooms of the independent shop at H V.17 (originally part of the big house) has a handsome wooden shrine (Fig. 5.12). The flat above the shop, H V.6, interconnecting with the Casa di Nettuno (Fig. 5.13), has its own hearth. The Casa a Graticcio (H III.13/14/15) has been treated as the classic example of multiple occupancy (Figs. 5.14–15). One upstairs flat at the back, accessible from the courtyard within, had its own wooden shrine containing two lares (not to mention a Jupiter, Athena, Aesculapius, two Fortunae, Harpocrates, and a Bacchant).[55] The front flat, accessible from without (H III.13), has both its own wooden shrine and a hearth. There has been considerable work on collecting evidence of lararia,[56] and it would be worth investigating what they can tell us about patterns of habitation.

Can we distinguish archaeologically between the extended family and the slave family? On other grounds it seems to me unlikely that the extended family was anything but exceptional in Italy under the Empire. The whole Augustan legislative program promoting the family and controlling manumission suggests to me that by this period slavery and

Figure 5.11 Casa del Bicentenario, Herculaneum, upper floor, with lararium painting. This is situated immediately above the fauces (entrance no. 15) and presumably belongs to the apartment accessible from no. 14.

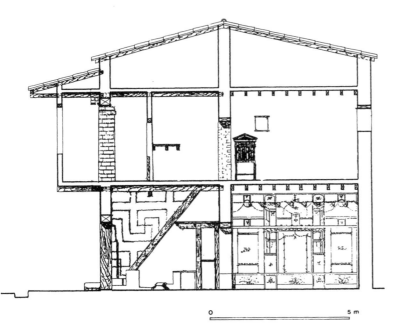

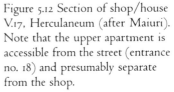

Figure 5.12 Section of shop/house V.17, Herculaneum (after Maiuri). Note that the upper apartment is accessible from the street (entrance no. 18) and presumably separate from the shop.

Figure 5.13 Casa di Nettuno ed Anfitrite, Herculaneum, view of upper apartment.

Figure 5.14 Casa a Graticcio, Herculaneum, with upper balcony.

Figure 5.15 Isometric drawing of Casa a Graticcio, Herculaneum (after Maiuri). Note two separate apartments, the front one accessible from the street, the rear one accessible from the courtyard. Wooden fittings (beds, cupboards) are drawn in as found.

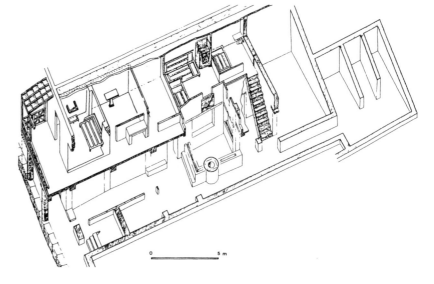

manumission operated as an alternative strategy to the extended family, even if the Romans possibly regarded the latter as their *mos maiorum*. But how would one demonstrate or exclude the presence of the extended family? One interesting pattern is that of the late-republican villa, seen in the Villa dei Misteri or Settefinnestre (Figs. 3.19–20), where we find up to four suites of rooms, each comprising a smaller inner room and a larger reception room (cubiculum and triclinium), symmetrically disposed around a central hall (see Chap. 3). Each suite can act as a separate reception unit; one might imagine the paterfamilias in one, and adult—even married—children in others. But it is equally possible that the others act as guest suites, or even as seasonal alternatives for the master.

Another possible approach is through close attention to the distribution of beds in houses. Surprisingly many traces survive of these: At Herculaneum the preservation of wooden bed-frames is quite common (including, in one famous instance, a baby's cot). Even at Pompeii some fragmentary wooden beds survive, though more common are traces of the frame left in a heap of *lapilli*. Indirect evidence also survives. It was quite normal, especially in more modest bedrooms, to build the bed head into a niche in the wall, clear traces of which can be found. In the grander bedrooms, too, the bed space may be marked out decoratively, by a contrasting "carpet" of mosaics, by a break in the wall decoration, or even by an alcove with lowered ceiling for maximum privacy (presumably what the younger Pliny refers to as a *zotheca*).[57] Would analysis of the beds point toward the distribution of married couples/children/slaves/etc. within the house?

Apart from one exceptional child's bed (see Fig. 5.15), there seems to be no archaeological indication of where children of whatever age may have slept. The young, at least in well-off households, presumably slept, as Tacitus complains,[58] with servile nursemaids and tutors. Married couples ought to be easier to trace. The literary evidence repeatedly suggests that they slept together. To "sleep apart" (*secubare*) is an exceptional circumstance that requires explanation, as when Tiberius and Julia quarrel;[59] when a rhetorician refers to pregnancy as an occasion for sleeping apart "without compromising modesty";[60] or when Tibullus and his mistress or Ovid's Hercules and Omphale sleep apart (explicitly in separate beds) on the eve of sacrifice.[61] By contrast, Tacitus sees it as part of strange Jewish mores that men and women eat and sleep apart ("separati epulis, discreti cubilibus"), and he snipes at the implications for adultery.[62]

In theory, then, beds for married couples ought to be detectable. But though there are many beds on which couples *could* have slept, there is no clear differentiation between single and double beds such as we know. In Figure 5.16 the distribution of widths of thirty-five beds is tabulated; a similar exercise with modern beds would show two distinct peaks at 90cm and 135cm. Without unambiguous evidence of double beds, there seems little chance of identifying households with more than one married couple.

Both the possibilities and the limitations of using a bed count to reconstruct the population of a grand house are brought out with great clarity by Strocka's new publication of the Casa del Labirinto (Fig. 5.17).[63] The house offers four main areas where people may have slept: at the front, the main atrium (27) and the secondary atrium (3); at the back, the magnificent reception suite overlooking the peristyle (39–46) and the annex with a separate entrance at no. 8. The main atrium offers one room with a niche

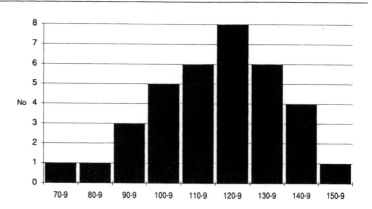

Figure 5.16 Distribution of bed widths. There is no standard width for either wooden frames or bed recesses.

for a double bed (30), and four single(?) bedrooms at 24, 25, 28, and 29. The secondary atrium has certain bedrooms at 8 and 14, a probable one at 2, and a possible one at 6. Stairs in room 2 lead to an upper apartment with an unknown number of rooms. The annex has a double(?) bedroom at 49 and an unknown number of upper rooms. The grand reception suite has two carefully contoured cubicula flanking the oecus Corinthius at 42 and 46. From this evidence, Strocka cautiously reckons the population of the house at seventeen to thirty in its high period, and fourteen to twenty-four in its final phase, when he argues that the distinguished family of proprietors was absent and a humble family of tenants had taken over.

What emerges from Strocka's analysis is not only the extraordinary difficulty of estimating for beds, using only signs of their incorporation in the architectural and decorative scheme of a room, but the uncertainty of the basic assumptions about who slept where, assumptions from which we could proceed to populate the beds we can detect. The insecurity of such assumptions reaches its worst in the grandest area of the house. In the final phase, Strocka guesses, these areas were uninhabited because reserved for the use of the absent proprietors. But even in the house's high period these rooms present a difficulty. Were the two elegant cubicula flanking the oecus Corinthius a matching set for the master and mistress of the house? In the summer, maybe, or for daytime use; but, continues Strocka, "that the Paterfamilias and the matrona cut themselves off permanently in this way from their children and relatives, I find hard to imagine."[64]

That is precisely the nub of our problem: We ourselves find the picture of parents isolated from their families by the lonely splendor of a peristyle an alienating thought. Did the Roman? Tacitus's Maternus, philosophizing with friends in his cubiculum and shaking his head over the corrupting influence of foreign nursemaids on children, might have been less surprised. Room 42—with its mosaic floor of the labyrinth that gives its name to the house, and its position on the axis of the peristyle—can be confidently identified as a key room. And although we instinctively shy from imagining people living and sleeping in the alarming exposure of such magnificent reception areas, we can use our reading of the ancient sources to guard against and control such instinctive assumptions (see Chap. 3). But the architecture of the house cannot of itself provide an answer: It cannot tell us whether the two cubicula that flank the prime reception room

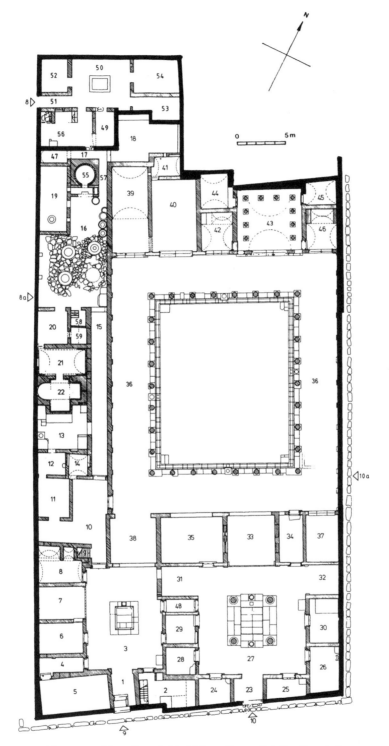

Figure 5.17 Plan, Casa del Labirinto, Pompeii (after Strocka).

were for master and mistress separately, or for master and his wife in one, and either a son (or brother) and his wife, or an honored guest, in the other. Nor can it tell us how, whatever the designer's intentions, subsequent generations of inhabitants actually used these spaces.[65]

———————

THAT the archaeology of Pompeii and Herculaneum should offer us precise insights into the composition of the Roman family and the balance of children versus slaves seems too much to ask. On the other hand, it does appear to offer vivid evidence of other important aspects of domestic life. The modern fascination with the nuclear family is linked to the conditions of modern domestic life; the mother-father-children unit is so apparent because of its isolation within the home. Not only do we live without other relatives, but we live away from the world of work, without servants, apprentices, slaves, workers, and other friends or dependents. In consequence, we now exclude the latter categories from our concept of the family, and privilege the nuclear family as a focus of research into the past.

Pompeii and Herculaneum offer an example of the sort of domestic context within which we must accommodate the Roman family. In all sorts of ways it is not what our experience of the family leads us to expect. The total number of households in Pompeii is surprisingly low, the average number of rooms per house surprisingly high. If we want to envisage a town of something in the order of ten thousand inhabitants, we must assume a high average, about seven to eight persons, per house. We may also be struck by the wide range of house sizes, whether measured in terms of ground-floor rooms, from one to over thirty per house, or in terms of area, from under $25m^2$ to over $2,500m^2$. This points to a wide range in size of household and to the implication that, common though small units may have been, a majority of the population lived in what we would regard as big households.

But this is by no means the same as saying that Romans lived in big families. On closer inspection, our households turn out to be potentially housefuls, where the owner or user's family and slaves mix with a fluctuating assortment of dependents, freedmen, workers, friends, and lodgers. To concede so much may appear to undermine the value of the archaeological evidence for reconstructing the Roman family. If our only interest is to generate statistics for average family size, that is certainly so. But for understanding the physical setting of the family, and consequently the way the family environment was conceived, it is of considerable importance. If we take the paterfamilias as we normally envisage him, the householder in his atrium house, with wife, children, and slaves, I doubt whether Pompeii could produce more than six hundred to eight hundred such families. Yet these must be surrounded by a great penumbra of persons of varied status, much harder to define as family groups. Some of course may be respected members of society, living with families in rented equestria cenacula; others will include the poorest and most marginal members of society.

Between the core of householders and the fringe of dependents, tenants, or lodgers, a spectrum of social and economic relationships is possible. At one extreme the trusted freedman may continue to live in his master's house as part of his familia; at the other, the stranger may rent an apartment for cash. Maiuri, whose excavations made him well aware of the penumbra, inferred a period of acute social change in both Pompeii and Herculaneum.[66] He assumed that the patrician family *ought* to be free of its squalid assortment of shops and lodgers, and that there had once been (as recently as the reign of Augustus) a time when that was so, but that the new economic conditions of the Empire, exacerbated by the effects of the earthquake of A.D. 62, had created a new commercial petite bourgeoisie and subsequent overcrowding. He saw in the tenement blocks of Ostia, already anticipated in the Palaestra block at Herculaneum, the eventual solution to the new social and economic pressures: multiple-occupancy rented accommodation.

The picture offered here is rather different. The "promiscuous crowd" of the traditional atrium house was not a novel or transitional phenomenon but rather its natural condition. The big house was simultaneously source and symbol of wealth: the "extras" living with the nuclear family were both a source of income and a sign of social power. The tenement block, by contrast, was a more efficient way of raising income, at the cost of being a less effective source of social power. It is worth noting that the one tenement block at Herculaneum was presumably the property of the municipality, put up to offset the costs of the *palaestra* development. Further study is needed to understand changes over time (does Ostia reflect the demise of the big house, and if so why?) and regional contrasts (how does the North African and Provençal evidence compare?).

Precisely because it is not simply a family house, the Pompeian house can be unexpectedly difficult for us to read. One of the most striking contrasts between the Pompeian and the modern house is the failure of the former to differentiate architecturally and decoratively either between male and female worlds or between those of adults and children. That is because, as in Ariès's big house, such modern differentiations disappear in what seems to us promiscuity, and the real contrasts turn around the public face of the house and its reception or business functions. The atrium offers a useful symbol of such promiscuity: Its function in adult male life for reception, business, and social and patronal relations is obvious enough. But it also emerges in the sources as the traditional place where the materfamilias conducts her life; Tarquin finds Lucretia and her maids in the atrium spinning after dark,[67] a custom attested in Cicero's day,[68] and there Columella's housekeeper operates.[69] And it is where, on the rare occasions we see children at play, they too are found.[70]

One of the merits of Ariès's *Centuries of Childhood* is his realization that part of changing attitudes to children in history is the physical environment of the home. If we want to understand the texture of domestic life in early imperial Italy, we will have to come to terms with the phenomenon of the big house and its implications: the lack of privacy and separateness for the parent-child unit; the ways in which slaves and freedmen formed an active part of the *familia* and in both economic and psychological terms could serve as an alternative strategy to children and family; and the social promiscuity of the big house.

CHAPTER 6

=========================== ❑ ===========================

HOUSES AND TRADE

It was one of those old town houses, a few of which are still to be found, in which the court of honour—whether they were alluvial deposits washed there by the rising tide of democracy, or a legacy from a more primitive time when the different trades were clustered round the overlord—is flanked by little shops and workrooms, a shoemaker's, for instance, or a tailor's . . . ; a porter who also does cobbling, keeps hens, grows flowers, and at the far end, in the ancient building, a "Comtesse."

Proust, *The Guermantes Way*

PROUST'S EVOCATION of a forgotten age preserved in the Hôtel de Guermantes, and his studied uncertainty as to whether the juxtaposition of nobility and trade represented an ancient tradition or its demise, point to one of the main ways in which experience of the postindustrial city leads to misreadings of the ancient city.[1] The Roman house was no island of privacy, protected by watertight barriers against the world of public life outside. It was porous, constantly penetrated by the outside world; and from its ability to control and exploit this penetration it drew power, status, and profit. The public entered the private in two guises that can be expressed in a number of antitheses: dignity versus vulgarity, pleasure versus utility, luxury versus profit. On the one hand there is the world of social exchanges that generates social and political power for the householder; on the other, the world of production and commerce that generates profit.

The symbolic contrast between "noble" patronage and "sordid" trade was made visible even in the nature of the openings that linked the house to the street outside: the narrow opening, artificially emphasised by the long corridor of the *fauces*, that leads to the atrium is designed to exclude and to mark the privilege of one who approaches for dignified purposes; whereas the wide opening of the *taberna* throws open the space inside and vulgarly displays its contents, promiscuously accessible except when the shutters are drawn against thieves at night (Fig. 6.1).[2] Both types of opening seek to tempt in the outsider: the shop openly so, but without dignity, in order to extract a profit; the *fauces* subtly so, by displaying a seductive vista, a glimpse of order, beauty, luxury, and privilege, which the lucky may achieve (Fig. 6.2).

This chapter explores the relationship between these two types of penetration. We misunderstand it, just as we misunderstand the relationship of public and private, because we do things differently. We distinguish the commercial from the residential; shops, workshops, offices, and factories from houses. The Roman town draws the lines elsewhere, and though spatial, architectural, and decorative contrasts were constructed between petty trade and dignified sociability, they might nevertheless coexist in the same house.

ELITE RESIDENCE

One feature of the tight nexus that bound together town and country in the Greco-Roman world was that the great landowners who dominated politically were dependent on the urban centers for their power and regularly resided, at least in part, within the city. That, as Max Weber appreciated, represented a significant contrast to the usual pattern in the cities of the medieval world, especially in northern Europe. There the separation of town and country led to the development of two competing elites, the barons of the countryside and the big merchants of the town. The Greek and Roman cities never evolved a specifically urban elite, and the success of metics and freedmen, men who either lacked citizen status or whose status was compromised by the taint of slavery, is a symbol of that failure.[3]

Many who reject the Weberian model of the ancient city prefer to reaffirm the scale and significance of commercial activity in the ancient city and to minimize the contrast to the medieval model. Frank and Rostovtzeff, impressed by the variety and liveliness of the nonagricultural activities implied by the archaeological record of cities like Pompeii, posited an emergent bourgeoisie,[4] a picture taken to extremes in the fantasy of a Pompeii run by fuller bosses at the center of a complex cloth industry.[5] Others have attempted to

Figure 6.1 Casa del Gran Portale, Herculaneum, frontage. The narrow house-entrance is strongly marked by brick pillars (this distinctive feature gives the house its name). To its right is visible the wide threshold of a shop front. The shop no longer connects with the house (the doorway visible in its side wall is blocked), though it may have been linked in ownership and operation.

Figure 6.2 Casa dei Ceii, Pompeii, view of fauces. The "throat" of the entrance passage underlines the separation of house from public world outside.

identify a quasi-elite in the freedmen Augustales, of whom Trimalchio serves as the fictional paradigm; but impressive though their wealth and dignity as priests of the imperial cult, their exclusion from local office showed the continuation of their subaltern status.[6]

To gloss over the differences between the antique and the medieval (the medieval being as hard to generalize about as the antique, if not more so)[7] is to abandon the best insights derived from Weber's bold comparative method. Paradoxically, one of the most valuable of these was his perception of the involvement of the rural elite in specifically urban activity. The towns of medieval and early modern England (which Weber knew from his reading of Maitland) make a particularly sharp contrast. The cleavage between urban and rural elite in England down to the beginning of the early modern period was pronounced. It was a major turning point for the English town when in the seventeenth century the country gentry started to take up residence there. Squalid and subject to plague, the medieval and early modern English town deterred the rural elite by the sheer unpleasantness of its habitat, over and above the undoubted political and economic divisions. "A clean town was something to be remarked on," observed Patten of the early modern English town.

> Running water (was) largely non-existent and internal sanitary arrangements primitive in the extreme. Outside in the streets, which were often the ultimate destination of these primitive sanitary arrangements, mire, filth and butchers' offal mingled on unpaved and undrained surfaces rarely swept or attended to by the town scavenger. (Patten 1978, 32)

The arrival of the country gentry as town residents was marked by cultural transformation, the spread of new London fashions, assembly rooms, coffee houses, theaters and spas; by the emergence of distinctive elite housing zones like the ostentatiously "classical" squares and terraces; and by economic transformation as new capital was injected into the urban economy.[8]

Such transformation was unnecessary in antiquity. The elite of a Roman city were perforce resident in the town for at least part of the year. A multiplicity of social ties involved them with the commercially active population. As private patrons, partly of freeborn clients but most conspicuously of freedmen, they were drawn into advising and supporting traders. As candidates for office, unless the electoral advertisements (*programmata*) of Pompeii are grossly misleading, they benefited from the support of groups of traders, whether or not these formally had the status of *collegia* (colleges): if the *quactiliarii* (felt makers) could declare their support for Vettius Firmus in his candidacy for the aedileship and underline their identity with a vivid depiction of felters at work,[9] then, whatever Vettius's own involvement in the felting trade, it is clear that trades could represent themselves as having a sufficiently powerful group-identity to be worth cultivating for political ends.[10] Once elected as magistrates, they were involved in the adjudication of commercial disputes, such as those illustrated by the dossier of the freedmen Sulpicii from Murecine.[11]

Socially and politically, contact with the commercial world of the town was inevitable for the elite. It stands to reason that the economic dimension was also vital. Both as patrons of freedmen engaged in trade and as property owners drawing rents from the lease of stores and shops, a substantial portion of the urban elite must have derived at least part of their income from trade, even if they did not actually run businesses. There is a good case for seeing urban real estate as a vital element in the income of the elite (this includes, of course, rental of apartments).[12] Compared to land, such investment was high risk, thanks particularly to the dangers of fire; but the returns were also high and perhaps there were other compensations, such as a spread of cash income through times of year when no agricultural returns were forthcoming. One may also hypothesize that such economic ties intermeshed with the social and political ties. Landlords in the countryside could enjoy social and political support from their tenants. Not the least of the advantages of property ownership in the towns must have been to extend a nexus of social and political influence along the lines of economic power. Traders were thus a simultaneous source of revenue and social position for their landlords.

Archaeological evidence ought to betray something of such links, and this chapter will look at the evidence of Pompeii and Herculaneum to illustrate the potential of archaeology in this respect. First, however, it is necessary to expose a number of questionable assumptions underpinning debate about these site, formulated in their most uncompromising fashion by this century's dominant excavator, Amedeo Maiuri.[13]

One great strength of Maiuri's excavations is that they were conducted in full awareness of their potential importance for revealing the social and economic fabric of a Roman town. On the one hand, as was perhaps inevitable under the *età fascistica*, he was concerned to find glorious monuments: the Villa dei Misteri and the Casa del Menandro were the jewels in his crown. On the other hand, he looked for social and economic change, influenced by historical debate and particularly by Rostovtzeff, who drew on close knowledge of the site in his account of the supposed rise of a commercially and industrially based bourgeoisie in early imperial Italy. Maiuri evolved a thesis of a major social and economic transformation of the area under the early empire, which came to a head after the earthquake of A.D. 62. The case was argued in *L'ultima fase edilizia di Pompei* (1942): The old patriciate was in decline, unable to stem the rising tide of commerce; its tasteful residences were invaded by industry or broken up into squalid shops and flats; the new men who pushed out their old masters displayed their vulgar taste in the new styles of decoration. The earthquake delivered the coup de grâce to the patriciate, who retreated to their country estates, leaving the field clear for the nouveaux riches.

> But it is also in this period [i.e., post-earthquake] that we witness the transformation of many upper-class houses [case signorili] into *officinae*, the intrusion of shops, *cauponae* and *thermopolia* into the interior of and along the facades of patrician residences, the splitting up of a single, grand, upper-class house into several modest dwellings, the change and perversion of taste in type and style of the decoration of the rooms, sacrificing beautiful and noble old paintings for banal and poor redecoration, in short the invasion by the mercantile class of the structure of the old Romano-Campanian patrician class of the city. (Maiuri 1942, 216–17)

The same thesis emerges repeatedly in Maiuri's numerous guide books and popular works on Pompeii. One may be struck by the warmth of his language, his sympathy for the taste attributed to the old patriciate, and his resentment at the "brutal invasion" of the commercial world:

> Shops . . . defaced the simple and severe architectural forms of patrician houses by plastering garish trade signs on the wall; they pressed against the sides of noble portals as if to launch a final and triumphant attack against the whole edifice after having completed the conquest of some of its less important rooms. (Maiuri 1960, 188)

His picture of Pompeian society read from the physical remains is certainly lively ("this motley crowd of enriched merchants, secondhand dealers, bakers, fullers, decayed patricians, and thrusting industrialists dabbling in politics," ibid. 138), but it rests on unwarranted assumptions. He has been criticized from a variety of angles. Careful study of the prosopography of the Pompeian elite has shown at least some of the picture of an invasion of the elite by "industrialists" to be sheer fantasy.[14] Andreau questioned his picture of the economic effects of a major earthquake: comparison with the well-documented effects of similar disasters in Catania (1693), Lisbon (1755), and Messina (1783, 1908) suggests that the picture of a commercial boom in the aftermath of a quake is most implausible. On the other hand, there are parallels for an exodus of the rich to their country estates and a crisis of accommodation leading to splitting up of grand houses into apartments, as well as for long delays in reconstructing the city's public and private buildings, stretching over twenty years and more.[15] On this basis, there is at least some plausibility in Mauri's suggestions. What is hard to estimate is the extent to which an exodus of the rich would have been likely in an ancient as opposed to modern town, with its very different conditions of political participation.

The fundamental obstacle to Maiuri's thesis, as has been stressed by a number of scholars,[16] is the inadequacy of the archaeological evidence on which it rests. Excavation that fails to penetrate below the A.D. 79 levels cannot allow genuine comparisons to the situation before the earthquake. Maiuri's case is anecdotal, not statistical. He points to the installation of new shops, yet of some six hundred Pompeian shops catalogued by Gassner, only twenty on her reckoning demonstrably postdate the earthquake.[17] Again, Maiuri points to fourteen cases of "industrial" establishments (half of them bakeries or fulleries) installed in the last phase in private houses, but this is no basis for inferences about the social fortunes of the houses' owners. In view of the fact that nowhere in Pompeii do we find establishments specially constructed for "industrial" purposes, bakeries and fulleries and workshops are bound to be discovered in the fabric of private houses. Given ownership of multiple properties, and patterns of death and inheritance, the decline of individual properties cannot be used as an index of the fortunes of the elite as a whole. To sustain Maiuri's thesis, it would be necessary to demonstrate an absolute decline over time in the number of elite properties in the city. The frequency of grand houses in the city decorated in later styles of painting tells strongly against this hypothesis; and to suggest that only "new men" lived in houses decorated in new styles, while old styles point to old families, is manifestly absurd.

There may well be considerable elements of truth in Maiuri's account of the development of the city. More careful and systematic investigation may confirm a tendency to split up properties, install flats in upper stories, and open shops in front rooms, though it goes hand in hand with the reverse process by which old shops are closed down.[18] But what is particularly interesting in the context of this discussion is the nature of Maiuri's model of Roman society and of his assumptions about the relations between the elite (his "patricians") and trade. As Ettore Lepore observed in a subtle and penetrating critique (1950), Maiuri's model is simply too rigid. What justifies the assumption that the old aristocracy was based purely on landed property, rather than being "simultaneously landed and commercial"? Why should only freedmen nouveaux riches have been involved in trade, and how, in view of the transitional social status of the freedman, can they constitute a class with interests in conflict with those of the old elite?

It is worth looking at some examples to see these assumptions at work. Maiuri's publication of his excavations in Herculaneum (1958) is a valuable test case because he was able to incorporate in detail in an excavation report the thesis of economic change previously evolved and selectively illustrated in his Pompeian studies. The handsome two-volume publication of the best part of six blocks of houses is also an essay in social and economic interpretation. The very structure of the volumes is significant. Rather than presenting his material topographically, block by block, as was traditional, Maiuri sorted the houses by social class. His classification recreates eight divisions, which are presented in a hierarchical order:

1. Patrician houses of traditional type.
2. Middle-class houses (*del ceto medio*) of traditional type.
3. Grand houses (*case signorili*).
4. Residential houses of nontraditional type.
5. Middle-class houses with attached shops/workshops.
6. Multiple-residence houses.
7. Mercantile houses and shops with dwellings.
8. Shops/workshops in a multistory block.

Implicit in this classification are two assumptions. One is that houses in which shops or workshops have been incorporated are socially humbler than those without; the second is that houses of traditional (i.e., atrium) construction are socially superior to those of nontraditional type. Thus all the houses in the bottom four categories include shops/workshops. Among the residential houses, traditional houses are preferred to nontraditional, with the bizarre result that the three largest and most opulent houses are put in the third class. Among the houses with shops, those of most traditional structure (class 5) are preferred to those of the least traditional structure, the Ostia-type multistory insulae (class 8).

Once these assumptions have been incorporated into the classification system, it reveals a whole series of misfits, and these are all taken as evidence for the thesis of social change and degeneration. The Casa Sannitica (H V.1), with its stately atrium (see Fig. 2.10), is the first specimen: it must have belonged in the early Empire to a family "del più nobile patriziato ercolanese" (Maiuri 1958, 198). But this is a surprisingly small house, with no peristyle. Its reduction to the traditional nucleus therefore demonstrates to Maiuri that it was shaken by the "grave crisis provoked by the increase of overseas trade in the patriciate of the city." Nevertheless, the rooms clustered round the atrium of this household in reduced circumstances managed to "keep themselves pure of mercantile invasion" (ibid. 204); that is, there are no shops in the facade.

The anonymous house H V.11 (see Figs. 6.3–4) is another relatively small house of classic symmetrical fauces/atrium/tablinum construction. The "nobility" of its tablinum, which is indeed decorated with rich paintings and a handsome marble inlay floor, confirms that it was originally an upper-class (signorile) residence.

But after upper-class occupation lasting possibly as late as the Claudian era, the profound transformation which the commercial life of the city had to undergo

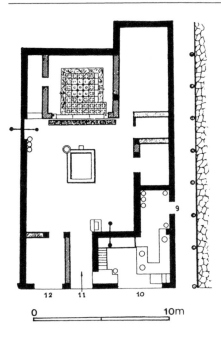

Figure 6.3 Plan, House V.11, Herculaneum (after Maiuri).

Figure 6.4 House V.11, Herculaneum, tablinum. The walls have rich fourth-style decoration, with mythological panels set against a red background, flanked by architectural vistas on a white background. The fine marble opus sectile floor forms a carpet in the center of spaces for couches (for a detail see Fig. 7.2). Note that the end wall of the tablinum in this small house is closed: the mythological painting is at the focus of the axial view from the entrance.

with the new arrangement of the Via del Foro, the grave crisis which the new currents of overseas commerce and earthquake damage produced in the class of the oldest patrician families of Herculaneum, and finally the need to withdraw from the noisy and plebeian commercial life of the Forum, were the multiple reasons which determined the decay of this house from an upper-class residence to the practical use of a lodging with shops. (Maiuri 1958, 248)

The evidence for the decline consists in the "conversion" of both front rooms of the house to shops, and the "vulgar patching" of the tablinum decoration, damaged in the earthquake, which indicates the level of taste and priorites of the final owner (ibid. 250).

But the prime specimen of degeneration is the neighboring Casa del Bicentenario

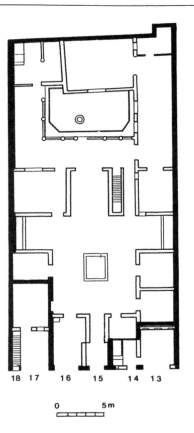

Figure 6.5 Plan, Casa del Bicentenario,
Herculaneum (after Maiuri). Note that
the exceptional length of the fauces
presupposes use of the frontage
for shops.

18 17   16   15   14 13

0   5 m

(H V.15, Fig. 6.5), a show house of the modern tourist trade and findspot of the much-discussed Petronia Justa dossier. Apart from the luxurious houses that engross the views from the seawall of the town, this is the largest excavated house; on the other hand, it has no fewer than four shops built into its facade. The thesis of decline is rolled out to account for this supposed contradiction. Built by a rich and noble family in the early Julio-Claudian period, with its magnificent atrium and richly decorated tablinum, it suffered toward the late fifties A.D. from the major social changes of the rise of commercial fortunes and the collapse of the old landowning aristocracy. The rooms fronting the forum were opened up as shops under freedmen or tenants. Ownership passed from the hands of a patrician to a rich freedman, and the house was split up into shabby flats. Its focus shifted from the noble quarters at the garden end of the commercial frontage, and there new flats were built and decorated. The lack of taste of the new owner is detected in the crude repairs to the beautiful Daedalus and Pasiphae painting in the tablinum and in the absence of the sort of handsome furniture to be expected in a patrician house at the time of excavation (ibid. 222ff.).

Throughout, Maiuri's assumptions are consistent and involve a simplistic correspondence between architectural and aesthetic features and the social standing of the inhabitants. Good-quality decoration reveals the social quality of the owners; crude repairs indicate vulgar owners. The traditional atrium points to "patricians," irrespective of the size of the house. The presence of shops is taken to be completely incompatible with the presence of "patricians": thus where we find shops, as in the anonymous H V.11, the "patrician" owners are assumed to have withdrawn; where we do not find them, the old "patricians" are envisaged as still huddled in their reduced circumstances, taking refuge from the surrounding tide of change.

All these assumptions are arbitrary. There is no reason a fine atrium should point to a patrician, let alone a landowning family. The Casa Sannitica is plausibly the reduced core of a once larger house; the anonymous H V.11 is not. What sort of patrician can have inhabited a house of these dimensions? What is the basis for the claim that the shops along the frontage of the Via del Foro are converted front rooms? The anonymous H V.11 stands on a street corner close to the forum; it is the classic location for a corner shop. No archaeological evidence is offered for the "conversion"; it is pure surmise, based on the logical chain of inference that a fine tablinum indicates noble inhabitants and that noble inhabitants exclude commercial usage. Similarly, no archaeological evidence is adduced for an earlier phase of noncommercial usage of the frontage of the Casa del Bicentenario. Its long fauces seem ideally designed to allow the incorporation of shops in the frontage and to set back the atrium. Without a detailed structural and archaeological examination, it is impossible to refute Maiuri's account of the house's development; but as it stands, it rests on a substructure of unexamined assumption.

An alternative set of assumptions deserves consideration: That wealth of architectural and decorative detail is indeed a pointer to wealthy owners but can indicate nothing whatsoever about the sources of that wealth, whether rural or urban; that good taste is no indicator of status and could be found among freedmen as well as aristocrats; and that the urban elite, best defined by their tenure of public office, drew revenue from trade and agriculture without discrimination and distanced themselves from commercial activity by the pattern of their lives (i.e., by not engaging in "sordid occupations" in person) without feeling any need to distance themselves physically.

What encourages the distinction between two sets of wealthy owners—freedmen involved in urban profit-making, and rural landowners living in patrician style—is the distinction between types of wealthy house, some of which shown signs of commercial activity and others of which wholly lack it. But this contrast can be accounted for in terms of geographical location; there is no need to superimpose a hypothetical contrast of social class. Of course there are some grand houses untainted by commerce, and others with shops in their facades. To take Herculaneum, there is a clear pattern whereby the largest houses with the largest peristyles along the seawall (i.e., Case dell'Albergo, dell'Atrio a Mosaico, dei Cervi, della Gemma, and del Relievo di Telefo, Figs. 6.6–7) are free from shops, while another group of smaller but nevertheless grand houses, with atria, peristyles, and fairly elaborate decorations, cluster on the main roads leading to the forum and have shops in their frontages (Case del Tramezzo di Legno, del Bicentenario, del Salone Nero, and del Colonnato Tuscanico). But can we plausibly attribute the contrast between the two groups to the social standing of their owners? The distribution of shops makes complete sense topographically: they cluster on the main thoroughfares

Figure 6.6 Casa dei Cervi, Herculaneum, aspect over seawall. The layout of this house and its neighbors is designed to optimize the view of the sea.

Figure 6.7 Casa dei Cervi, view from main reception room (5) down garden axis toward sea (see also Pl. 1). The vista was emphasized by the placing of marble statuary.

and thin out and disappear toward the periphery. There would be little point in trying to open up shops in any of the seawall houses. On the other hand, the potential for shops along the Via del Foro is obvious, and none of the three large houses that front it miss an opportunity.

This was precisely Maiuri's dilemma. He was unwilling to admit that such fine houses could have been built by anyone other than members of the elite, and was thus driven to posit the introduction of shops as a secondary stage. But where were the shops in the early Julio-Claudian period if not along the main streets? Was Herculaneum once a town without shops? Alternatively, if we admit that it had to have shops, even at the beginning of the first century A.D., and that they were bound to be along the main streets, why were grand houses ever built there? The answer lies at hand: the forum was the center of political as well as commercial life, and in any Roman town some (but not all) of the political elite could be expected to live in its close proximity. This might be supported by consideration of the distribution of electoral advertisements, which cluster along the main shopping streets, most conspicuously along the via dell'Abbondanza in Pompeii.[19] Programmata are scarce in Herculaneum, but there too they are found close to the shops of the via del Foro.[20]

Of course, the presence of programmata does not prove that the candidates named lived nearby (though della Corte frequently identified houseowners on that assumption alone), but it does illustrate the way in which the worlds of public life and commerce intertwined. If there was any contrast between the owners of the "main-street" houses and the seawall houses of Herculaneum, it is as likely to be between the politically active and those pursuing the life of leisure (e.g., visitors from Rome) as between the commercial class and the ruling elite. If we accept the attractive conjecture that the exceptionally rich Casa dei Cervi belonged to the family of M. Nonius Balbus, proconsul and patron of the town, whose funerary altar the house overlooked,[21] we may take it as an example of a household that stood above, if by no means outside, the operations of local politics.

But the strongest evidence against Maiuri's assumptions derives from the city of Rome itself. One might well argue that the elites of Pompeii or Herculaneum were a poor model of the likely behavior and attitudes of the high aristocracy of the metropolis. The gulf between a local decurion of Herculaneum and the senatorial elite of Rome, let alone members of those *gentes* (descent groups) who could properly call themselves patrician, is vast. And indeed, Rome is often regarded as a prime example of zoning, the Palatine representing the most exclusive residential quarter for the nobility, in contrast to predominantly plebeian areas like the Aventine. As Ovid puts it explicitly in his image of the abode of the gods as the Palatine of the heavens, the plebs lived elsewhere.[22] Whatever may have happened at a second-rate colony like Pompeii, let alone little Herculaneum, can we image a Scipio or a Cicero enduring the proximity of petty commercial activity?

The answer is that we must, since it is clearly indicated by both literary and archaeological evidence. A vivid picture of the gradual transformation of the Roman Forum, particularly in the second century B.C., is evoked by the annalistic tradition preserved by Livy.[23] As late as 210 B.C., when a major fire swept the forum, there were no basilicas, and behind the rows of shops, the Veteres on the south and the Novae on the north, were private houses.[24] They were constructed with the characteristic Maeniana or balconies from the houses behind projecting over the shops (see Fig. 5.14), from which people could watch the gladiatorial games below.[25] In the course of the next century, the private houses were gradually replaced by ambitious public buildings. In 184 B.C., Cato as censor bought up private property in the area known as "the Quarries" (Lautumia), immediately adjacent to the Curia in the northwestern corner of the forum, for his Basilica Porcia; the property purchased consisted in two atria or private houses, the Maenium and the Titium, together with four tabernae.[26] This sounds very much like the standard Pompeian pattern of a house flanked by two shops.[27] A little later, in 170 B.C., Ti. Sempronius Gracchus as censor constructed the Basilica Sempronia in the southeast of the forum, on the corner of the Vicus Tuscus behind the temple of Castor and Pollux; this involved the demolition of the house of no less a man than his father-in-law Scipio Africanus, together with its adjoining shops, including a butcher's.[28] Butchers' shops had been a feature of the early republican forum—it was outside one of them that Verginius saved his daughter from the advances of the decemvir Appius[29]—and Varro saw the replacement of the butchers by bankers (*argentariae*) in 310 B.C. as the first increase of dignitas in the forum.[30] But though butchers were excluded from the state-owned Veteres and Novae, they evidently continued to trade in privately owned shops nearby. The image of the great Scipio living with a butcher's shop at his front door should in itself be enough to refute Maiuri's assumptions about patrician houses.

The private houses that surrounded the third-century and earlier forum cannot be wished away on a commercial bourgeoisie, though evidently the shopkeepers lived there too, and there was one banker who caused public outrage during the Punic Wars by appearing at his *pergula*, the room above his shop, at midday, garlanded with roses for a drinking party.[31] Perhaps one day the levels below the Basilica Julia may be excavated to reveal how a Scipio lived. Meanwhile, we may turn for confirmation to the dramatic excavations currently being conducted at the foot of the Palatine by Andrea Carandini.[32] Along the stretch of the Sacra Via between the Atrium Vestae and the Clivus Palatinus, Carandini has revealed a series of private houses of considerable dimensions (c. 900m²), built astride what may be the ancient ritual boundary of the Palatine, the *pomoerium*, and dating back to a remarkably early period, possibly the sixth century B.C. (Fig. 6.8). These he identifies plausibly as residences of the republican nobility, inhabited with a striking degree of structural continuity down to the end of the first century B.C. If the hypothetical identification with the setting of Cicero's *De Domo Sua* is accepted, we may provisionally pinpoint not only the houses of Cicero and Clodius but those of powerful families like the Aemilii Scauri and Octavii. Two points relevant to the present argument emerge from the preliminary results. One is that the basic pattern of atrium construction with narrow fauces seems to go back to the archaic period. The other is that in all periods from the archaic to the late republican these large houses had shops incorporated in their frontages on the Sacra Via.

It would indeed be surprising if a thoroughfare as prestigious as the Sacra Via were not flanked with shops. This was a prime location, and by the late Republic the businesses must have been highly profitable. The large houses behind the shops similarly

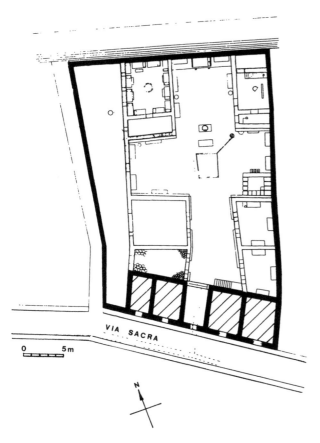

Figure 6.8 Plan, Rome, with aristocratic house at the foot of the Palatine on the via Sacra (reconstructed by Carandini). Large houses fronting the via Sacra date back to the sixth century B.C., and appear to incorporate shops from an early stage.

represented a prime location for the political elite, whether or not we count Cicero and Clodius among their number. Moving closer to the forum was an established technique of maximizing the popular following.[33] It does not follow, of course, that other Palatine houses, more secluded from the main roads, also included shops. But, like the literary accounts of the houses of Scipio and others on the forum, the excavations indicate that there was no perceived incompatibility between elite housing and the presence of petty commercial activity. It helps to explain the location of a grand house like the Casa del Bicentenario on the road leading to the forum of Herculaneum: it directly imitated a style current among the political elite of Rome.

URBAN PROPERTY IN THE LAWYERS

A model that predicts a basic spatial disjunction between the residential spaces of the elite and the commercial spaces of the petty trader must surely be rejected. In evolving an alternative model, it is desirable to pay close attention to patterns of property owner-ship in their legal setting and to explore the way in which these are reflected in the archaeological evidence. We saw in the previous chapter how relevant the case law of the jurists excerpted in the *Digest* can be to reconstructing a picture of the complex possibilities of habitation within the house. The lawyers were concerned with applying the principles of civil law to the practicalities of life throughout the Roman world. What they say is as relevant to Pompeii as to Ostia. This is no less true of what they have to say about the nonresidential use of the house. Indeed, this is a theme of some prominence in the picture of the house they offer, for legal disputes centered on property and wealth, and the productive capacity of a house was of crucial importance in disputes over ownership, inheritance, and liability.

A couple of considerations are in order. The first concerns the meaning of the term *insula*. The *Digest* consistently distinguishes two types of urban property, the *domus* and the *insula*. These are treated by archaeologists as technical architectural terms: *domus* referring to the classic, grand, single-occupancy residence, and *insula* inconsistently either to the multistory, multioccupancy, brick and concrete block, as at Ostia, or, quite differently, to the area isolated by four surrounding streets, containing many separate properties, as at Pompeii. But it is clear from the references both in the *Digest* and elsewhere that *insula* is not an architectural but a legal term for a unit of ownership. Just as the domus has a dominus or domina, so does an insula. The *dominus insulae* entrusts supervision of his (or her) unit of ownership to a caretaker, an *insularius*, just as the owner of a rural estate entrusts supervision of his villa to a *vilicus*.[34] That is obviously applicable to the situation at Ostia, but it should be equally applicable at Pompeii and Herculaneum.

The block defined by surrounding streets is not properly an insula unless it is a unit of ownership. This evidently was the case with the "insula Arriana Polliana Cn. Allei Nigidi Mai," where tabernae with their upper rooms (pergulae), "equestrian apartments" (*cenacula equestria*), and a house or houses (domus) were available for rent.[35] But a street block might also logically include several insulae. For instance, it is conceivable that the Casa del Bicentenario formed part of an insula that extended over (say) the group of shops and flats to its east (H V.17–29) and possibly also over the houses and shops to its west (H V.8–12; see Fig. 6.9), with which there are traces of previous interconnecting doors. The problem with housing of the Pompeian type is that it is virtually impossible to demonstrate such *legal* boundaries. Perhaps the block I have suggested round the Casa del Bicentenario was three separate insulae or blocks of ownership. Or perhaps it had once been a single insula but had by A.D. 79 been split up into several. Archaeology cannot give an answer to questions about legal ownership. But we can bear in mind the legal background and remember not to assume that every physically separate unit was a legally independent, owner-occupied unit.

We must next consider the implications of what the lawyers reveal about the complexities of the relationship between patterns of habitation and patterns of ownership.[36] It is sheer innocence to populate all the houses of Pompeii with owner-occupiers. A house is a piece of property, an asset (and liability) to its owner, to be used in many ways by a variety of people—for profit, or as a benefit to dependents, as well as for residence and reception. Such complex possibilities for the legal fortunes of a house make it quite

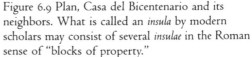

Figure 6.9 Plan, Casa del Bicentenario and its neighbors. What is called an *insula* by modern scholars may consist of several *insulae* in the Roman sense of "blocks of property."

illegitimate to infer from the splitting up, renting off, and changing usage of a house that its owner has fallen on hard times. If Cnaeus Alleius Nigidius Maius, one of the outstanding elite of Pompeii, *princeps coloniae* and giver of games, rented out shops, flats, and houses in a block he owned, it does not mean that he was desperate for money or that he had left the city in disgust, but that he was realizing the value of a unit of property that had come into his hands by whatever means, inheritance, sale, or even as dowry with his wife.

Finally, the occurrence of tabernae in the legal sources could be studied with profit. Shops (which frequently overlap with businesses, *negotia*) are seen as a valuable source of rental income. The usufructuary of a house might be anxious to establish his claim to rent out the shops the testator had run himself.[37] The context in which shops are most frequently considered is that of the *actio institoria* in the fourteenth book of the *Digest*. Shops are normally envisaged as run by slaves or freedmen who act as *institores* (legal agents) for the owner, so committing him to legal liability for their financial contracts.[38] You might use the same slave to run two businesses, say a cloak business and a linen cloth one, or to run two branches of the same business, one at Buccinum and the other across the Tiber.[39] A shop left to you in a will may come as a package, with its slave-*institores* and the rest of its equipment (*instrumentum*), including the stock.[40] Of course, you might also leave a shop to a freedman or slave, such as the blacksmith's shop left with its equipment to Lucius Eutychus and Pamphilus (who is thereby manumitted) for them to run.[41]

These are only intended as examples of a highly complex picture. There is still room for more thorough investigation that would look at shops and urban property in general in legal, literary, and epigraphic sources, and attempt to relate the results to the archaeological remains. But the possibility to which this legal evidence points for Pompeii and Herculaneum is that the many separate physical units of various size may have made up a much smaller number of units of ownership. Clusters of shops, flats, and houses may have formed, as *insulae*, units of ownership that were valuable sources of rental income. Such clusters could have formed the basis not only for a variety of economic relationships, ranging from rental, through indirect running of business through freedmen, to direct running through *institores*, but also for a variety of social ties of obligation and political support. Although freedmen were clearly prominent in the trade of the area and may indeed have emerged as important property owners, both through their own efforts and as beneficiaries of their masters' wills, it is likely that the ruling elite represented by the members of the local councils were also major owners and exploiters of urban property. There is no need to see in such urban property-ownership evidence of a decline of a hypothetical elite that originally owed all its income to the land.

Modern boundaries of work versus residence, business versus leisure, dissolve, as I have argued (Part I), in the Roman house. Any analysis that attempts to distinguish the residential units of Pompeii from commercial or industrial ones must founder on this objection. But this is not to say that there are no such boundaries *within* the house. A distinction on which the lawyers place some emphasis is that between the profitable and the pleasurable use of space. Thus they draw a sharp distinction between household expenditures that are useful and those that are merely for pleasure (*impensae utiles* and *impensae voluptariae*). Useful expenditures are those that improve the value of a property, such as adding a bakery, a shop, or a storeroom; those for pleasure improve the decoration but not the returns of the property, such as gardens (*viridaria*) and fountains, marble veneers (*incrustationes*), pavements (*loricationes*), and wall paintings (*picturae*).[42]

The lawyers are here strictly concerned with property as an economic asset and so speak of the *utilitarian* improvements in positive terms; thus, they are not concerned with the social enhancement of a property. They do however, as we shall see, acknowledge elsewhere that "voluptuary" enhancements are both expensive and highly desirable, though the moralizing rejection of luxury may lead them to take a harsh view of the matter.[43] Thus Ulpian takes a high moral tone with regard to "luxuries," disallowing extravagant claims for repairs to decoration on a collapsed party wall.[44] The lawyers show no disapproval of shops, except such houses of ill-repute as a *popina* (drinking house) or gambling den.[45]

RESIDENTIAL AND NONRESIDENTIAL SPACE

With these considerations in mind, we may return to the samples from Pompeii and Herculaneum and look more closely at the distribution of profitable versus pleasurable use of space. Archaeological evidence from across the Empire needs to be examined before we can build an adequate model of the relations between the elite of a Roman city and its trade. Naturally Pompeii and Herculaneum may have been atypical in this as in other respects, and the earthquake of A.D. 62 will be one factor to be borne in mind. What is still needed is a wide-ranging investigation of the links between shops and grand houses in the numerous published sites of the Roman world, from Delos and Ephesus to

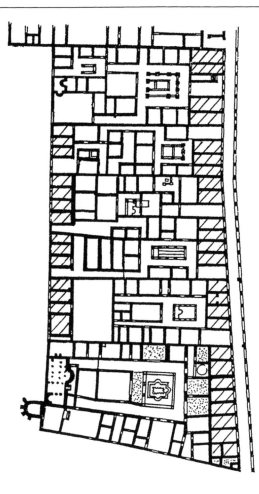

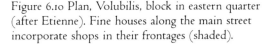

Figure 6.10 Plan, Volubilis, block in eastern quarter (after Etienne). Fine houses along the main street incorporate shops in their frontages (shaded).

Glanum and Silchester, and above all the towns of Roman Africa.[46] The well-published excavations of Volubilis (Fig. 6.10) suggest strongly the same sort of admixture of the commercial and residential as at Pompeii.[47] But pending more systematic investigation, the evidence of Pompeii and Herculaneum is at least sufficient to cast considerable doubt on traditional assumptions about the way a Roman elite was likely to distance itself from commerce.

This is an area in which some helpful statistical work has already been undertaken. Eschebach was concerned with charting the different categories of usage of space, and his color-coded plan offers a vivid picture of the importance and diffusion of the nonresidential across the houses of Pompeii, though it incorporates assumptions about the classification of houses as residential or otherwise that are too rigid.[48] Jashemski's dramatic excavations of soil surface and roots in a variety of gardens revealed the (hitherto unsuspected) importance of horticulture within the walls, and she was well aware of the social and economic significance of her findings.[49] Raper made a more thoroughgoing attempt at a statistical approach.[50] Using models of analysis derived from urban geographers, he put Pompeii on a grid and compared the distribution of different types of usage across it. The pattern that emerged confirms the visual impression derived from Esche-bach's plan: a confused jumble of shops, workshops, crafts, horticultural plots, and houses across the whole city, with no real attempt at segregation or concentration beyond the tendency of shops to line main roads and horticulture to cluster on the margins, at the farthest distance from the forum. As Raper (1977) observes, the spread of the commercial is pervasive: "The commercial structures tended to be constant in their association with private houses and mansions suggesting a continuum of indiscrete usage of space" (208). While several squares display public usage to the exclusion of all else, none with any significant degree of residential usage are without at least some commercial usage.

Broadly similar findings emerge from the analyses of the contributors to the new *Pompei. L'informatica* volumes. La Torre in particular shows that though there are contrasts to be drawn region to region, the overwhelming pattern is of a mixed distribution of the various types of commercial and artisanal activity, whether bakers, fullers, taverns and inns, or even (if credibility stretches this far) brothels in among the residential areas of the city.[51]

All these studies, however, have been concerned with examining the distribution of commercial activities within the city, a central concern of urban geographers of the modern city, and not with its location within the house. For this purpose it is not enough to observe the geographical scatter of nonresidential activity. It is necessary to have more precise information about the relationship between different types of use of space and about the inferences we are entitled to make when we find evidence of nonresidential activity. Here we are hampered by the limitations of what archaeology can tell us and above all by the imprecision of the archaeological reporting.

Three broad categories can be distinguished. Shops, with their wide openings on the road, are easy enough to distinguish on architectural grounds, though they require more careful excavation and reporting of the finds than has often been the case. These shops cover a range of activities, from retail only to production and retail; many are for the sale of food and drink.[52] Second, there are the open areas for horticulture; these too are easily recognized on a ground plan, though it requires the techniques of excavation pioneered by Jashemski to distinguish viticulture, floriculture, market gardening, etc. The third category, of various trades and types of production dubiously labeled "industrial," is both more diverse and hard to identify and quantify. Some establishments, such as those of bakers, fullers, dyers, metalworkers, or lampmakers, can be securely identified and measured.[53] In other cases the finds point to the presence of the craftsman, but because there is nothing to distinguish his house architecturally, his nonresidential activity is hard to measure. Thus the supposed cabinetmaker of the Casa del Fabbro (I 10.7) is identified by an ample set of tools, though no workshop is visible in the house. There are also cases where architecture and finds point to some sort of workshop, without revealing the nature of the activity. Finally, there is a penumbra of types that are hard to categorize, like the occasional stable-yard (e.g., I 8.12). There were also surely *hospitia* ("hotels" gives a misleading impression), the identification of which remains conjectural.[54]

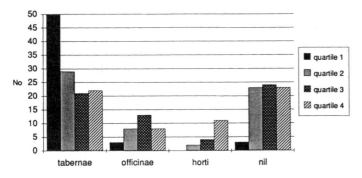

Figure 6.11 Houses with nonresidential usage, by quartile. Shops (*tabernae*) are almost universal in the bottom quartile, but also frequent in other quartiles. Bakeries, fulleries, etc. (*officinae*), tend toward units of middling size. Horticultural plots (*horti*) are necessarily large. The proportion of houses with none of these activities (nil) is equal in the top three quartiles.

The moral is that, as in any archaeological survey, activities that are physically distinctive are likely to be well represented, others underrepresented. That is, many houses that are not registered as including nonresidential activity may in fact have been the workplace of craftsmen. But for statistical purposes, the safest procedure is to start with units that *certainly* included nonresidential activity and to ask in what ways they distinguish themselves from those whose function is ambiguous. This in turn may assist in sorting out the ambiguous cases.

The total sample included 122 houses (over half) that either are or incorporate shops (*tabernae*); 32 are workshops (*officinae*) or include areas given over to some trade; 17 include horticultural areas (*horti*). Some houses (13) fall into more than one of these categories, but fewer than a third have no sign of economic activity. The three types of activity are unequally distributed across the house sizes (Fig. 6.11). There is a clear and comprehensible pattern here. The smallest units are virtually all shops; three are described as workshops, but at this level the distinction is minimal. Only three units are excluded; and these (VI 11.1/2; VI 14.29; H III.4) are extremely likely to have functioned as workshops too. Much the same applies to slightly larger units; only three more among houses under 100m^2 rate as neither shops nor workshops. But it is not the case that only the smaller units have a commercial side; well over a third of the houses in the top two quartiles also include shops. Horticultural plots go to the opposite extreme: only in the top quartile are they at all common. This is the natural result of the size of a horticultural plot (138m^2 is the average); because these are normally attached to not insubstantial houses, the average total unit size is high (482m^2). Officinae lie in between the two patterns, and are surely (for reasons outline above) understated. But because the types of artisanal space that show up unmistakably (bakeries, etc.) tend to require a moderate amount of space (the average is 76m^2), they tend to cluster in the medium-large range.

It is striking how widespread nonresidential activity is among houses of all sizes. Even in the 31 percent that appear immune, there may well have been a fair amount of unrecorded activity. We should remember too that many of the larger houses that apparently lack shops in fact had them in front rooms which have been blocked off and are inaccessible from the house. These could even so be owned, and either rented or controlled, by the occupants of the house. The overall picture that emerges is of a wide penetration of economic activity. While there may be a substantial difference between the use of space for economic—that is, profit-making—activity and its use for social, residential, and reception function, it does not follow that we are dealing with two distinct categories of building, residential and nonresidential. Workshops and reception rooms, profit-making and luxury, might sit alongside each other in the same house. Indeed, they might blur into each other. At what point does the *materfamilias* spinning and weaving with her maids cross from the domestic to the industrial?[55] The location of production in the house is not accidental but results from its social location within the structures of the familia.

The interconnection of economic and residential functions can be further tested by focusing on those houses that have atria and peristyles. These architectural features are, as we have seen (Chap. 4), closely associated with the reception function—a point that is strongly reinforced when we come to look at the correlation of these features with decoration (Chap. 7). It is therefore particularly interesting to see whether in atrium/peristyle houses, in which we presume there to be higher-status reception activity, there is a relative avoidance of lower-status, profit-making activity.

Undoubtedly there are some situations in which reception and profit making should be regarded as alternative uses of space. Certain economic activities, like horticulture, baking, fulling, stabling, etc., require large areas. Such activities are common in large houses without atria. In the top two quartiles, that is, in those houses with ample room architecturally, 37 houses (32 percent) lack atria. A good many of these were substantially involved in economic activity of one sort or another: 7 have large horticultural plots, and 13 have substantial areas given over to various economic activities, including a bakery (I 12.1/2), a supposed weaver's workshop (H V.3–4, the Casa del Telaio), a *garum*-making establishment (I 12.8), and two stables (VI 15.16, 20). There is also an interesting group of houses without atria built round a four-sided peristyle that look like possible hospitia (H IV.17/18; I 12.6; VI 15.23; perhaps also I 11.9/15 and VI 11 4/15–17).

That is to say, there were plenty of profit-making establishments in which reception activity was a low priority. That is particularly obvious in the case of horticultural plots. In an urban site it is virtually impossible to achieve a plot large enough to sustain simultaneously a vineyard or vegetable garden *and* an elegant peristyle garden. One must move out to the countryside to the great villas with *partes urbanae* and *partes rusticae* before the two become compatible. Equally, the sense of activities competing for space is made visible by those cases where economic activity displaces reception areas. A classic instance is the fullery in the atrium/peristyle structure of the Fullonica Stephani (I 6.7, Fig. 6.12). A large tank stands in the atrium, actually occupying the potential position of the impluvium, while the peristyle garden is occupied by the complex series of basins required by the fulling process. Rather than seeing, with Maiuri, in the transformation of residential space a sign of the decline of the city in the postearthquake period, we may take it as a reminder of the fluid boundaries between private space and work space and the potential of the house to adapt its usage over the passage of time.

The importance of change over time is also visible in the Casa del Labirinto (VI 11.8–10, Fig. 5.17).[56] The presence in this exceptionally fine house of a bakery with four mills—certainly in excess of the requirements of domestic consumption—raises the question of how easily the activities of a bakery could sit alongside high luxury. The fact that other bakeries in the town are not attached to grand houses is enough to arouse suspicion. The structural history of the house reveals that the bakery must indeed have been installed in the final phase of the house; in particular, it involved blocking off access from the main reception suite to the handsome private baths built only thirty years before.[57] This sort of major change is exactly what the lawyers would reckon an *impensa utilis*, an expenditure that would bring profit not pleasure, and that an usufructuary with the right of dwelling would not be allowed to undertake. Because it curtailed the reception function of the house, it is reasonable enough to infer that it marks some significant change in usage, and it may well be that the earthquake of A.D. 62 triggered a withdrawal of the proprietors from habitation and a new phase in the hands of tenants.[58] Or it may be that one owner died and his (or her) heirs decided to make different use of the property. Whatever the human story behind it, the house certainly illustrates the way in which pleasure and profit could compete for space.

But though there are cases in which profit and pleasure were at odds, there were plenty of others where they sat alongside each other. Economic activity does not necessarily "degrade" a house; a significant number of the grandest houses combined economic with reception functions. The Casa degli Amorini Dorati (VI 16.7) supports a number of linked shops and workshops; the Casa del Menandro (I 10.4) includes its own stable-yard (Fig. 6.13). The important distinction is not between houses with a reception function and those with an economic one but between the houses with an economic function and

Figure 6.12 Fullonica Stephani, Pompeii. A large basin for fulling occupies the previous space for the impluvium of the atrium.

Figure 6.13 Casa del Menandro, Pompeii, Pompeii, stable-yard. This has its own
back entrance and is separated from the reception areas of the house by a
long corridor (see Fig. 3.2).

those with an economic *and* a reception function. A marked contrast emerges between
those houses with atria and those without in which horticulture or other profit-making
activity is attested (see below, Table 8). Those with atria tend to be larger, both in terms
of area and number of rooms, and, as we will see below, far more elaborately decorated.
The implication is that there was nothing to stop a grand house with a reception function
from supporting economic activities as well.

If we turn to the samples for Regions I and VI of Pompeii and select only those in
the top quartile that have both an atrium and a peristyle and at least some decoration
surviving, a group of thirty houses emerges. Of these, thirteen do not have any form of
commercial usage, yet they are very difficult to distinguish as a group from the seventeen
that do. The average size is virtually the same ($798m^2$ for the noncommercial, $823m^2$ for
the commercial); both groups have an average of seventeen ground-floor rooms, of which
a similar proportion are decorated (average eleven rooms for the noncommercial, ten for
the commercial); and the same proportion have mosaic floors (average three rooms in
both groups). Even the average area of their open space enclosed by peristyles is almost
identical ($121m^2$ in the noncommercial, $122m^2$ in the others).

Is there any reason here for supposing elite avoidance of the commercial among the
thirteen? Again the critical factor is location. The large houses that front on busy thoroughfares—the via dell'Abbondanza, via Stabiana, and via di Nocera—tend to incorporate shops, those remote from main roads lack them. There is a distinct group in the heart
of Regio VI of splendidly decorated houses away from the thoroughfares (e.g., in Insula

9 the Case del Meleagro, dei Dioscuri, etc.), and this is indeed the area that on Raper's analysis scores exceptionally high for residential usage and low for commercial. But even if some of the elite did cluster here, it is manifest that others were scattered throughout the city in less secluded surroundings.

MY ARGUMENT has sought to break down some of our assumptions about the ideological and physical distance between the elite of the Roman town and commercial activity. My concern has been with attitudes, not with the economy. None of the evidence discussed here undermines the proposition that agriculture was dominant in the economy or that agricultural interests were primary among a landowning political elite. Nor does it suggest the emergence of an urban bourgeoisie that regarded itself as economically, socially, and culturally distinct from the landowners. But it may come some way toward explaining how towns and trade could flourish in a world dominated by agricultural interests and why a situation of antagonism and conflict between bourgeoisie and landowners did not arise. The Ciceronian gentleman could afford to despise trade, while at the same time stimulating it by his luxurious lifestyle, staffing it by the importation of slaves and their subsequent liberation, providing it with premises within his own properties, even his own home, milking it of profits, and turning to the tradesman for political support.

To Maiuri the physical evidence of Pompeii and Herculaneum, with their often surprising juxtaposition of rich and poor, beautiful and commercial, luxurious and squalid, suggested patrician cities in decline. But the same evidence can point to quite different conclusions. We must start by thinking away the assumptions of the industrial city of the modern Western world, with its patterns of social contact and interaction. We must reconstruct a world in which the rich frequently lived in close contiguity with their dependents, slaves and freedmen, clients and tenants, the sources of their economic and social power. In this respect, it may not be the Roman world that proves to be strange but our own. Investigation of the cities of preindustrial Italy could teach us much—from the *vicinie* of the medieval Genoese clans vividly described by Jacques Heers (1977) to the *palazzi* of Renaissance Rome with their ground-floor arcades occupied by shops.

Even today such patterns are not unknown. Strangely enough, a corrective to Maiuri's assumption can be found in contemporary Naples. So much, at least, is suggested by the contrasts drawn by the Naples-born novelist Luciano De Crescenzo, through the mouthpiece of his twentieth-century Neapolitan Socrates, Bellavista, defending Naples with its basement slums (*bassi*) and tangle of interconnecting washing-lines, in contrast to the sanitized Milan:

> Have you ever reflected that Naples is the only great city in the world that is without exclusively popular quarters? The ghettos of the subproletariat, typical of the heavily industrialised cities, like Turin or Chicago, have never existed in

our city. In Naples, the working class lived in the basements, the nobles on the so-called "primo piano nobile" and the bourgeoisie on the upper floors. This social stratification of a vertical type has obviously favoured cultural exchanges between the classes, avoiding one of the worst evils of class, that is the ever greater cultural divergence between the poor and the rich. (De Crescenzo, *Cosi parlò Bellavista* [1980], 100)

CHAPTER 7

LUXURY AND STATUS

> Our friend, Lucius Lucullus, that great man, made what passed as a very neat reply to
> criticisms of the magnificence of his Tusculan villa: he had two neighbours, uphill an
> eques Romanus, downhill a freedman; considering that they had magnificent villas, he
> ought to be allowed what others of lower rank got away with. Don't you realise, Lucul-
> lus, that even their aspirations are your responsibility? The abuses of the leading men
> [*principes*] are bad enough; but what is worse is the way they have so many imitators.
> History shows that the leading men in society have always dictated its character. When-
> ever there has been a transformation of morals and manners [*mutatio morum*] among the
> social leaders, the same transformation has followed among the people [*populus*].
>
> Cicero, *de Legibus* 3.30–31

CICERO'S CONCERN over the social and moral effects of the behavior of the Roman elite
stands in the mainstream of Roman moral thought. From the elder Cato onward, articulate Romans voiced their anxieties about the upsurge of luxury. It was, of course, in the
first place an elite phenomenon: the prime profiteers of war and provincial exploitation
were the principes. But though the immediate concern of moralizers and legislators was
doubtless for the disruption luxury caused within the ruling class, they perceived the
damage as affecting their whole society. Cicero is unambiguous: "the whole society is
normally infected by the desires and vices of the leading men."[1]

Authors of the early imperial period took up and reiterated the same thoughts, especially in discussions of the censorial function of the emperor. Emperors were conscious
of and exploited their perceived function as moral exemplars: Augustus set the style,
winning the praise of Ovid for his examplary destruction of Vedius Pollio's luxury house
in the heart of Rome.[2] And Tacitus credits the frugal Vespasian with putting an end,
through personal example, to the moral decline that reached its peak (or nadir) under
Nero.[3] But although such passages share the assumption that luxury spreads socially
through imitation, we may prefer to imagine that it was only the upper orders of wealthy
senators and equestrians on whom the emperor could conceivably have any impact as role
model.

Here the elder Pliny is an important witness. He was, as is notorious, obsessed with
the impact of Roman conquests and triumphs on society in spreading moral corruption,
like the taste for pearls or for vessels of fluorspar.[4] His model of Roman society is not
without differentiation, and in one fine passage he sets clear limits to the social spread
of a contagion. The skin disorder that broke out under Tiberius among the kissing
classes who exchanged embraces at the morning salutation only affected the *proceres*, the
upper orders, and did not spread to the common people, the plebs: he elaborates, not to

the *servitia* nor to the *plebes humilis aut media*, that is to say, to the slave class, the poor, or the rich outside the upper orders (*Natural History* 26.3). But this limitation is specific to the spread of skin disorder. Elsewhere, in his far from coherent protests against the introduction of the gold ring as a status symbol to mark the equestrian order, he complains that legislation under Tiberius attempting to restrict the wearing of gold rings after common tradesmen and barkeepers had used them to protect themselves from magistrates only encouraged the spread of the phenomenon among those of servile origin (ibid. 33.32–33). Silver shoe buckles, paradoxically regarded as less trite and therefore more desirable than gold ones, became a luxury among women of plebeian status (*luxu feminarum plebis*), while embossed silver sword hilts attained fashion among common soldiers (ibid. 33.152). Earrings formed of clusters of pearls called *crotalia* (castanets) were the aspiration of even poor women (*pauperes*), and Pliny acknowledges the potency of "luxury" in providing status markers, quoting the women as saying that "a pearl was a woman's lictor in public" (ibid. 9.115).

The model of society offered by both Cicero and Pliny is consistent. There was, and they felt ought to be, a divide between the upper orders—*summi viri*, principes, proceres, or whatever—and the plebs. Naturally luxury had its origin and most dramatic manifestations among the upper orders of senators and equestrians; but not the least alarming of its characteristics was the tendency to spread downward, to Lucullus's freedman neighbor, to the barkeepers with gold rings, to the common women sporting what was doubtless no more than costume jewelry. But this model runs counter to a picture sometimes cherished by Roman historians. The vast riches squandered by the elite of the late Republic and early Empire, and the contrast with the undoubted squalor experienced by the poor, tempt us into polarizing the culture of the elite and that of the masses. It is easy (and perhaps for us morally satisfying) to dramatize this contrast.[5] But to ignore the social diffusion of luxury is to miss something important both about the structure of Roman society and about the way in which luxury operated within society.

If Cicero and Pliny were right, the patterns at work in Roman society were by no means historically isolated or insignificant. In the course of indexing a collection of English seventeenth-century documents, Joan Thirsk was "struck by the frequency of reference to small consumer goods like brass cooking pans, cambric, gold and silver thread, hats, knives, lace, ribbons, ruffs, soap and tape." Tudor moralists had regarded the introduction of these foreign novelties with horror; based often on cheap materials, these fashion goods involved the export of English bullion to pay for foreign labor. But home production soon came in, and both the rapidity with which these initially elite fashions spread and their degree of social dissemination are startling. Within two years of the first appearance of silk stockings on the legs of a courtier in 1575, they were offered for sale by a shop in Kirkby Lonsdale. Worsted proved a cheaper alternative to silk, and the stocking-knitting industry expanded rapidly, catering not only to the middle but to the laboring classes. That consumer goods reached a mass market was due to the differentiation in the quality of goods procured. Low-quality versions of elite fashions, often manufactured in the country, were sold to the humble. Such "projects" in the seventeenth and eighteenth centuries created a mass market before the advent of the industrial revolution and multiplied opportunities for employment. They stimulated the economy without involving any change in work methods or the unit of production. Many features of Thirsk's picture, the moralizing, the rapidity of change of mores, are reminiscent of the Roman scene; and they point to the importance of examining the social diffusion of "luxuries" and consumer goods.[6]

But before we accept the Ciceronian model, we require documentation. However emphatically Cicero states that the morals of the elite penetrate the whole fabric of society (the passage quoted above continues with much more in the same vein), it is always possible that he was sufficiently isolated from experience of the "lower orders" to be a misleading witness to their lifestyle. The rich, successful freedman and his urge to "ape" the aristocracy could not be missed; Trimalchio symbolizes what was a longstanding Roman obsession. But what of the majority of poor freedmen, or the poor but honest *ingenuus* whom Juvenal's satirical tradition idealizes? Not only do we require to know whether Cicero's picture is true; we need to know in precisely what degree it is true, how far through society the imitation of the elite extends. And we need to know how the picture develops over time, how far the supposed increase of luxury leads to greater social diffusion.

The material for answering these questions exists. Because luxury is part of material culture, archaeology can follow its traces. Moreover, the artifact as social symbol is one of the most prominent concerns of contemporary archaeology in other fields.[7] Both materials and methods to construct a sociology of Roman luxury lie readily to hand.

One essential preliminary is to clarify our definition of *luxury*, since confusion can arise from its alternative senses. One sense, typical of usage in Roman authors, is essentially moralizing. Luxury is what goes against the natural order, what is morally shocking and depraving in its effect. This definition we find unsympathetic, since from our own perspective what the Romans found depraving may be a normal part of life. Thus Friedländer pointed out how the spread of mechanical refrigeration had rendered Roman protests against iced drinks absurd.[8] There can be, that is to say, no absolute standards of luxury, only standards relative to the availability of given commodities within a society. For us, luxury is often explicitly relative: the "de luxe" version is only recognizable as such by comparison to "standard" models.

But a relativist definition of luxury leads in its turn to difficulties. If luxury is in its nature relative, how can one ever speak of the social spread of any given luxury? For in becoming common, pearl earrings must cease to be regarded as luxurious at all. To avoid this difficulty, it is essential to focus on luxury as a social process rather than on the individual items that may be categorized as "luxurious."[9] As a social process, luxury functions as the attempt to mark or assert a place within a network of social relationships by the display or consumption of material goods; in this process, the goods are valued in proportion to their relative inaccessibility outside the social circle that is employing them.

Luxury as process involves not only the dimension of differentiation between different groups within society but the essential dimension of change over time. It is precisely its potential to provoke imitation that defines a luxury, yet the more it is imitated, the less

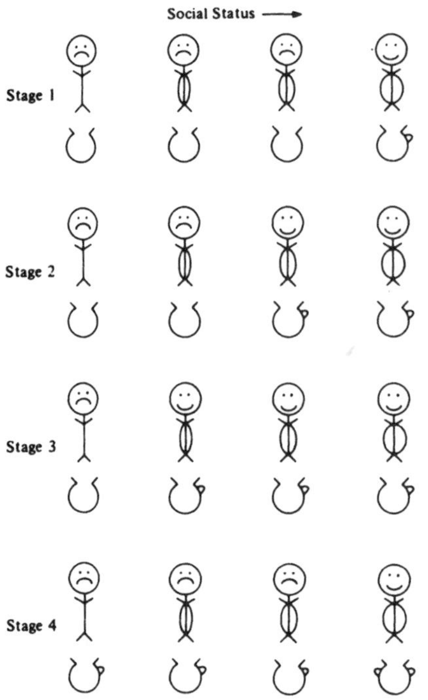

Figure 7.1 The social diffusion of luxury items (after Miller). The columns, from left to right, represent progression through social strata, from poorest to richest; the rows, from top to bottom, represent progression through time. The pot, with or without handles, may be taken to represent any type of material goods.

luxurious it becomes. It is only over the passage of time that luxury can be apprehended. The luxury is defined both by its novelty (and thus restricted access) and by the demonstration of its power in the growing spread of imitation. It therefore requires continuous innovation. The relationship between the two dimensions of social difference and change over time is graphically illustrated in Daniel Miller's study of pottery in India (Fig. 7.1). The sequence in his diagram symbolizes not only the progressive dissemination of luxury goods across the social strata, in the desire to imitate the well-being of the rich, but the effect this has on the rich, who are driven to further innovation to maintain distance from the poor. Were we to identify the four social strata of the diagram with the Roman ranks of lower plebs, middle plebs, equites, and senators, we could take it to represent both sides of the argument between Cicero and Lucullus.

But in addition to observing change over time, we should observe that the *rate of change* is not constant. It is driven by the degree and extent of social competitiveness and mobility. In a stable society, the rate of innovation and diffusion will be low, so the same luxuries may mark the dominant class over a long period of time. But in an unstable and highly competitive society with strong elements of upward social mobility, diffusion will be wide and innovation rapid. As fast as the leaders seize new symbols to assert their power, as did Lucullus with his villas, they will be emulated by those below. The wider the emulation spreads, the more debased the object of emulation becomes, and the greater the pressure grows on the leaders to innovate further, so distancing themselves from their imitators.[10]

It is precisely such an unstable society that we witness in the Ciceronian and early imperial period. Whether the abolute standards of luxury attained by the Romans were high is irrelevant; nor does it matter to distinguish at what level specific goods or patterns of behavior rate as luxuries. The points of interest are the extent and speed of diffusion of new status markers, and the rate of innovation at the top.

Numerous types of artifact reveal this process. We may think of the marvelous imitations of embossed silverware by the Arretine potteries, the scale of diffusion of Arretine ware, and the speed with which its production spreads to debased provincial versions. We may think of the spread of honorific statues, and particularly the funerary commemorations so characteristic of the Roman Empire—and here the most lamentable consequence of the disciplinary separation of history and archaeology has been the divorce between the study of funerary epigraphy and that of the monuments which so eloquently comment on the status of the commemorand.[11] House decoration, which is here investigated, represents only one among many possibilities; but it represents an especially rich field for investigation both because of the importance the Romans attached to houses as status symbols and the exceptional pains they took to decorate them, and because of the systematic way in which the Vesuvian catastrophe has preserved a substantial body of evidence. If the evidence is limited to a given period and region, it is by chance to the period in which Romans believed their own luxury to have reached a peak (or nadir), and in the region of Italy most immediately affected by the fashions of the Roman rich.[12]

PAINTING BY NUMBERS

The present chapter aims to test the social emulation model by using the sample of houses from Pompeii and Herculaneum to measure the extent of diffusion of wall painting. Statistical measurement of the diffusion of art is something that has recently been tried by art historians concerned with the early modern period. The reduction of art to numbers appears crude in comparison to the refined judgments of traditional aesthetics, but it does serve a vital purpose in controlling the impressions that inevitably arise from an anecdotal approach. A study of seventeenth-century Delft by John Montias has shown that 66 percent of the householders possessed at least one painted canvas, and that the average number of paintings per household was eleven.[13] It was even relatively common for artworks to hang in peasant households in the Netherlands. Dutch art may be a special case, but a study of Metz in the same period by Philip Benedict shows France not far behind.[14] Two-thirds of the French households prove to have paintings, though the inventories on which this information is based are slightly skewed as a sample, and the proportion may consequently be reduced to 58 percent. The mean per household is 5.5 canvasses, predominantly religious in Catholic houses, but not in Protestant ones. Social class affects the distribution: 90 percent of nobles had canvasses, 80 percent of the learned professions, slightly more of the merchants and officials, and nearly 55 percent of artisans, bourgeois, and laborers. These numbers are by no means so banal and predictable as they might appear; before the investigation was made, it was confidently asserted that outside the Netherlands, paintings belonged exclusively to the crown, the nobility, and the church.

No comparable figures are available for Pompeii, and two factors would make a precisely similar exercise impossible. In the first place, the art of Pompeii is very different from the canvasses of the Netherlands or Metz. Lavish though it is, room decoration is in a different league from easel painting and has as much in common with wallpaper as with canvas. More significantly, we lack the essential paper documentation from which Montias and Benedict were able to move. A corpus of inventories can supply both precise information about the social standing of the owners and a full record of their possessions. Neither is attainable via the archaeological record. What the database generated by the samples investigated in this book permits is the correlation of evidence of decoration with other measures of the standing of a house—its size, architectural features, and usage—and hence to gain a controlled picture of the diffusion of decoration across the full range of the housing stock.

Postindustrial society brings its own culturally conditioned assumptions about the social diffusion of art. A survey of modern France cited by Zeldin indicates that in 1974 over half the population had no pictures or reproductions of art in their homes; about 20 percent had reproductions; 26 percent originals by amateurs; 23.5 percent posters; but a mere 8 percent originals by professional artists.[15] But it is not merely that we are led by contemporary conditions to expect the diffusion of art to follow lines of restricted diffusion defined by social class. We expect distinctions of *taste* to mark those social groups. Such is the assumption underlying Pierre Bourdieu's massive study of "distinction," based on a survey by questionnaire enabling correlations to be drawn between occupation, income, and education on the one hand, and preferences in music and art, not to speak of furnishing, clothes, and lifestyle, on the other.[16] But the gains to be won from employing on antiquity the sort of statistical procedures by which we analyze our own minutely differentiated society lie not only in the opportunity of discovering analogous differentiations in the past but also in discovering the limitations of the type of analysis that makes self-evident sense to us.

The discussion of the population of Pompeian households (Chap. 5) has already shown that there can be no simple equation between the range of *housing*, from poorest to richest, and the range of *inhabitants*. The promiscuous composition of the big house suggests that the larger the house, the wider the social range of its inhabitants. We cannot, then, treat an analysis of houses in the same way as an analysis of inventories in wills, or of responses to questionnaires. But that does not mean that the enquiry is less interesting. Precisely because the Roman house provided an important environment in which social relations were constructed, the luxuries of decoration played a vital role in structuring that social environment. What our evidence permits us to measure is not the spread of *taste* across social classes but the spread across an urban society of the strategy of using art to structure the social environment, to mark privilege and prestige in a promiscuous world.

I. Casa dei Cervi, Herculaneum. The main reception room (5), with a commanding view over the garden, is marked by a pediment above its entrance decorated with mosaics and shells (a). The room itself is decorated in fourth style in black-ground with red-gold architectural elements on a highly polished surface (b).

2. Casa degli Amorini Dorati, Pompeii. The main reception rooms surround the elegant four-sided peristyle (a). Note the superior elevation of the end portico, and its central pediment. The yellow decoration of the room of gilded cupids, overlooking the peristyle, has the unusual diagonal pattern of "tapestry" style (b).

3. Casa del Sacerdos Amandus, Pompeii. The small peristyle garden has only two colonnades; the other two sides are painted on the walls with engaged half-colums (a). The third-style decoration of the triclinium has four mythological panels, including one of the Cyclops Polyphemus and the nymph Galatea (b).

4. Casa dell'Efebo, Pompeii. A cubiculum (room 12) with simple white-ground decoration (b). Decorative borders in yellow surround three panels on each wall. The central panel is framed by an aedicula of columns. The side panels have cupids as central motifs; the central panels have mythological scenes. Detailed is a scene representing Narcissus and Echo (a).

5. Casa del Principe di Napoli, Pompeii. A portico overlooking the garden leads to a small room, with elaborate but unsophisticated decoration (a). To the left opens the main reception room of the house, with a fully blown fourth-style decorative schema of columns in perspective and mythological scenes in the centers. (b).

6.   Caupona di Sotericus (I 12.5), Pompeii. The front part of the house (a) has the characteristic features of a food/drink establishment: a bar opening on the street, storage bins behind in the courtyard. In the rear is a small garden/yard, overlooked from a room with third-style decoration, including a mythological painting of Perseus (b).

7. Casa di Fabius Amandio, Pompeii. The view from the entrance of this little house shows the fauces-atrium-garden sequence in miniature (a). The walls of the atrium are decorated in elaborate fourth style, with landscapes at the center of red panels and architectural vistas between the panels (b).

8.   Casa dell'Atrio a mosaico,
Herculaneum. A suite of linked
reception rooms faces west over the
garden. The central and largest
room is decorated in blue (b), with
monochrome mythological scenes at
the center of each wall, here of the
Punishment of Dirce, tied beneath a
bull by Zethus and Amphion (a).

DECORATION AND LUXURY

What exactly does the presence or absence of decoration tell us about a house? To traditional Roman morality, painted walls and mosaic-carpeted floors spelled luxury. When decorated plaster first appeared on Roman walls, seemingly in the early second century B.C., it was a luxury that could provoke outrage: Cato could boast that none of his walls had stucco, and threatened to expose the corruption of those who had *villae expolitae*.[17] Later refinements in turn struck contemporaries as outrageously indulgent: Lucullus's "picture-gallery" decorations attracted censorious comment at the end of the Republic,[18] Augustan rhetoricians declaimed against decorations that imitated landscapes and seascapes, and still in the Flavian era the elder Pliny protested against entrusting art to walls, which could not be removed and saved in case of fire.[19] Even sober lawyers took a moralizing view. Not only did spending on wall decoration count as the opposite of a useful expenditure; lawyers disapproved of allowing excessive costs for damage compensation for such paintings. So, according to Capito in the Augustan period, one might have extremely expensive decoration on a party wall, but if a neighbor demolished it, one could only reclaim for the price of plain plaster.[20] Ulpian in the third century was also of the opinion that only moderate costs could be allowed in this situation, because one should not pander to luxury.[21] On the other hand, it was acknowledged that decoration could so enhance the value of a house that it might actually be bought for its adjuncts, marbles, statues, and painted pictures, and such was the value of a *pictura* that it could be an exception to the rule that everything attached to somebody's property belonged to that property.[22]

Luxury presupposes wealth, and naturally decoration must indicate wealth; but, as I have tried to suggest in the first part of this book, decoration points to something rather more specific. A rich man does not decorate all areas of his house indiscriminately, from triclinium to kitchen or slave's bedroom. On the contrary, the function of decoration is to discriminate and to render the house fit for the pattern of social activity within it. The language of private decoration draws on the language of public life; it reflects the reception function of a house and the expectations of contact with visitors from outside. Decoration (or its absence) should tell us in the first place about the social use of space; this will have its implications for the social position and wealth of the inhabitants. This working hypothesis may now be tested against the evidence available.

Measuring the luxury of decoration is bound to be somewhat arbitrary. Wall decoration in particular presents us with a bewildering variety: in its present condition of preservation, from the washed-out and crumbling to the immaculate; in period of execution, over the two centuries or so covered by Mau's four decorative styles; and in elaboration of detail and fineness of execution, ranging from the crudest daubings on rough whitewashed plaster to extraordinary confections of breathtaking artistic skill. Moreover, walls often tell a complex history over the course of decades and even centuries: of decoration and redecoration, of adaptation and repair, especially in the wake of the earthquake damage that preceded the eruption. No statistics can do justice to the complexity of the individual variants. For purposes of comparison of a large group of houses it is necessary to simplify, sometimes drastically. Even so, enough of the contrasts can be caught to form the basis for valid comparisons. Here the inventory of *Pitture e Pavimenti di Pompei* is of great assistance. Because each photographic-record number is accompanied by a verbal description of detail and an assignment to chronological style, a considerable level of detail is preserved on a systematic basis. Indeed, one might almost measure the decorative elaboration of a house by the length of its entry in *Pitture e Pavimenti*; in the finely decorated houses, not only is there physically more to record and describe, but its description requires a higher degree of verbal elaboration. In fact we can use less crude measures, but it is worth noting that the samples chosen for study here represent a considerable proportion of the whole compilation: the Regio I sample occupies 166 of the 256 pages of volume 1; the Regio VI sample, 194 of the 376 pages of volume 2. The samples have been chosen because of the relative wealth of information available.

One can measure wall decoration in different ways in order to answer different questions. First, it is possible to give a rough measure of the presence and extent of decoration in a house by counting the number of rooms decorated with anything more elaborate than bare plaster. For this purpose I have reckoned as a room any space that is given a separate number on the house plan, including public areas, corridors, etc. (and it should be noted that this is a more generous definition than that used to define rooms in order to measure house size). The value of this room count is limited. Obviously a house with two magnificently decorated rooms might be preferable to one with ten crudely decorated rooms in a state of poor repair. But within its limitations, such a count offers a highly convenient measure of simple extent of decoration. Second, the vast majority of these decorated rooms can be assigned within a consensus of expert opinion to one of the four decorative periods, and it is revealing to count the distribution of rooms between the styles. For this purpose I have followed the assignments of *Pitture e Pavimenti* (and have ignored fragments of an earlier phase preserved in a decoration of later period, and, equally, later repairs and patchings in decoration of an earlier period).

Quality is much harder to quantify. I have not presumed to make an arbitrary judgment of decorative quality of each room or even each house.[23] It is, however, possible to take note of certain outstanding features. One such feature that is characteristic of Roman painting of the imperial (but not republican) period is the mythological painting: a formally constructed scene, in a hellenizing idiom, of a subject from Greek mythology (still lifes, landscapes, vignettes of animals, etc., fall outside my definition). What makes the distribution of these "mythologicals" potentially interesting is not only their frequency (and the care with which excavators have recorded and preserved them) but their close connection with the luxury world of the Roman elite and the works of art pillaged from Greece in the late Republic. Similarly, mosaic floors and designs of polychrome marble (Fig. 7.2) point directly to the luxury of the elite (moralists protested at such *lithostrota*).[24] Mosaics, like mythologicals, have been counted according to the number of rooms in which they occur (or are recorded as having occurred).

Because mosaics and mythologicals are relatively restricted in diffusion, it would be

Figure 7.2 House V.ii, Herculaneum, opus sectile marble floor
(see Fig. 6.4 for context).

nice to have some measure that allows for qualitative distinctions across the spectrum of diffusion. Comparisons among different styles of painting would be dubious, but the fourth and final Pompeian style is both sufficiently common in its occurrence and varied in its range of elaboration to allow some tentative comparisons, though I have restricted the exercise to a single sample area, Regio I.

It remains to be seen what emerges from the data collected and what inferences can be drawn. I shall look in turn at (1) the pattern of diffusion of decorative features; (2) the relationship of decoration to social and economic activity; (3) changes over time; and (4) the relationships between different social levels.

I. The Diffusion of Decoration

We may begin by remarking the sheer extent of wall decoration in our samples from Pompeii and Herculaneum. Even excluding certain types of decoration that fall outside the art-historical classification of the four styles, as well as those that are rather different in function from such decoration, like lararium paintings and decorated shop-counters (and to these I shall return),[25] there remain in the whole sample 137 houses, or well over half (59 percent), with at least one decorated room or area, with some 740 decorated rooms or areas between them (average 5.4 rooms each). But this is certainly an understatement of the picture in A.D. 79. First, we must remember that we are only looking at ground floors. But where upper floors survive, it seems that decoration was normal (Fig. 7.3). Thus, in the Herculaneum sample, rooms survive in a state of good preservation above six houses (H III 13/14; V 6/7; V 8; V 15; V 17; V 22), all of which have decorated walls, and even in the Pompeii Regio I sample, upper rooms survive above five

Figure 7.3 Casa di Nettuno e Anfitrite, Herculaneum, bedroom in upper floor. The walls are decorated in the fourth style with red panels and white-ground architectural vistas.

houses (I 7.18; 10.1; 10.4; 10.18, all these four very close to each other; and 11.9/15, the Casa del Primo Piano), and again all are decorated. In many houses where only fragments of walls from upper stories are standing, traces of decorated plaster can be seen. There can be little doubt that if the survival of upper floors was less fragmentary, the picture of the extent of decoration would be further extended.

Second, we must allow for the sheer disintegration of evidence. In Regio I of Pompeii and in Herculaneum, finds are relatively well preserved; as far as one can tell, though the condition of numerous walls has deteriorated, sometimes dramatically, there is still no room where the decoration has been completely obliterated. In the Regio I sample, 71 percent of houses have some decoration. But the Regio VI sample has suffered very badly over the years, particularly in the smaller houses, and its drop in proportion of decorated houses to 50 percent might well reflect a reduction by 20 percent or more through simple neglect. (Insulae 10 and 11, excavated over 150 years ago, have surviving decoration in only 8 out of 23 houses.)

But even though the figures for Regio VI are likely to be an understatement, there is a clear pattern in the distribution of houses with some sort of decoration. Figures 7.4 and

7.5 examine their distribution across the size quartiles. The chances of finding decoration in the smallest units are slim (the reasons will be examined in due course); on the other hand, it is very rare for the largest houses (Quartile 4) to be completely undecorated, and because four out of the five cases occur in Regio VI, loss of evidence is the most likely explanation. In the middle two quartiles the likelihood of decoration increases with size, except in Regio I, with its steep rise in the second quartile. In fact, there is a cutoff point at about 100m^2; below this size decoration is unusual—fourteen houses (17 percent) in the whole sample—but above that point the chances of decoration increase rapidly. It is particularly in this middling range that Regio VI seems to be badly underrepresented. This results in a misleading impression of the contrast between the grand houses and the small (see above, Chap. 4).

Just as the chances of being decorated at all rise with house size, so does the number of decorated rooms/areas. The average number of decorated rooms in those houses with surviving decoration in the first quartile is 1.5; in the second, 2.5; in the third, 4.3; in the fourth, 8.6. It would be strange if this were not the case, since we have already seen that the number of rooms increases with the size of the house. But it is certainly not the case that decoration *always* rises in proportion to number of rooms. On the contrary, there are very large houses with little decoration (or at least little surviving), and relatively small ones with nearly every available space decorated. Extent of decoration thus becomes a measure of status display when taken in conjunction with size of house and number of rooms.

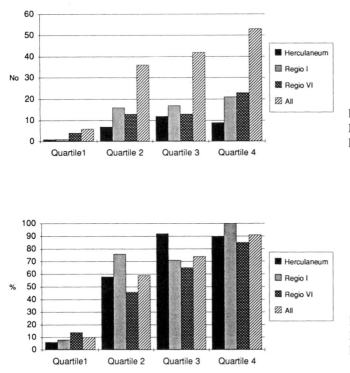

Figure 7.4 Distribution of houses with at least one decorated room (number of houses).

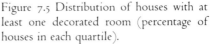

Figure 7.5 Distribution of houses with at least one decorated room (percentage of houses in each quartile).

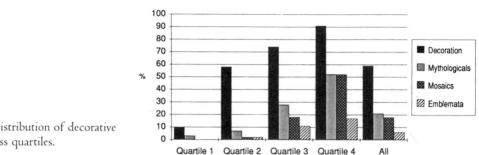

Figure 7.6 Distribution of decorative features across quartiles.

The distribution of the special features of mythologicals and mosaics is much more restricted than that of wall decoration in general (Fig. 7.6). Less than a quarter of houses overall have mythological paintings, less than a fifth mosaic floors. But these special features correlate strongly with house size, so they are found in over half the houses in the top quartile, but become exceptional in the bottom quartile. Even rarer are the rich panels of mosaics or polychrome marble which may form the centerpiece (*emblemata*) of the floor of a particularly important reception room. Again, the distribution is tilted toward the larger houses.

Not all grand houses necessarily contained either mythologicals or mosaics. Those in Herculaneum, like the Casa del Salone Nero (H VI.13), that are richly decorated in other respects suggest that it was by no means necessary for a prestigious Roman house to contain mythologicals. There seems indeed to be a slight contrast between Pompeii and Herculaneum, which emerges from comparing the distribution of mythological paintings and mosaics in the three samples. In Herculaneum, only 17 percent of the houses in the sample have mythological paintings, as against 23 percent in Pompeii Regio I and 24 percent in Regio VI. On the other hand, mosaics are found in 25 percent of the Herculaneum sample, but in only 14 percent of Pompeii Regio I and 17 percent of Regio VI. It would appear that the houses of Herculaneum express their distinction by mosaics in preference to mythological paintings, and it is of course possible that there were contrasts in fashion between the two towns.

Two points emerge clearly from analysis of the distribution of decoration. The first is that there is a predictable correlation between size of house and lavishness of decoration. The larger the ground area of a house, the more likely it is to have decoration, the more numerous the decorated rooms it will tend to have, and the more luxurious the features among them. Decoration and house size both operated as status markers, and consequently correlated. But the second and related point is that we are not dealing with a dichotomy—between grand and richly decorated houses of the "elite" on the one hand, and the undecorated houses of the tradesmen on the other—but with a continuous spectrum. The same status markers that are found in the very grandest houses also occur, albeit more rarely and in more modest quantities, in quite small units; and between largest and smallest lies a large middle ground. Houses in the bottom quartile (and in fact houses smaller than 100m^2) only exceptionally have decoration of any sort, though even among these, mythological paintings can be found. Houses in the second quartile regularly have some but not much decoration, and little of special quality. Houses in the third quartile are regularly and fairly extensively decorated, and sometimes have special features like mosaics and mythologicals. In the top quartile, it becomes remarkable if a house lacks decoration; it is normally abundant, and in at least half the cases there are special features.

II. DECORATION AND FUNCTION

Two overlapping modes of explanation for the absence of decoration are possible. One is economic: either the inhabitants simply could not afford to decorate, or they were tenants or dependents for whom the landlord did not think it worth decorating.[26] The other is functional: the purposes the house or unit served were such that decoration was either inappropriate or superfluous. The two explanations could converge: Vitruvius's picture of the appropriate housing for different social levels lays heavy emphasis on function and assumes that the lowlier plebeians would both find rooms for the reception of visitors unnecessary and need rooms suited to rustic and other functions.[27] However, rather than follow Vitruvius in assuming this convergence, it is worth examining the evidence to see what light it casts. We have seen that the architectural features of atrium and peristyle offer a useful index of reception function (Chap. 4), and that evidence for economic activity of different types is found in houses of all sizes (Chap. 6). How does decoration correlate with these indicators?

Shops are a good starting point. Units in the bottom quartile, and generally those under 100m^2, are rarely decorated. But it has also emerged that units in the bottom quartile are almost universally shops or workshops. There is no clear case of a unit under 100m^2 that does not include a shop, workshop, or in one case (I 8.12) a small garden plot. Can we distinguish whether function or poverty was responsible for their lack of decoration? Two tests are possible. One is to compare these units with the shops that are frequently incorporated in the frontages of larger units. The houses in the sample (123 total) include a total of 143 shops; 73 (51 percent) of the shops form part of units under 100m^2, 70 (49 percent) belong to larger units. Of these 143 shops, only 29 (20 percent) are decorated in any fashion; among these, 9 belong to units under 100m^2, 20 to larger ones. It would appear that shops forming part of larger units did have a better chance of decoration, and therefore that poverty (or the indifference of the landlord) was a factor. But it is also clear that among shops of any sort, decoration was uncommon.

The second test is to compare the sort of decoration found in shops with that found elsewhere. It soon emerges that it is far from being the type of drawing-room decoration to be found in a private house.[28] Sometimes the shop counter is the focus of embellishment; five of the twenty-nine "decorated" shops merely have decorated counters. In three cases decoration is limited to lararia, which I have excluded from the reckoning for decoration elsewhere (I return to this below). In three shops (I 6.12; VI 16.32; H IV.17) the decoration consists of a fairly crude phallic or Priapic scene of a type and style not normally met inside houses (Fig. 7.7). In general, shop decoration is cruder in execution than its residential counterpart, and in the rare cases in which decoration of the standard residential type is met, it occasions surprise. Thus in Herculaneum, a shop (H V.17, Fig. 7.8) neighboring the Casa del Bicentenario pleasantly decorated in red and yellow

Figure 7.7 Shop IV.17, Herculaneum. Above the counter, now much faded, is visible decoration in the form of "a Priapic figure, shamelessly and monstrously ithyphallic, who performs with one of his hands a ritual apotropaic gesture" (Maiuri, 1958, 437).

Figure 7.8 Shop/house V.17, back room. The red/yellow-ground fourth-style decoration with white-ground architectural vistas is a widespread fashion in Herculaneum (compare Figs. 2.27, 6.4, 7.3).

Figure 7.9 Caupona VI 10.19, Pompeii, tavern scenes. The style of decoration is consciously distanced from that of domestic spaces, though the division of the wall into panels is standard.

with a handsome backroom surprised Maiuri: "The decoration on the ground and upper floors is rather high-class [piuttosto signorile] and seems more suitable for a family of good class [di buon ceto] than for a retail outlet."[29] Here as elsewhere Maiuri is too ready to assume that nice decoration can only have been put up by those "di buon ceto"; but his remark underlines the rarity of meeting a nicely decorated shop. It is possible in this case, and certain in others, like the shop farther down the street at H VI.16,[30] or the third-style backrooms of I 6.10 and 12, that the decoration dates to a period before the conversion of the room to commercial use. But even a taberna can serve a reception function, and one should take note of the tavern at VI 10.1/19, with its drinking room surrounded by scenes of gambling and daily life (Fig. 7.9), and its little backroom with paintings of Aphrodite fishing and Polyphemos and Galateia; one should also note the bar or "clubroom" with very similar mythological scenes at VI 14.28.[31]

Shops then suggest strongly that both function and lack of resources explain the absence of decoration. A similar pattern emerges in those houses that include artisanal or horticultural activities. Examination of architectural features (Chap. 4) suggests that economic activities ought not be seen as an *alternative* to a reception function. The real contrast seemed to be between establishments with a productive function that did and did not have architectural features pointing to a reception function *alongside* any economic function. The distribution of decoration among these houses confirms this pattern to a remarkable extent. This is most apparent if we look at those houses in the top two quar-

TABLE 7.1
Decoration of horiticultural and industrial houses in top 2 quartiles

	No.	Avg. area sq.m	Houses decorated	Rooms decorated per house	Houses with mythologicals	Houses with mosaics
Horticultural						
with atrium	7	664	6	8	4	3
no atrium	9	410	5	1	1	0
Industrial						
with atrium	11	610	11	8	7	3
no atrium	13	278	7	2	0	0

tiles, that is, those unlike the shops and workshops of the bottom two quartiles in which there might not even be room for atrium construction. Table 7.1 suggests that the presence or absence of decoration is closely tied to the reception function implicit in the impluviate atrium.

Whatever the economic activity, the houses with atria have at least some surviving decoration, and on average in a large number of rooms (8 per house); mosaics and mythologicals are common. Those houses without atria may have some decoration, but it is sparser and poorer. The exceptions prove to be anomalous. The only atrium house in these quartiles that apparently lacks decoration is VI 9.1 in Pompeii. Classified as a *hospitium* (guest house) with attached stables, it was excavated in the mid-nineteenth century and has lost its decoration; it originally had a mythological scene of Io. By contrast, the only nonatrium house that does have a mythological painting is I 9.3/4 (Casa di Successus). It has a colonnade overlooking its garden, which may in consequence be an ornamental garden rather than a horticultural plot, as I originally assumed in classifying it.

The evidence for horticulture and industry points in the same direction as that for shops. Function is critical for the distribution of decoration. Decoration played a vital role in social life, but it was superfluous to most economic activity. The presence of economic activity in a house by no means precludes decoration, but where decoration is found, it surely points to social activity alongside the economic.

One of the most striking points to emerge is the value of the atrium as an index of the sort of social activity that gives rise to decoration. If we consider the whole sample (Fig. 7.10), it is clear that atrium houses have a much better chance of being decorated than those without atria, and exceptional features like mythologicals and mosaics cluster in them in a very marked way.

It is inevitable that decoration should be more common in atrium houses, given that it is rare in smaller houses and that, for structural reasons alone, a majority of the small houses could not have atria. But size is not the only factor at work. There are, after all, both small atrium houses and large nonatrium houses. Yet atrium houses, however small, almost always have decoration; of the eleven that lack it, eight are in Regio VI of Pompeii, where the destruction of evidence is worst, and it is safe to assume that most of these were in fact decorated. On the other hand, in nonatrium houses, though the

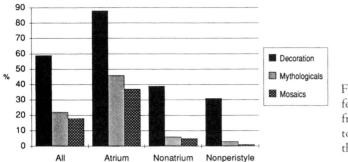

Figure 7.10 Distribution of decorative features by house type. This contrasts the frequency of decoration in atrium houses to those without impluviate atrium and to those with neither atrium nor peristyle.

presence of some decoration is not uncommon, fine decoration (mythologicals and mosaics) is extremely rare; and when we except those houses (notably in Herculaneum) in which a peristyle functions as an alternative to an atrium, fine decoration disappears almost completely. The exceptions deserve remark, particularly three taverns with mythological paintings on their walls in Pompeii Regio VI (VI 10.1; VI 14.8; VI 14.28), and the highly unusual Sacello degli Augustali at Herculaneum, with a large mythological painting in its central shrine. The one house with neither atrium nor peristyle to boast a mosaic floor is the no less unusual Casa del Bel Cortile at Herculaneum (H V.8), with its central courtyard and stairwell (Fig. 7.11), and its enormous reception room (5.50 by

Figure 7.11 Casa del Bel Cortile, Herculaneum, view from main room to courtyard and stairwell. This unusual feature takes the place of the normal atrium or peristyle. Note the blocked door on the right, formerly opening onto the peristyle of the Casa del Bicentenario.

10 meters). This is not adequately accounted for by Maiuri (384ff.), and I would suggest that it be seen as the meeting place of some corporate body like a collegium.

III. The Chronology of Diffusion

The data from our sample points to a remarkable diffusion of decoration through the housing stock of Pompeii and Herculaneum and to the sort of imitation of the Roman elite which Cicero describes, however attenuated this becomes. But it refers to a single point in time, the year A.D. 79. We are looking at the accumulated results of a cultural explosion dating back to the second century B.C. and apparently already past its apogee by the reign of Titus. The richness of experimentation and the speed of development over this period is stunning, and certainly in the case of wall decoration was not sustained in later centuries. It would be of great benefit to build back a chronological element into the analysis, partly because one cannot stop at commenting that a house is decorated. The decoration might be fairly fresh, as in the Casa dei Vettii; or it might date back as much as two centuries, as in the Casa del Fauno. Should that make a difference to our estimation of the current inhabitants in A.D. 79? But more interestingly, it would be valuable to look at the chronology of the process of diffusion. If the luxury of the elite spread outward in society, how swiftly did the ripples move?

Here at least we are on well-worked terrain—well-worked to a fault. In the late nineteenth century, August Mau, by basing his research on systematic examination of what was effectively a sample—the current excavations of his day (mostly in the Regio VI sample used here)—was able to establish a firm chronological framework for the phases of decorative fashion. Mau's framework of four styles, based on the assumption that Pompeii reflected Roman fashions as described by Vitruvius, has proved its value by its relevance for analyzing mural decoration of the same period not only from all over Italy but increasingly from the provinces. Many modifications in detail have been made since, but the consensus remains firm that the first or "masonry" style evolved in the second century B.C.; that the second, "architectural," style came early in the first century B.C. and flourished in the last generation of the Republic; that the third style came in with the Empire; and that a fourth style, in many respects merely an extension of the third but also harking back to the second, took over in the Julio-Claudian period, perhaps in the reign of Claudius.[32]

Social and cultural history does not operate with the sharp and precise caesurae of political history, and in dating the diffusion of a cultural pattern it is not even desirable to work with a more precise dating framework than sketched above. The point should also be made that the style of a piece of decoration only strictly gives us a *terminus post quem*. It has been demonstrated repeatedly that earlier styles were imitated, repeated, echoed, restored generations later.[33] A fourth-style decoration *cannot* have been executed under the Republic; but a second-style painting *may occasionally* have been produced in the first century A.D. With this caveat in mind, we may ask what is the relative diffusion of the four styles.

The difficulty in this enquiry lies in the survival of evidence. It is well known to all that the fourth style is enormously more common in Pompeii than the first or second, but that is inevitable: it is the most recent. Earlier decorations have frequently been replaced, and fragments of the older styles can still be seen under or embedded in decorations of the imperial period. There was extensive rebuilding as well as redecoration; numerous walls, once decorated in earlier styles, have certainly been demolished, and it is not until the true excavation of Pompeii starts—which will dismantle walls and examine beneath floor levels—that a credible picture of preimperial Pompeii can be reconstructed.

To this extent our hands are tied, and a count of the relative frequency of the four styles can tell us nothing. But though we cannot measure frequency, we can observe something of the extent of social spread.[34] It is possible to contrast the types and sizes of houses in which decorations of the various styles survive. That is to say, because the survival rates of earlier styles are likely to be lower than those of later styles, we can attach no importance to absolute numbers. The relative frequency of examples of the fourth style does not in itself prove an absolute increase. However, if decoration has spread more widely through the housing stock, we would expect the *proportions* to change. First-style decoration ought to be infrequent in small houses compared to larger ones; fourth-style decoration should be *proportionately* more common in small compared to large houses. Similarly, there should be a proportionate rise between first and fourth styles of the frequency of decoration in nonatrium as compared to atrium houses. This is, in fact, precisely what we find.

Of course, these observations would be undermined if there were reason to suppose that earlier phases of decoration were less likely to be preserved in one size or type of house than another. One problem is that of changing property boundaries. The house in which a first-style decoration was first put up may have been rather different in size and type from that in which it survives. Thus the fine first-style fauces of the Casa Sannitica at Herculaneum lead into what is certainly an atrium of early construction (see Fig. 2.10); but Maiuri is probably right to conjecture that the original house was much more exten- sive than the house of A.D. 79.[35] In this case the occurrence of first style in a small house would not prove that small houses were decorated in the second century B.C. (but it would be an instance of an atrium house decorated in the second century B.C.). Though property boundaries change over time in both directions, and small houses are amalga- mated into large, as well as large being split up into small, the general tendency is to fission rather than fusion. Numerous small and medium houses of imperial Pompeii and Herculaneum are the result of progressive subdivision. To take another clear example, the magnificent Casa del Criptoportico (I 6.2/4), which must have been one of the largest and finest houses of later republican Pompeii, was split into two properties (Fig. 7.12). In one, the cryptoporticus with its luxurious baths was reduced to a storage area; in the other, the handsome suite of the Sala degli Elefanti that once opened onto the porticus has become the rear room of a house in the process of fourth-style redecora- tion. But this process of fission should tend to exaggerate the proportion of early styles in smaller houses.

Second, it is conceivable that the survival of earlier decorations is not random in the sense we would require. The most obvious distortion would be if wealthier owners in larger houses more frequently redecorated their walls, while poorer owners more often

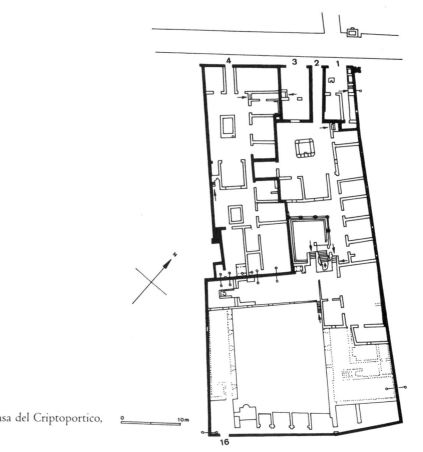

Figure 7.12 Plan, Casa del Criptoportico,
Pompeii.

made do with out-of-date decoration. In fact this is not the case; indeed, the largest house
in Pompeii or Herculaneum, the Casa del Fauno, preserves the most complete and
extensive first-style decoration we have, while the best specimens of second style come
from opulent villas outside Pompeii: Oplontis and the Villa dei Misteri. Of course, it is
possible that "old" families set a higher premium on "old" styles of decoration, yet it is
hard to imagine that the humble systematically destroyed what the rich so lovingly
preserved.

Let us examine the data. In Herculaneum, first- and second-style decoration is too rare
to be revealing, and the lack of a volume of *Pitture e Pavimenti* means that strict compara-
bility is not possible.[36] For this purpose, then, the sample is restricted to the two Pompeii
regions. The accompanying charts analyze the houses, by quartile size (Fig. 7.13) and
house type (Fig. 7.14), in which rooms predominantly decorated in one of the four styles
occur.

Even when all allowances have been made for the limitations of our evidence, the
pattern is too marked to leave room for much doubt. The republican styles cluster in a

very pronounced fashion in the largest houses. The smallest house in the sample with first-style decoration is 125m², the smallest with second-style is 140m². There is, that is to say, no sign of shops and workshops at the lower end of the scale having been decorated in the republican period. The same applies to shops incorporated in larger units; just one (VI 14.11) has first-style decoration, and that presumably dates from a period when it was a room in the adjoining house (VI 14.12), which has first-style decoration in its vestibule. Even third style is exceptional among shops: four cases among all shops in the sample include two that were previously private rooms within the Casa dei Quadretti Teatrali (I 6.10, 12). By contrast, fifteen shops in the Pompeii sample have fourth-style decoration, and though it may still be the case that shop decoration remained unusual, it is clearly only toward the end of its history that decorating fashion penetrated to shops.

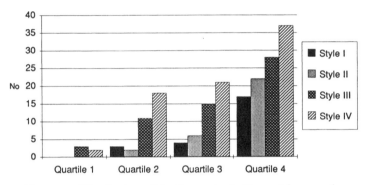

Figure 7.13 Distribution of the four styles in Pompeii by quartile.

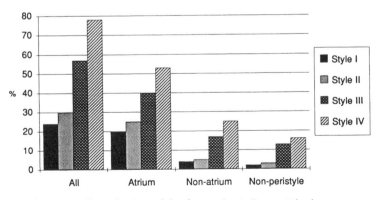

Figure 7.14 Distribution of the four styles in Pompeii by house type, contrasting houses with atria to those without and to those with neither atria nor peristyles.

TABLE 7.2
Proportionate distribution of the four styles

	Quartiles 1–3 (10–345m²)	Quartile 4 (350–3000m²)	Nonatrium houses	Atrium houses
Style I	1	2.4	1	5
Style II	1	2.8	1	5
Style III	1	1	1	2.4
Style IV	1	0.9	1	2.1

It would also appear that the decoration of small to middling houses (i.e., those in the second and third quartiles) was unusual, though not unknown, under the Republic. In the top quartile there is a steady increase in numbers of decorated houses from style to style, but no sudden leap. But in all other quartiles the pattern changes dramatically between republican styles (I and II) and imperial (III and IV). So if we look at the proportion of decorated houses in the first three quartiles as against those in the top quartile, we find that it changes dramatically between the republican and imperial periods (Table 7.2).

While under the Republic, decoration is two to three times commoner in the top quartile than in all other houses put together; under the Empire the balance becomes equal. This is strongly supported by the distribution of the styles between nonatrium and atrium house. The proportion changes, not gradually from one style to the next but suddenly between second and third styles: from 1:5 under the Republic, to 1:2 under the Empire. We have seen a close association between decoration and the reception function implicit in the atrium. It now emerges that the spread of decoration beyond atrium houses is much more marked in the imperial than the republican period.

The evidence points very strongly toward a progressive spread of decoration. Even in Cicero's day, wall decoration had spread well beyond the villas of the rich into the fabric of urban Pompeii.[37] But there is still some justification for referring to it at this period as an "elite" cultural phenomenon.[38] The Empire brings what might be described as a quantum leap. Fourth-style decoration was surely yet more common than third, but it extended a tendency toward social diffusion established in the first generation of the Empire.

IV. FROM LUXUS TO KITSCH

Few would wish to deny that the culture of the Roman elite was luxurious. But when we come to discuss the decoration of hundreds of rooms in dozens of houses in second-rate Campanian towns, ranging from the breathtaking to the crude, simple, and banal, can we still meaningfully speak of luxury? We naturally think of the architecture of a house with an ornate, four-sided peristyle like the Casa del Menandro as luxurious, but might refuse to use the same language of its modest neighbor, the Casa del Fabbro, with its single brick-pillared portico looking out over a modest garden patch (Figs. 7.15, 16),

Figure 7.15 Casa del Fabbro, Pompeii, axial view. The roof above the atrium has not been restored. Note that the house plan is far from symmetrical (see Fig. 3.24), but a small shrine on the garden wall (now overgrown) provides a focus framed by the tablinum.

Figure 7.16 Casa del Fabbro, Pompeii, portico. To the right the two main reception rooms look through the portico to the garden. At the end is the kitchen area and stairs up.

let alone a bar/tavern like the Caupona di Sotericus (I 12.3), with its atrium full of storage bins and its minute backyard (Pl. 6). Of course, there is a great gulf between the luxury of the elite houses and the modest aspirations of the small. But what matters is to understand that they do not belong to different cultural universes. It is precisely the cultural language of the elite that the others are imitating, even if by doing so they reduce it to the banal and everyday. The worsted stockings of the English working classes, we have seen, owed their inspiration to the silk stockings sported on the calves of outrageous courtiers; but both luxury and outrage had been watered down to a scarcely perceptible dose. Modern wallpaper has its origins ultimately in the silk hangings of the aristocracy and more immediately in the large and elaborate paper murals of the mid-nineteenth century; the advent of steam machines in 1858 made possible the cheap and repetitive patterns that were to flood the market.[39]

It is by looking at the fourth style of wall decoration that we can see this pattern most clearly. I have argued above (Chap. 2) that the decoration of the imperial period represents a great increase in range of quality and expressivity in comparison to the relatively limited styles of the Republic. Between the best and worst of the first style there is not much difference, except in technical quality of execution, and even with the second style, the range is little more. By the time we reach the fourth style, the range is huge, between simple white-ground walls divided with red stripes and embellished if at all with the sketchiest of vignettes, to richly colored and minutely worked masterpieces like the classics of the Casa dei Vettii. It might be argued that there was an overall decline in quality from the late-republican and Augustan peak (Villa dei Misteri etc); indeed, Schefold was so disparaging about the quality of Flavian painting as to use expressions like "vespasianischer Kitsch."[40] But while progressively more of low quality was produced as demand expanded, the distance between the top and bottom of the market widened.

The fourth style may be analyzed, I have suggested (see Figs. 2.13–21), as incorporating a series of hierarchies or ranges of choice, affecting color, decorative framework, and motifs. Thus, if we concentrated on the central field of the wall alone (though socle and upper register introduce their own variants) we can distinguish a range of dominant background color, from the simple white, through the frequent red and yellow (often combined), to the rare blacks, blues, and greens. Then, in terms of elements used to articulate and to divide the wall into separate panels, there is a range from simple lines; through border patterns, mostly of the "bordi a tappeto" or "embroidery border" type; to embellishments such as candelabra and columns; to the elaborate architectural vistas that take a life of their own in this style. Finally, in terms of motifs with which to embellish the central field created by these borders, there is a progression from little vignettes, of swans, griffins, cupids, tragic masks, sacred objects, and so on; through more ambitious roundels and small panel-paintings, the roundels often containing faces, the panels still lifes, little landscapes, villa scenes, etc.; to reach a climax with the larger and more elaborate panel paintings, above all of mythological scenes. (This account is a simplification of a complex and varied reality, but one designed to bring out something of that complexity.)

Both the unity and the range of the fourth style lie in the way that decoration, however grand or humble, can be drawn from this same repertoire. Precisely the same terminology can be found repeated in the careful descriptions of fourth-style decorations in *Pitture e Pavimenti*; the richest decoration is distinguished by its use of more of the standard elements, so that description becomes longer. As a very crude illustration, we can look at the fourth-style rooms in just one of the samples, that in Regio I. Thirty-six houses there have between them 115 rooms decorated in this style. Of these, 5 are shop paintings and 10 garden paintings, which fall outside the idiom described above; the remaining 100 rooms can be compared with regard to the hierarchies of color, framework, and motif. A room may have (and the more elaborate the decoration, the more this is so) several features within each range, for example, both embroidery borders and architectural vistas, or both vignettes and mythologicals; hence the totals do not add up to 100.

Of background colors (Fig. 7.17), white is the single most frequent (40 rooms); red and yellow together (they are hard to distinguish because frequently combined) account for more than half (55) of the rooms; blue/black/green are rare (11). Among dividing elements (Fig. 7.18), easily the commonest is the decorative border (81 rooms), while candelabra (35), columns (23), and architectural vistas (33) are each found in a third or fewer of the rooms. The conventional account, which regards the architectural vista as the characteristic of the fourth style, is to this extent misleading; in fact, the decorative border is the most predictable element, and it is on this that the most promising recent research concentrates.[41] Finally, among motifs (Fig. 7.19), vignettes (71 rooms) far outnumber roundels and panels (43), and of course mythologicals (16); only 9 rooms are completely without traces of any of these. Again, it is with vignettes, rather than the mythological paintings that have engrossed attention, that serious analysis of the fourth style must start.

This analysis, complicated though it looks, oversimplifies the varieties of fourth-style decoration. But it serves well enough to illustrate the way in which certain elements are equally common in houses of any size (white, red/yellow backgrounds, decorative borders, vignettes) and form the staple, so to speak, of this style, while others are relative rarities tending to cluster in the largest houses (blue/black/green among colors, columns and vistas among dividing elements, panels and mythologicals among motifs). But one point that emerges is that it is by no means true that the smallest houses always have the simplest decoration, and the largest the most lavish. Thus the charmingly decorated little Casa della Venere in Bikini (I 11.6) swells the figures for mythologicals in the second quartile, while the Casa dell'Efebo (I 7.10–12) is exceptional among large houses in the frequency of its white-ground rooms and swells the figures for the top quartile (Pl. 4).

A larger sample and a more sophisticated analysis of the component elements would be necessary for better understanding of the fourth style. All that this analysis seeks to demonstrate is that the fourth style has a unified repertoire; that great and small houses draw on the same idioms, and that richly decorated houses distinguish themselves by the employment of more and richer elements. "Banalization" does not mean that all fourth-style decoration is worse; but it does mean that as "down-market" versions proliferate, the top of the market has to distinguish itself by increasing richness and elaboration. To

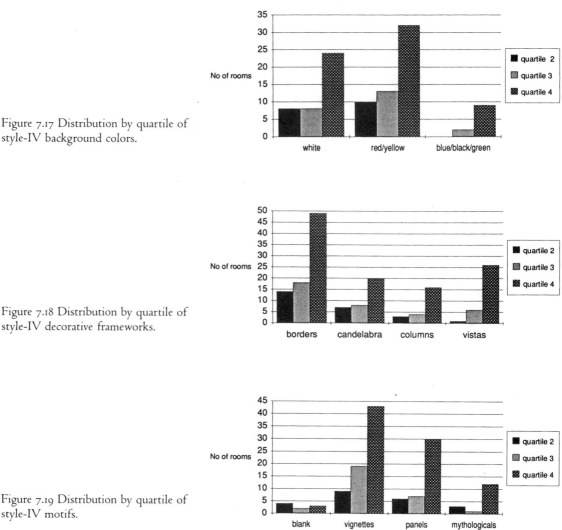

Figure 7.17 Distribution by quartile of style-IV background colors.

Figure 7.18 Distribution by quartile of style-IV decorative frameworks.

Figure 7.19 Distribution by quartile of style-IV motifs.

modern taste such baroque or fantastical decoration may seem excessive, and there is a temptation to prefer the simple delicacy of Augustan third style, or even some of the simpler versions of the fourth, like the gilded griffins and cupids of the Casa del Fabbro. But our own judgments are beside the point. From the social point of view, the remarkable phenomenon is that a former luxury was able to develop to the level where it could penetrate so thoroughly into the domestic environment of a town.

How we should explain the growth of the range of this repertoire in terms of the relationship between artist and patron is of subordinate importance. One might argue that as the demand for decoration spread to the less well-off, the ateliers of decorators responded by reducing the quality of a former luxury; or that the ateliers deliberately introduced simpler and cheaper schemes of decoration in order to tap a wider market. From the point of view of the present analysis it makes little difference (and both explanations may be simultaneously true). The point is that the fourth style is well adapted for a market that ranges, as we see in Pompeii, from the rich to the poor: wall decoration is no longer the preserve of an elite.

———————

PAUL ZANKER, in one of the finest studies of Pompeian housing of recent years, showed how potent was the aristocratic villa as a model for the lifestyle of even quite modest houses in Pompeii.[42] Here we find gardens with miniature waterways, *Euripi* and *Nili*, adorned with statuary shrunk to the scale of gnomes, nymphaea with miniature dining couches, disproportionate garden paintings evoking imaginary gardens—all testimony to the way in which Lucullan luxury created the image of success and happiness to which even those with slender resources aspired. The argument of this chapter is to extend yet further Zanker's model.

Take the cluster of small houses nestling alongside the handsome Casa di Paquius Proculus (Fig. 7.20). At the other end of the row the Casa del Sacerdos Amandus (I 7.7) is very much a middle-range house (c. 230m^2), toward the bottom of the third quartile of our sample, with atrium and a pretty peristyle with colonnades on two sides, and six rooms nicely decorated in the third style, the largest including a (now familiar) group of mythological scenes, Polyphemus and Galateia, Perseus and Andromeda, the fall of Icarus, and the Apples of the Hesperides (Pl. 3). The Casa di Fabius Amandio (I 7.3) is considerably smaller (c. 125m^2), close to the minimum at which an atrium is feasible; but tight organization makes possible not only an atrium but a miniature garden (without colonnades). Both these and five rooms have third-style decoration, and four of the rooms have simple mosaics on the floor (Pl. 7). Between these two houses is a workshop (I 7.5), probably owned by I 7.7, and perhaps previously part of it. At 80m^2 the ground floor has only space for a central yard and two rooms (Figs. 7.21, 22). Both of these are decorated, again in the third style; even the bird and cherry panels on the simple white-ground walls of the smaller of these (Fig. 7.23) can be closely paralleled in a luxury villa like Oplontis (Fig. 7.24).

It would be pure speculation to try to pinpoint the status of the individual inhabitants or owners of any of these three houses. What the statistics do allow is to identify the broad context of inhabitants of houses of these sorts. By no stretch of the imagination could we see in them members of an elite. The members of the ordines of the city, both decurions and Augustales, wealthy landowners and traders, ought to be found in the top 10 percent, or at the most generous 25 percent, of the houses. Too many of the indicators of wealth and prestige cluster in the houses in the top quartile to make it plausible to look lower down the scale for an elite, even a local one. Nor on the other hand can we be looking at the poor. Too many other houses lack decoration, at least on the ground floor, let alone atria, to allow us to populate such handsome premises with them, unless as

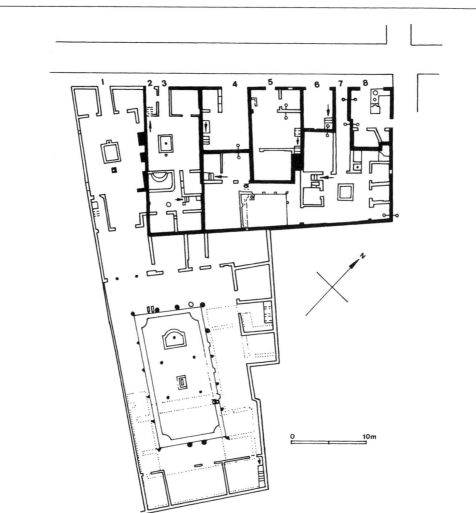

Figure 7.20 Plan, Casa di Paquius Proculus and its neighbors
(I 7.1–7), Pompeii (after *CTP*).

Figure 7.21 House I 7.5, Pompeii. A central court gives access to two rooms
(doorways visible to left and right), both with fourth-style decoration.
In the far corner of the court are visible a hearth and stairs to rooms above.

Figure 7.22 House I 7.5, room (a). The decoration comprises bird and fruit motifs
in the center of white panels with simple red frames.

Figure 7.23 House I 7.5, room (a), detail of bird and fruit.

Figure 7.24 Villa of Oplontis (Torre Annunziata), detail of decoration of passageway (81) to piscina. Although slightly more detailed in execution, the style of this bird and fruit motif in the grandest surviving Campanian villa is no different from that in house I 7.5.

lodgers and tenants of upper flats. Necessarily, we are dealing with a large and disparate group between elite and poor. I hesitate to use terms such as *middle/lower-middle class* or *bourgeoisie/petite bougeoisie* because of their profoundly anachronistic connotations. In the elder Pliny's terms, they were the *plebs*; not the *plebs humilis* but the *plebs media*. To judge by the nomenclature of almost all the documentary evidence we have from the Campanian towns, a high proportion of them are likely to have been of servile origin; to judge by the archaeological evidence, they were extensively involved in the trade, craft, and commerce of the city.

Among such relatively prosperous plebeians, habits of luxury house-decoration, derived from conscious imitation of the Roman elite, spread. The distribution of the four styles suggest strongly that although decoration was by no means uncommon even under the Republic, it was under the early Empire that the major diffusion among plebeian households got under way. This would appear to be a period of increasing prosperity for the city, and the spread of decoration does surely reflect a rise in prosperity among such people. But decoration represents more than display of wealth. Together with architecture, it is a method of fashioning space adequately for the social activity it is expected to contain, and specifically for the reception of visitors, and hence a way of displaying, or laying claim to, social rank. Vitruvius's sketch of the social ranks for which the architect builds might lead us to expect, beneath the level of public figures, lawyers, and financiers, a large mass of people "of common fortune" who paid their respects to others and did not receive their own visitors. That picture tends to be refuted by the evidence of Pompeii and Herculaneum, where even small flats above shops may share in their touches of luxury.

But social spread brings with it banalization. I have tried to show how in the fourth style even the decoration of modest houses draws on the same repertoire as that of the great show houses. The ultimate model for them all is the Hellenizing culture of the senatorial elite of the later Republic and early Empire. But as the imitation spreads out and becomes banal, so its social function shifts. At a remove, it may import something of the lifestyle of the prosperous and successful into a humble home. But more than that, I would suggest, it brings a sense of belonging: of membership in a society in which ideology and culture are defined by the elite. Particularly for those whose claims to Roman identity were new and tenuous, the manumitted slaves, it must have been necessary to surround themselves with visible symbols of their Romanness. To become a Roman, a slave must pass through rebirth by imitation; the master supplied the model. However foreign the trappings of luxury may have been in origin, the fact that the aristocracy, which had always set the model within Roman society, had made them their own converted them, paradoxically, into symbols of the Roman.

Behind the explosion of new fashions in domestic luxury that Pompeii and Herculaneum would appear to document, there seem to me to lie a complex of factors of social and economic change that are by no means confined to Campania. One is a an extraordinary rise in economic prosperity, and specifically urban prosperity, in late republican and early imperial Italy that was the direct result of conquest. A second is a massive expansion of the Roman citizenship, with its implications for the redefinition of what being "Roman" actually signified. A third is a cultural revolution among the elite that has its roots in intense competition, in the need in a rapidly changing political scene to assert claim to social leadership, and to stay one step ahead of competitors as the new status symbols became progressively banalized.

Together these factors generated a social and cultural revolution that spread not only through the cities of Italy but with surprising speed into the provinces.[43] Particularly in Gaul, the dramatic advance in diffusion of Roman painting from style I, restricted to three sites near the coast in Provence, to the cautious advance of style II to ten sites more widely spread in the south, to the bold spread of style III to thirty sites stretching as far west as Bourdeaux and as far north as Arras, may be taken as a mirror of the advance of Roman power and culture between the second century B.C. and the beginning of the first century A.D.[44] Understanding of the process of Romanization in the provinces must start with interpretation of cultural change in Roman Italy. Pompeii and Herculaneum offer precious evidence toward that interpretation, and just as they have been successfully exploited to construct a paradigm of the chronology of decoration, they offer a potential paradigm of its sociology. But the value of the paradigm offered here can only be tested by extending the investigation outside Campania.

CHAPTER 8

□

EPILOGUE

In succession
Houses rise and fall, crumble, are extended . . .
Houses live and die: there is a time for building
And a time for living and for generation
And a time for the wind to break the loosened pane . . .
T. S. Eliot, *East Coker*

To visit a Roman house in the extraordinary state of preservation made possible by the eruption of Vesuvius is like seeing the set of a drama; and the desire is natural to re-populate this set with its dramatis personae. Playing games with names, and giving each house the name of an "owner," even if we could do it satisfactorily, is not enough. We want, more than a cast list, to know what sort of people lived what sort of lives in these surrounds.

Just occasionally, answers to our curiosity peep through. One source that betrays, however obliquely, something of the lives of the inhabitants is the occasional find of business documents, normally in the form of a bundle of wooden tablets coated with wax. There have been two major finds of this type in Pompeii: one from the house of Caecilius Jucundus (V 1.26), the dossier of a banker, has been thoroughly studied;[1] the other, from a suburb of Pompeii called Murecine, revealing the business activities of two freedmen *mercatores* (merchants), Sulpicius Cinnamus and Sulpicius Faustus, largely at the neighboring colony of Puteoli, is still under intensive study.[2] Both of these dossiers throw light on, and raise troublesome questions about, a range of financial, commercial, and legal transactions. But a third and less familiar group of documents from Herculaneum, the Tabulae Herculanenses, have a particular relevance to the themes of this book; they bear on the inhabitants of some of the properties here studied, and allow a glimpse of private lives, of relationships within domestic groups and between neighbors, and of men and women seeking to establish their own status in this competitive and fluid society.

The Herculaneum Tablets form not a single dossier but a group of dossiers from at least three houses (Fig. 8.1).[3] They were close neighbors (Fig. 8.1). One dossier comes from the Casa del Bicentenario (H V.13–16), the findspot (somewhat vaguely) being given as the southeastern part, an upper apartment overlooking the peristyle; a second from the upper apartment at H V.22, located this time in a wooden chest in room D, overlooking the street above the shop at H V.19; and a third dossier from the grand house just across the road, the Casa del Salone Nero (H VI.11). They emerged from the excavations immediately before the Second World War and spent the war mouldering in storerooms;

Figure 8.1 Herculaneum, view over Insula V frontage toward forum. Of the three dossiers discussed, that of Cominius Primus was found in the upper apartment nearest on the left, that of Petronia Justa in the casa del Bicentenario behind it, and that of Vennidius Ennychus in the Casa del Salone Nero beyond. The last building in the row at the edge of the excavations is the Sacello degli Augustali.

they were finally published in the University of Naples journal that started with the return of peace, *La Parola del Passato*.[4] Unfortunately, the records of which documents came from which house were not always well kept, and some are "of uncertain provenance."[5] One striking feature of the discovery of separate dossiers from closely neighboring houses is the implication for what we have lost. It must surely be something about the way the houses in this particular area of the site were preserved—to a high level, including substantial parts of upper floors—that enabled the dossiers to survive. We should infer that such baskets of documents were a widespread phenomenon, not the isolated one of which the survival rate gives the impression.[6]

The richest and most famous dossier is that from the Casa del Bicentenario. Some seventeen tablets, each originally consisting of several wooden sheets tied together, pertain to a single legal case, the status of Petronia Justa.[7] The dispute had taken the participants twice to Rome, in A.D. 75 and 76, to the tribunal of the urban praetor in the Forum of Augustus. At issue was whether Petronia Spurii filia Justa (as she called herself) was freeborn (*ingenua*) as she claimed, or the manumitted slave (*liberta*) of Calatoria

Themis (and consequently to be addressed as Calatoria mulieris liberta Justa). We cannot tell who was in the right, let alone who won the case. We cannot even be sure whose dossier it was, and consequently who lived in that apartment overlooking the peristyle. Scholars tend to find the case in favor of Calatoria Themis, and there is a good chance she was telling the truth. But a case in court on a matter of status turned not, as we naturally assume, on documentary demonstration of the facts, but on the ability of the contestants to marshal support from such of their family, friends, and neighbors who were prepared to stand up for them and make testimony under oath. It is this feature that makes the case so revealing of domestic life.

Our expectation is to find a society composed essentially of freeborn families like our own, modified by the presence of slaves, periodically manumitted and so enabled to start up, with luck, their own freeborn families. But the modification of family structure that flows from slavery and manumission penetrates far more deeply, and the boundaries between slave and free are far more fluid, than we might imagine. Slavery and biological reproduction intertwined as strategies for making a family, and the difference between a daughter and a slave girl might indeed be a legal nicety.

The agreed facts of the case were that Justa's mother was Petronia Vitalis, the manumitted slave of Petronius Stephanus, husband of Calatoria Themis. Justa, however, had not been brought up by her own mother but by Stephanus and Themis. The status of an *alumna* (foster child) was often uncertain; the natural parents might reclaim her and vindicate her freeborn status when she came of age, offering compensation to the foster parents for the costs of upbringing (*alimenta*). The Augustan grammarian Melissus, born free at Spoletium, was abandoned as a baby when his parents fell out; as a foundling he was brought up and well educated, then given, with the status of a slave, to Maecenas; but when his mother then tried to assert his freeborn status, he preferred to remain the slave of the powerful figure who had befriended him, a loyalty that earned him rapid manumission, introduction to Augustus, and promotion to a librarianship.[8] Vitalis, for whatever reason, had allowed her baby to be fostered by her patron, and in due course had reclaimed her and offered the normal compensation for costs of upbringing.[9] But Stephanus and Themis then proved too attached to Justa to let her go easily. "Why grudge the girl," others had heard Stephanus ask Vitalis, "when we treat her as a daughter?"[10]

Technically, Justa will have been born a slave to Stephanus if her birth was before her mother Vitalis's manumission, free but illegitimate (as admitted in "Spurii filia") if afterward. Either way, it is likely enough that Stephanus was the father. So it may be both that Stephanus treated her as a daughter because she was his natural daughter and that he treated her as a slave because she was his legal slave, as daughter to his slave Vitalis and as his alumna. The boundaries are extraordinarily fluid. That fluidity, combined with lack of documentation in the form of birth registers, must have made, in this and many other cases, clear proof of status unattainable.[11] Hence the importance of the voice of the community expressed through the depositions of witnesses.

Two voices survive in support of Themis's case. One is that of her freedman M. Calatorius Marullus, who claimed to have been manumitted together with Justa (TH 24).

Illiterate, he was not necessarily a convincing witness. The other is that of a free man (who may well, from his name, have been an ex-slave), Sex. Vibidius Ampliatus (TH 23). He claims to have been intimate with the household of Stephanus and Themis, to have enjoyed *domesticitas* with them, a rare and striking word indicating domestic intimacy of some sort. It might even signify that he lived in the same house, under the sort of arrangements explored above (Chap. 5). According to his testimony, he had been present when some transaction took place that proved for him that Justa was a liberta.

Rather more voices survive on Justa's side. There are the two men who were present when Stephanus claimed to treat Justa "as a daughter," and concluded (with more good-will than logic) that she was an ingenua; these are Publius Arrius Publi filius M[anceps?], himself freeborn, and Q Talmudius Optatus, probably an ex-slave (TH 19, 20). Then there are two men who, like Vibidius Ampliatus, also (if the documents are correctly restored) enjoyed *domesticitas* with Stephanus and Themis, and who witnessed Stephanus declaring that he had a single slave girl to manumit, Vitalis, after which he manumitted her; these are the freeborn Marcus Vinicius Marci filius Proculus and another whose name is lost (TH 17, 18). But the most telling testimony is that of C. Petronius Telesphorus (TH 16). He swears that Vitalis was his *colliberta*, manumitted, that is, by the same patron, Petronius Stephanus, that Justa was born free, and that he himself had negotiated with Stephanus and Themis the repayment of the cost of upbringing and the restitution of Justa to her mother Vitalis, and consequently knew her to be freeborn.

The testimony of Telesphorus must have been singularly damaging to Themis. When the case first went to Rome in December A.D. 75, Calatoria Themis was represented by a tutor, who stood bail for her (TH 14); the tutor, at that date at least, was Telesphorus himself. When the case returned to Rome three months later, in March A.D. 76, Calatorius Speudon, presumably freedman of Calatoria Themis, stood bail on her behalf. Her own tutor was testifying against her, and backing the story of Justa.

If Justa won her case, as I imagine, and kept this bundle of documents to prove her status, it was not so much because she actually was born free, the bastard daughter of an ex-slave, as because her influence and credit within the domestic and neighborly circle in which she moved, revolving around the household of Stephanus and Themis, could mobilize enough voices to speak up for her. (On the contrary, if she in fact lost, it will have been because more voices than now survive outweighed those of her backers.) In this world in which the demarcation between slave and free is so easily transgressed, social standing hung on legal definitions of status; but the application of legal definitions in turn might hang on a network of social relationships between the various players.

One important factor might be relationships between neighbors. But neighbors do not always get on, as the basket from the flat at V.22 vividly reveals. L. Cominius Primus, whose name dominates the extensive dossier (at least thirty-four tablets), moved in the same circles as Stephanus and Themis; he appears in the Petronia Justa dossier as witness, along with Petronius Stephanus, to a document now lost (TH 29), while several people with the name M. Calatorius act as witnesses for him.[12] He also has dealings with L. Venidius Ennychus, the protagonist of the third dossier in the Casa del Salone Nero, who witnessed a couple of his documents.[13] But he was apparently capable of sharp quarrels. We find him testifying under oath that his front doors have been stoned by a band of slaves belonging to Caria Longina and another.[14] There must be more to this incident than drunken rowdiness, though what he had done to upset Caria Longina we do not know. But his most frequent quarrels are with neighboring landowners to the agricultural properties he owns.

In A.D. 69, while Italy is torn by civil war (one tablet, TH 77, is dated to 26 January, eleven days after Galba's murder, a traumatic event the scribe momentarily forgets, first writing Galba's name in the date, then replacing it by Otho's), Cominius is arguing over the boundaries between his estate, the fundus Numidianus, and that of his neighbor, L. Appuleius Proculus. Ti. Crassius Firmus is appointed as arbiter of the dispute (Appuleius complains Cominius has been cutting down his boundary stakes), and with the aid of the surveyor L. Opsius Herma marks and records the boundaries anew (TH 76–80). Another neighboring landowner to this estate was Ulpia Plotina (TH 79), with whom Cominius has repeated transactions, through Plotina's slaves Venustus and Felix who sign a number of receipts.[15] With her he seemingly does business without problems. The fundus Numidianus then returns in the year after the controversy with Appuleius in a marriage dispute (TH 87). The estate, it appears, was held by Cominius as dowry for his wife Paullina, whom he is now divorcing, and consequently he is selling the estate. Nor is this the end of disputes: P. Petronius Agricola denounces Cominius over some problem involving his vines and orders him not to touch any more of what he has "sown or seeded" until the dispute is settled (TH 86). Cominius, it seems, was not an easy man to get on with.

With the third main dossier, that of L. Venidius Ennychus in the Casa del Salone Nero (Figs. 8.2–3), we return to problems of status. Ennychus, to judge by his characteristic Greek cognomen, is very likely an ex-slave, and based on this Maiuri assumes that he must be the freedman procurator of this handsomely appointed house rather than its proprietor.[16] That is typical of the assumption, repeatedly challenged in this book, that dignitas of architecture and decoration points to a freeborn owner of high social standing, and that freedman status is reflected in poor taste and squalid circumstances. The same assumptions led to the supposition that the landowner Cominius Primus (assumed to be freeborn) must be the proprietor of the fine Casa del Bicentenario rather than the squalid ex-slaves of the circle of Stephanus and Themis. How strange to find Cominius's dossier firmly located in a cenaculum above three shops, however nicely decorated. But the dignitas of Venidius, at least, was underestimated.

In the first of the tablets from his dossier to be published (TH 5), dated to A.D. 60, Venidius testifies that a daughter has been born to him by his wife Livia Acte. Initially this was taken by the editors as a *professio*, the registration of a free birth. But later a supplementary document emerged (TH 89) that led to reassessment. Here Venidius is declaring that under the terms of the lex Aelia Sentia he and his wife Livia Acte have a one-year-old daughter (*filiam anniculam*), whereby they fulfill the requirements to be Roman citizens. Venidius and his wife, in fact, belonged to the legal category of *Junian Latins*, a category recently shown to have been gravely neglected, slaves freed informally without fulfilling the full legal requirements for Roman citizenship, particularly the

Figure 8.2 Casa del Salone Nero, Herculaneum, main reception room. The grandiose black-ground decoration, articulated by golden architectural elements, is comparable to that of room (5) of the Casa dei Cervi (Pl. 1). Note the absence of mythological paintings or other decorative motifs in the centers of the fields, here as elsewhere in Herculaneum.

Figure 8.3 Casa del Salone Nero, Herculaneum, view of peristyle from the "black room." The Venidius Ennychus archive was found in a "rustic quarter" in this area.

minimum age of 30.[17] Such individuals could enjoy the benefits of freedom and could use the *tria nomina*, the standard, triple-name form characteristic of a citizen; but they were not citizens, fictional Latins rather than Romans, and their property reverted to their patron automatically at death. A Junian Latin could convert to full citizenship by declaring formally before a Roman magistrate a marriage for the purpose of begetting children and then demonstrating the survival of a child to the minimum of one year of age, a procedure termed *anniculi probatio*. Venidius emerges as a case in action of such promotion.[18]

Venidius's rise did not stop there. In a further document (TH 83), Venidius testifies before L. Annius Rufus, known from elsewhere to have held the duumvirate of the colony, that he merits the "right to honor" (*ius honoris*) and that he is prepared for Annius to pick—from ten men named by himself from among the number of the decurions or Augustales—a *disceptator* or arbiter to investigate his case. In the next document (TH 84) he declares himself ready to appear before Festinius Proculus as arbiter. The honor to which he claims the right ought not be public office, since freedmen were expressly excluded, but rather a place among the Augustales as priest of Augustus, one of the prime expressions of social dignity for freedmen opened up by the early Empire.[19]

Gradually Venidius begins to emerge as a social personality, and the unlikelihood of his owning an ostentatious house recedes. Indeed, if he was successful in his claim to promotion, his house would have proved well-situated, for the meeting place of the Augustales was almost certainly at the opposite corner of the same block, only a few doors down (H VI.21).[20] Perhaps we should see an allusion to his status in the paintings on the street facade of his house, to the right on entering the main door. The painting advertises a bar: four jugs, with their prices in *asses* below. Above these is the image of a laureled priest, with scepter and patera for sacrifice, and the words AD SANC(tum), "At the sign of the holy man." Conceivably the bar draws its identity from the priestly status of its owner, Venidius.

The above is pure conjecture; but what is now confirmed is that Venidius was successful in his petition for the right to honor. During the excavations in the 1960s of the corner of Insula VI nearest to the forum, a batch of marble plaques emerged elegantly inscribed with lists of names. They fitted precisely into other fragments identified as the album, or official notice board, of the collegium of the Augustales.[21] They belong to the context of what must be the *sedes Augustalium*: a dedication records the feast given to the decurions and Augustales in celebration of the election of the brothers Aulus Lucius Proculus and Junianus to this privileged group.[22]

In the new fragments, the name L. Venidius Ennychus is clearly recorded. Particularly striking is the company he keeps in the list. The same characters who are seen doing business with each other in the tablets emerge as fellow members of a privileged club with all the snob value of membership in a City of London Livery Company. A few names above Venidius are C. Petronius Stephanus and C. Petronius S[. . . .], perhaps the Petronius Stephanus father who appears with the other Stephanus on a list of signatories, apparently unconnected with the Petronia Justa case (TH 50, 102). Then there is M. Nonius Hermeros, who sold Venidius a slave girl, Olympias, guaranteeing that she was healthy and had a good record (TH 62). Further down is C. Messienus Nymphicus, co-signatory with Venidius of a couple of documents (TH 2, 99), and one of the witnesses in the Petronia Justa case (TH 23). And there is another member of the extensive clan of the M. Calatorii to which Calatoria Themis belonged, and with whom Cominius Primus did business, this one called Acratus.

The names on the part of the list on which Venidius appears have a formal feature in common. Those on the preceding part of the album all display the formal signs of freeborn citizens, filiation and tribe: C(aius) Nasennius C(aii) f(ilius) Fal(erna) Priscus. The Augustales were divided into panels, and the first is the most prestigious, the *centuria Claudia ingenuorum*. Those on the list after Venidius display the formal signs of manumis-sion: A(ulus) Lucius A(uli) l(ibertus) Regillus. But those on Venidius's panel have nei-ther the signs of ingenuity nor of manumission: L(ucius) Venidius Ennychus. The editor of the list assumed that they too must be freedmen, but it seems unlikely that on so formal a document the proper status indicators of a whole group should be omitted. Venidius's group then appears to enjoy an intermediate status, between free birth and manumission. Since we know what Venidius's status was, that of Junian Latin promoted through anniculi probatio to full citizenship, it would appear that the others too, Pe-tronius Stephanus among them, enjoyed a similar status. It would also appear that it was in some way better to be a promoted Junian Latin than a freedman; while lacking the pride of a father's name, the ex-Junian also lacked the stigma of a former master's name.

The more we meet these characters linking up with each other, the more a picture emerges, not so much of individuals but of a social context. They form a tight-knit business community. These were the people Venidius had dealings with; they were also the club to which he wanted to belong, from which he had to be able to name ten men, one of whom picked by the duumvir could be relied upon to support his application for membership. He could celebrate his election by giving them all a formal dinner, doubt-less at considerable cost, and then join in the feasting when future members were elected. He had the pride of seeing his name elegantly incised on the roll of honor. And doubt-less, like so many Augustales at Pompeii, he would have planned a handsome tomb on a road outside the city that declared his success. To die in volcanic catastrophe, without burial, without honor, perhaps in the tangled heap of bodies down by the harbor, was a cruel fate.

How then are we to relate these tantalizing glimpses of a community to the stage set of houses on which they played their parts? We have the set, a large part of the cast list, but only the tiniest fragments of the script. Amedeo Maiuri, a towering figure in the excavation of the sites, endlessly energetic, learned, and imaginative, was conscious enough of the society of free, slave, and ex-slave that populated the houses he exposed. Indeed, while excavating, he found time to edit the section of Petronius's novel, the *Satyrica*, known as the Cena Trimalchionis, which as Maiuri saw comes as close as we can get to providing a sample of the sort of social drama imaginable in a successful freed-man's house. If I have attempted in the chapters of this book to draw links between the social world revealed by the literary sources and the material world of the sites, I have followed in Maiuri's footsteps.

The crucial difference may lie not so much in methods, though I have tried to bring to my aid some of the insights derived from half a century's study of other societies, as in the viewpoints shaped by the societies to which we ourselves belong. The peak of Maiuri's active career belongs to the late twenties, the thirties, and the early forties of this century: to the età fascistica. Mussolini exploited, ruthlessly but skillfully, the potential of Italy's imperial past to create a model for the new imperialist Italy.[23] Archaeology benefited massively from the injection of state funds that generated the dramatic revival of imperial Rome, from the Imperial Fora of Rome and Augustus's Ara Pacis, to the stunning sites of Ostia, Pompeii, and Herculaneum, and much else. Maiuri, whether consciously or not, served the ideology, creating memorials to the magnificence of the Italian past.

But he also found himself forced to subvert it. Recalcitrantly, the Italian past in its very moment of glory refused to be "Italian." The population of the sites exposed, from Rome and Ostia to the Bay of Naples, perversely declared itself to be excessively un-Italian: servile and alien. Augustus—the ultimate model of fascist imperialism—by the very laws that seemed to guarantee racial purity, in restricting and morally policing the manumission of slaves, enabled and endorsed the vast influx of newcomers into the citizen body that is so remarkable a feature of at least the century that followed. Characters like Venidius owed their status to Augustus's laws, their pride to a priesthood that bore Augustus's name. Maiuri saw this, and was disturbed; the thesis of economic crisis, commercial invasion, and degeneration of taste is a protest against the betrayal by the Roman past of the racially purist ideals attributed to it. Finding "degeneration," he was driven to posit an earlier stage when society was pure: the golden age of Augustus.

The defeat of fascism, and the longer battle against racism, have transformed the ideologies through which we approach and interrogate the past. In a postimperialist world troubled by the problems of ethnicity and integration of immigrant populations, we may still turn to the Roman world for a success story, not this time of conquest and enslavement but of coping with the unexpected consequences. Venidius Ennychus in his handsome black salon, looking so much as if he *belongs*, becomes a symbol not of the collapse of a respectable Italian town but of the success of a new social system. From our own vantage point, we can appreciate that social integration is achieved through cultural transformation. The subject toward which this book has been moving, however tentatively, is the cultural transformation that carried and enabled a social revolution in Rome and allowed the social structures of republican Rome to adapt and absorb the consequences of conquest.

My main focus has been the ways in which domestic architecture and decoration could be used in constructing the social identity of the inhabitants. I have argued that the dramatic rate of innovation in wall decoration between the mid-second century B.C. and the reign of Nero was accompanied by an equally dramatic extension of the use of such "luxuries," geographically outside Rome and socially outside the ruling elite. I have argued that this innovation and spread was driven by emulation, not simply the internal competition within a closed elites but the aggressive competition from outside that elite, whether by members of the local elite of Italy and the provinces, anxious to penetrate the power and privileges of the center, or by members of socially suppressed groups, particularly ex-slaves, no less ambitious, and under the early empire no less successful, in penetrating the elite.

Social systems that distribute power in a network of human relations are dependent on symbolic systems that mark, articulate, and express that power. Like social systems, symbolic systems are not fixed; one of the rules is that they change through time, and that it is by changing the vocabulary of the symbolic system that new groups establish their own place and power. The face of power and the image of success change constantly; fashion, in all its ephemerality, matters, because by its very innovation it constitutes a new challenge for leadership. If fashions of wall decoration changed fast for two centuries and absorbed considerable resources, to a scale which in ancient economic conditions could only have been financed by imperialism, that is because much was at stake: the leaders of fashion were struggling to stay ahead under the pressure of constant challenge, while those who followed struggled no less to establish a sense of belonging in a society that perpetually threatened to reject them.

Far from being surprised to find Venidius Ennychus, ex-slave, ex-Junian Latin, now proud citizen and Augustalis, at home in his smart house, we might recognize that it is the existence of such men that underpins the evolution of a language of social dignity. How could you tell that somebody in first century A.D. Pompeii or Herculaneum *was somebody*? Many of the signs were traditional, or gave the carefully cultivated appearance of being so: the nomenclature of Roman citizenship, or the atrium construction of the traditional Italic house. Many more were new, the *honor* of the Augustalis, the right of a seat of honor in the theater, the honorific statue erected in a public place with lengthy praise of merits, the tomb on the public highway echoing the funerary forms of eastern potentates and Roman dynasts; and in private the dignity of porticoes and peristyles, rich with marble statues, mythological paintings, and mosaic floors. Such a vocabulary of symbols, by its blend of tradition and innovation, proclaiming continuity with a historical past and simultaneously allowing new moves by new players, constituted the language in which individuals could articulate their claim to belonging and their self-esteem. The language Venidius used was one generated at the center of power; the imperial freedman Callistus, whose power and wealth derived from his loyal service to the emperor, was famous for a mansion that outshone in luxury the palaces of the old nobility.[24]

The luxury of the early Empire, I have been suggesting, which we find so vividly documented in the houses of Pompeii and Herculaneum, is the cultural language through which in their daily and domestic lives people staked their claims to standing as Romans. What it might mean to be "Roman" was anything but fixed and certain. During the two centuries that leave their imprint most distinctly on the sites, the definition of the Roman was at its most fluid. At the end of the second century B.C., Pompeii was still an independent city-state, allied indeed to Rome and contributing to its military imperial effort, but defining itself culturally as non-Roman, with the Italic dialect of Oscan still its language of public life. But while in language, standard measures, and legal status of citizenship second-century Pompeii was not-Roman, in other respects it was clearly drawn into the ambit of Roman military, political, and cultural influence. The spread in Italy during this period of a material culture we call Hellenistic is one of the surest measures of Romanization.[25]

The demand in the early first century B.C. by Italian communities for membership of the Roman citizen body was partly a demand for recognition of the cultural fact that, for many, to be Italian was to be Roman. Acknowledgment of this principle in the outcome of the Social War of the 80s B.C. (which in Pompeii's case meant conquest and conversion to a Roman colony) led to rapid acceleration of the process of cultural assimilation. As the material culture changed, it became a more confident sign of membership of the dominant (Roman) culture. The very success of the local elites of Italian towns in using material culture as an instrument of their own assimilation rendered them in turn pervious to penetration by newcomers. As the gulf between "Roman" and "Italian" became progressively invisible, particularly from the reign of Augustus, so the challenge lay in closing the gap between the "Roman" and the "servile and alien." The picture offered here, rather than one of a native Italian patriciate swamped by the social and economic changes brought by alien intruders, is of a chain reaction of cultural self-definition and redefinition.

Romanness was not given but constructed: built and rebuilt over the years in the tangle of superimposed structures whose sequences are now so hard to disentangle. The houses of Pompeii and Herculaneum everywhere bear evidence of change; changing property boundaries, changing uses of space, changing fashions in house decoration and self-presentation. But while this makes the archaeology messy and hard to read, so long as we wish to separate out the stratigraphy and distinguish different periods as if they were different entities, it is a fair enough reflection of social reality. The inhabitants of Pompeii and Herculaneum of A.D. 79 lived in an environment fashioned by the changes of the past, which they themselves were in the course of changing.

The eruption of Vesuvius has done us a double favor. First, by cutting off the process of change in mid-flow, it has trapped the evidence of its pace. We know from the historical accounts that the period of the late Republic and early Empire was a period in classical antiquity in which transformations of particular consequence took place; Vesuvius, in catching this transformation at a high point, gives us a glimpse of how the change affected the material culture of domestic life. Here the pace of change implicit in the restless innovation in domestic decoration seems to me significant.

The second favor is to preserve a picture across a full social spectrum. A frequent suspicion about Roman literary sources is that, as products of an elite, they may give us an imbalanced picture of the Roman world, preserving only their own high culture and not the popular culture or cultures of the majority. Although at one level there is truth in this, the implied dichotomy is simplistic and perhaps a projection into the past of the cultural conditions of the postindustrial West. What seems to me to emerge from the Vesuvian towns is the inappropriateness of the attempt to separate out two worlds.

Massive social contrasts are apparent, in the gulf between the most magnificent mansions and the humblest tabernae or cenacula. Yet the gulf is constantly bridged, by contiguity and mutual dependence. We have seen, not so much a gulf between "rich families" and "poor families," but the promiscuity of the big household, in which rich and poor, and indeed male and female, young and old, inhabit the same spaces, separated by social rituals rather than physical environment. We have seen the (to Roman eyes) "sordid" world of trade and commerce intertwined with the world of luxury and grandeur. And we have seen the long ripples by which the luxuries of the elite spread through the housing stock, whether in the imitation of the idioms of decoration, or of the vistas of the good life offered by the view through the front door.

To argue for such intertwining is not to make a social idyll of the early Roman empire—this is not a world in which either equality or democracy meant much—but it is to suggest something about the culture of the elite familiar to us from literary sources. The paradox of luxury is that, in trying to set apart an elite in the use and display of material culture and lifestyle, it renders the elite penetrable. The idiom developed by the successful to mark their distinction is appropriated by those who envy their success. Spreading across social ranks and across provinces, it becomes a way of marking the world as Roman.

APPENDIX

======= ❏ =======

LIST OF HOUSES SURVEYED

NOTE: in the course of the survey on which most of my observations are based I visited every room in every house in the Herculaneum and Pompeii Regio I survey areas, and about a third of the houses in the Regio VI area. The purpose of the observations was interpretative rather than scientific: to come to an understanding of the material involved, the nature of the excavation and preservation, and to learn to "read" such houses. The data on which the statistics are based are partly derived from published sources and reflect the unreliability of those publications; my own observations have been important for checking, correcting, and attempting to make sense of what has been published. In particular, figures for ground area are based on published plans, not on measurement, and should be treated as indications of order of magnitude, adequate only for comparative purposes. Precise figures would be desirable, but this would require professional surveying.

SAMPLE I

POMPEII REGIO I, INS. 6–12.
A full photographic catalog of all wall decorations in all the houses in Regio I is now available in Pugliese Carratelli (1990).

INSULA 6: published in Spinazzola (1953) 115–16, 257–81, 437–593, 765–85; Maiuri (1929).

1   Taberna with back room, c. 50m². No decoration.

2/16   C. del Criptoportico, c. 1200m². Atrium, peristyle with 2-sided colonnade, 12 rooms, plus cryptoporticus with bath suite. Stairs up to rooms above front and side. Fine style-II decoration and mosaics in cryptoporticus, points to grander early phase (see below, no. 4).

3   Officina di Vero, c. 50m². Workshop with back room, stairs up. Simple white-ground decoration. Supposedly the office of a surveyor, inferred (implausibly) from a groma found among several other metal tools.

4   C. del Sacello Iliaco, c. 400m². Atrium, back court, plus 12 rooms. Stairs up to rooms above front, side, and back. Triclinium and cubiculum suite in fine style II (sala degli Elefanti) formerly opened on cryptoporticus (see above, no. 2). Extensive redecoration (6 rooms) in style IV partially completed (cf. Strocka 1984a).

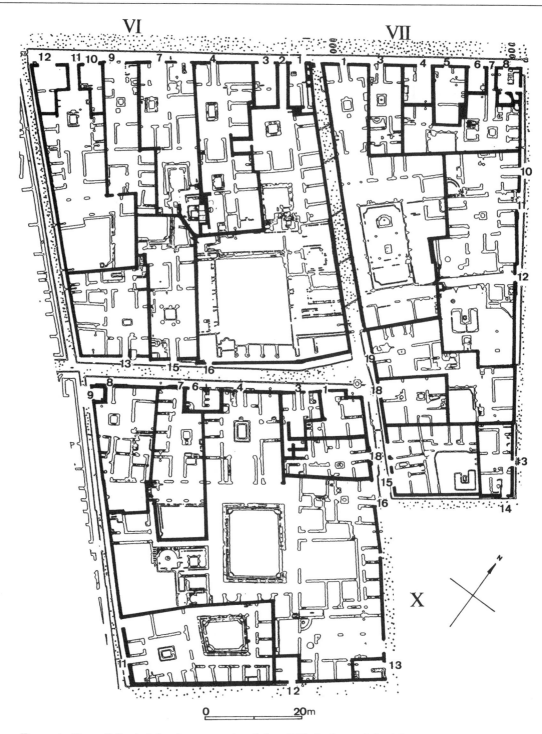

Figure A.1 Pompeii Regio I, Insulae 6, 7, and 10 (after *CTP*). In this and the following plans, boundary walls as defined for the purposes of this survey have been filled in, others left unfilled. There is, however, normally no structural difference between boundary walls and others, and their definition, which changed over time, is sometimes uncertain. Plans traditionally represent the state of houses as exposed, that is, broadly as in A.D. 79.

5/6   Officina/taberna with back room, stairs up from street at no. 6, c. 30m^2. No decoration.

7   Fullonica di Stephanus, c. 325m^2. Atrium, peristyle with 3-sided colonnade, 7 rooms. Stairs to rooms above front and back(?). Decoration in style II in triclinium overlooking peristyle, style IV elsewhere (atrium and 3 rooms). Basins and vats for fulling occupy atrium and peristyle (see Moeller 1976, 41–43). See Fig. 6.12.

8/9   Taberna ("thermopolium") and house, c. 250m^2. Sales area/atrium/peristyle (colonnades on 2 sides). Architecture points to smarter phase earlier, but no surviving decoration. Opening at back into house no. 11 indicates joint ownership and perhaps direct control of taberna. This is relevant to unusual absence of decoration in an atrium house.

10   Taberna with back room and stairs up, c. 40m^2. Style-III decoration in back room from earlier phase as part of no. 11 (confirmed by blocked door).

11   C. dei Quadretti Teatrali, c. 500m^2. Atrium, peristyle with 2-sided colonnades, 9 rooms. Notable style-III decoration in atrium with theatrical scenes, plus 5 other rooms decorated. Rich finds include bronze statuary, silver cups, and gold jewelry and coins. No. 11 likely to have owned whole block nos. 9–12. Partially converted for use as bathroom and restroom for present custodi.

12   Taberna (*officina ferraria*) with back room and stairs to upper rooms, c. 50m^2. Finds of ironware, including 30 keys and 30 sickles, point to ironmonger's business. Style-III decoration in back room (as no. 10). Present use as office for custodi.

13/14   C. di Stallius Eros, c. 275m^2. No. 13 entrance to atrium/tablinum/back garden with 2-sided pseudo-colonnade and garden painting, 10 rooms, stairs up at back. Stairs up from street to upper apartment at no. 14. House in ruinous condition when excavated, decoration rustic or faded, assumed uninhabited.

15   C. dei Ceii, c. 300m^2. Fauces/tetrastyle atrium/tablinum/peristyle with 2-sided pseudocolonnade and imposing garden paintings, 6 rooms, stairs up front and back of atrium. Handsome style-III decoration throughout except porter's room in front, basic white-ground. Republished in Michel (1990). See Fig. 6.2.

INSULA 7: published by Maiuri (1927) 7–83, (1929) 354–430; decoration in Maiuri (1938).

1   C. di Paquius Proculus, c. 790m^2. Atrium, peristyle with 4-sided colonnade, 13 rooms, plus cellars below; stairs to rooms above front and back of atrium. Notable mosaics, esp. in atrium, tablinum, and triclinium with emblemata. Decoration in several styles in atrium, tablinum, peristyle, plus 4 reception rooms. See forthcoming publication by German project.

2/3   C. di Fabius Amandio, c. 125m^2. Atrium, lightwell/garden, 5 rooms, slip-room opening on street at no. 2 (falsely *officina sutoria* [cobbler's shop] in lists, but finds only of weaver's carding combs). Stairs up at front over slip-room (perhaps replacing earlier stairs from street); stairs up at back. Elegant style-IV decoration except in rooms with stairs; garden painting in garden area, mosaic panel in end room. See Pl. 7.

4   Taberna/officina, c. 50m^2. Two rooms and stairs up. No decoration. Finds of pottery have suggested *officina vasaria* (potter's shop).

5 Officina, c. 80m². Central space plus 2 rooms, stairs up at back. Numerous finds of bronze, crystal, bone, marble. Style-III decoration in both rooms. Possibly linked to no. 7. See Figs. 7.21–23.

6 Taberna, single room, stairs up, c. 20m². No decoration. Finds include pen box, mirror, comb; i.e., inhabited.

7 C. del Sacerdos Amandus, c. 230m². Atrium, peristyle with 2-sided colonnade, 9 rooms, stairs up in atrium and at back. Style-III decoration in 6 rooms, incl. mythologicals in 2, mosaics in 2. Finds incl. statue of Isis. See Pl. 3.

8/9 Bar ("thermopolium") with back room, c. 35m². No decoration or finds recorded.

10–12 C. dell'Efebo, c. 660m². Atrium, peristyle with single colonnade and notable outdoor triclinium, 17 rooms. No. 10 divided off as separate unit by wooden doors. Stairs up in nos. 10, 11. Connects to no. 19 at bottom. Extensive style-IV decoration, incl. mythologicals in 3 rooms, opus sectile in main triclinium. Numerous finds incl. marble statuary and bronze Ephebe. See Pl. 4, Figs. 2.21, 4.5.

13/14 *Caupona* (tavern), c. 100m². Five rooms and stairs up, supposed brothel above. No decoration. Unpublished.

15–17 Officina (degli scrittori murali), c. 240m². Garden (no colonnade) with outdoor triclinium, 12 rooms, stairs up. No decoration. Unpublished.

18 Taberna (di Nireaemius), c. 125m². Atrium, 6 rooms, stairs up to (surviving) upper room. Style-III decoration in 3 rooms, plus upstairs. Finds of minor domestic objects. See Fig. 2.17.

19 House, c. 330m². Atrium, peristyle with 2-sided colonnade, 12 rooms, stairs up front and back of atrium, back of peristyle. Style-III decoration in most areas, mythologicals in 4 rooms. Finds incl. silverware. Linked to no. 11 by steps, but apparently separate unit.

INSULA 8: recently studied by Castiglione Morelli del Franco (1989).

1–3 C. di Stephanus, c. 550m². No. 1 bar with back room, linked to atrium of no. 2, as is taberna at no. 3. Atrium, peristyle with 4-sided colonnade, 5 rooms, 2 stairs up in atrium. Style-IV decoration in 2 rooms. Beneath peristyle, accessible from side door no. 19, are extensive cellars with complex plant for cloth dyeing: cf. Moeller (1976) 35–36.

4–6 C. della Statuetta Indiana, c. 390m². Tabernae at nos. 4, 6 linked to no. 5. Atrium, peristyle with 3-sided colonnade, 11 rooms. Various decoration in 3 rooms.

7 Taberna (supposedly *pistrinum* [mill]), single room, c. 20m². No decoration.

8/9 Caupona, c. 290m². Bar with back room at no. 8, linked to house at no. 9 with atrium, peristyle with single-sided colonnade and outdoor triclinium, 4 rooms. Style-III decoration throughout, incl. mythologicals and emblemata in 2 rooms.

10 Hospitium(?), c. 200m². Built around peristyle with 2-sided colonnade, 5 rooms plus kitchen beneath garden of no. 9. Style-IV decoration in 1 room. Upper rooms, possibly accessible from elsewhere (no. 5?). Note that interconnections—blocked doors, etc.—suggest that nos. 4–10 may have formed a single block of property. Identified by Maiuri (1953/54) as *officina vasaria* on basis of cartoon of potter at work.

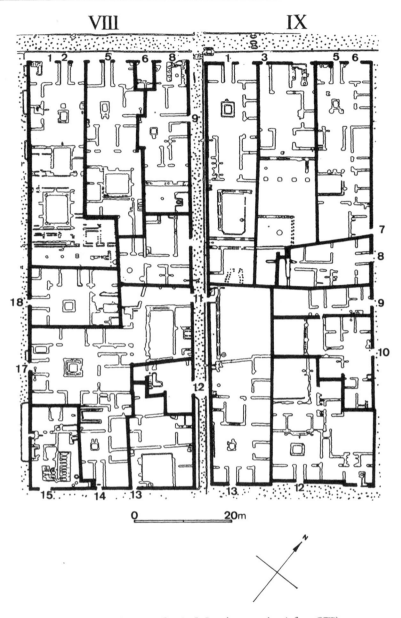

Figure A.2 Pompeii Regio I, Insulae 8 and 9 (after *CTP*).

12   Stable-yard, c. 90m². Note break in pavement permitting entry of carts. Yard plus back room and stairs up. Skeleton of horse or donkey and agricultural implements. No decoration.

13   Officina (di Granius Romanus), c. 215m². Courtyard with single colonnade, 8 rooms. No decoration.

14   C. di Epidius Primus, c. 190m². Atrium and back garden (no colonnade), stairs up by door. Traces of style-II and -IV decoration in 3 rooms.

15/16   Caupona and officina (di Fufidius Successus), c. 175m². No. 15 bar with back room, leads to large workshop with kiln and plant for production of pigments(?). No. 16 leads to 3/4 indeterminate rooms/spaces, with stairs up. No decoration. Deserves further study.

17/11   C. dei Quattro Stili, c. 500m². Atrium (entrance at no. 17), peristyle with 2-sided colonnade, 14 rooms, stabling at back (no. 11). Stairs up at front of atrium(?) and in peristyle. Extensive decoration in 11 rooms and areas in each of 4 styles, incl. 2 rooms with mythologicals.

18   C. dell'Atrio Dorico, c. 225m². Atrium, 8 rooms, stairs up at back. Doric stucco work in atrium, style I decoration in 1 room.

INSULA 9: partially published but no excavation reports.

1/2   C. del Bell'Impluvio, c. 475m². No. 2 taberna, links to no. 1 atrium, peristyle with 3-sided colonnade, 8 rooms, stairs up at back of atrium. Five rooms decorated in styles II and III, 1 with mosaics. Below back of peristyle is workshop complex, accessible from side door no. 15.

3/4   C. di Successus, c. 490m². No. 4 bar with back room, links to no. 3. Nonimpluviate atrium, uncertain peristyle/horticultural area with single colonnade, 6/7 rooms, stairs up in atrium. Decoration in style IV in 4 rooms, incl. one with painting of boy and bird (puer Successus).

5–7   C. del Frutteto, c. 425m². No. 6 taberna with stairs up and back room, linked to no. 5 atrium, peristyle with 2-sided colonnade, 9 rooms, stairs up at back of atrium. Back entrance at no. 7. Fine style-III decoration and mosaic floors in 6 rooms, incl. 2 with mythologicals, 3 with emblemata, attractive "garden" paintings illustrated in Jashemski (1979) 74–78. Decoration published in Maiuri (1952b).

8   Officina textoria(?), c. 170m². Nonimpluviate atrium, 7 rooms. Traces of style-I and -II decoration in 2 rooms.

9   House/workshop, c. 120m². Circulation space, stairs up, 4 rooms and backyard. Unclear link to no. 10. Collection of pigments found here (or in no. 10, 11, or 12?). No decoration. Note that nos. 9–12 are listed elsewhere as a single unit and *may* have been such.

10   House/workshop, c. 220m². Circulation space, stairs up, backyard with single colonnade, 8 rooms. No decoration.

11/12   Caupona (di Amarantus) and house, c. 420m². No. 11 bar with 2 back rooms and yard, links to no. 12 atrium, peristyle with 2-sided colonnade, 8 rooms. Style-IV decoration in 2 rooms. Supposedly a brothel.

13/14   C. di Cerere, c. 500m². Atrium, peristyle with single colonnade, 10 rooms. Extensively decorated in style II, plus 2 rooms in style III; mosaics in 6 rooms, emblemata in 2. Decoration published in de Vos (1976).

INSULA 10: published by Maiuri (1933) and Elia (1934) 264–344. Elia's excavation report is perhaps the most careful from Pompeii published to date. The insula is subject of a thorough reassessment by a British team; see Ling (1983) for an interim report. See Fig. A.1.

1   Taberna (workshop/dwelling), c. 90m². Circulation area with stairs up, backyard with kitchen, 3 rooms. Style-III/IV decoration in 3 areas.

2/3   Caupona (di Coponia), c. 80m². No. 2 bar with back room, linked to dwelling at no. 3, circulation area with stairs up, 3 rooms. Some crude ("style IV") decoration in one room.

4   C. del Menandro, c. 1700m². No. 4 entrance to main reception area, atrium, peristyle with 4-sided colonnade, stairs up at front of atrium, 12 rooms, 4 storage spaces, etc., bath site with own atriolum and 3 bathrooms; garden and kitchen area plus 2 rooms and cellars behind baths. Reception areas decorated throughout in styles II, III, and IV. No. 16 entrance to secondary service area with separate atrium and backyard, 9 rooms on ground, more above; nos. 15 and 17 (shop entrance) give access to same area; simple style-III decoration in atrium area only, but traces of decoration also in upper rooms. No. 14 access to stable-yard with 4 rooms/areas. Finds numerous, including exceptional silver service. See Figs. 2.4, 3.1–2, 3.9–10, 3.21, 6.13.

5/6   Officina, c. 40m². No. 6 workshop with treading stalls for fullery (Moeller 1976, 43), plus back room. No. 5 external stairs lead to rooms above; supposedly brothel, on dubious basis of casual graffiti. No decoration.

7   C. del Fabbro, c. 310m². Atrium, peristyle with single colonnade and wooden outdoor triclinium, stairs up at back, 6 rooms. Style-III decoration with mythologicals in reception rooms overlooking peristyle; simple style IV in other rooms. Numerous finds, including hoard of silver coins, pieces of marble, and sets of tools (hence identification as cabinet maker; but the variety and state of the tools point rather to a collector of scrap). See Figs 2.15–16, 2.17, 3.24, 7.15–16.

8   C. di Minucius, c. 270m². Atrium, secondary court with stairs up, back garden, 7 rooms. Identification as weaving establishment on basis of loom weights and graffiti; cf. Moeller (1976) 39, doubted by Jongman (1988) 163. Simple style-III and -IV decoration in 3 rooms. Finds include large range of minor domestic objects.

9   Taberna, single room, c. 10m². No finds or decoration.

10/11   C. degli Amanti, c. 470m². No. 10 workshop linked to dwelling. No. 11 entrance to atrium, peristyle with 4-sided colonnade on 2 levels, stairs up at front of atrium and back of peristyle, 13 rooms plus storage spaces. Elegant style-IV decoration in atrium and 8 rooms, incl. 1 with mythologicals; style-II remains in one room. Scarcity of finds suggests robbing, probably in antiquity, consistent with tunneling holes. See Figs. 2.13, 3.7–8, 4.17.

12   Officina, single room with stairs up, c. 25m². Wrongly identified as *latrina publica* (the latrine is next door) by Eschebach and *Pompei. L'informatica*. No decoration or finds.

13   *Popina* (bar, labeled as "thermopolium"), single room with stairs up, c. 25m². Finds incl. range of pots and pans. No decoration.

18   C. di Aufidius Primus, c. 120m². Atrium, stairs up, backyard, 5 rooms. Simple but elegant style-III decoration in atrium wing and upstairs rooms. No finds reported. Currently used as gardening store.

INSULA 11: unpublished. Mapping in Eschebach very unreliable; correct in *CTP*. Cf. Hoffman (1984) 111–14 on house types in this block.

1/2   Caupona, c. 190m². No. 1 bar leads to circulation space, 4 rooms. Style-IV decoration in central area and 2 rooms. Clearly linked at back to no. 2, wide shop-entrance and indistinct arrangement of 2/3 rooms behind, 1 with slight traces of decoration. (The confusion resulting from lack of publication is clear in Eschebach's entry, followed by *Pompei. L'informatica*: no. 2 is wrongly recorded as linked to no. 3, though Eschebach rightly distinguishes no. 1 from nos. 10–12, the thermopolium of Euxinus.)

3   Taberna, c. 65m². Main room with stairs up, 2 back rooms. Slight traces of decoration in back room and upper room.

4   Taberna, single room, c. 10m². No decoration.

5/8   C. di Lollius Synhodus, c. 325m². Large atrium with stairs up, backyard and indistinct arrangement of 5 rooms, presumably for commercial plant; back entrance at no. 8. Traces of style-IV(?) decoration in 1 room.

6/7   C. della Venere in Bikini, c. 170m². No. 7 shop and back room, linked to no. 6 atrium, small back garden, 5 rooms, stairs up. Elegant style-IV decoration in fauces, all rooms (not shop and back room), and garden, incl. 3 rooms with mythologicals. Publication by Australian team forthcoming.

9/15   C. del Primo Piano, c. 460m². Main entrance at no. 15, nonimpluviate atrium, stairs up, peristyle with 2-sided colonnade, 13 rooms plus 2 latrines. Back entrance at no. 9, adjacent stairs up to 3 surviving upper rooms. Decoration in various styles in 5 rooms, incl. 1 with mythologicals. Prominent lararium in garden. Hospitium?

10/11   Caupona of Euxinus, c. 400m². No. 10 entrance to large horticultural plot, stairs up at back, 1 small room with rudimentary decoration. Linked to no. 11 bar and 3 back rooms, 1 decorated (style-IV). Linked to no. 12, here treated as separate unit (note distinct horticultural plot), but doubtless common ownership. Publication by Jashemski (1967), (1979) 172–76.

12   C. di Euxinus, c. 340m². Nonimpluviate atrium, 5 rooms, large horticultural plot. Style-II/III decoration and mosaic floor in 1 room. Decoration published in de Vos (1975) 63–78.

13   Unnamed house, c. 170m². Nonimpluviate atrium with stairs up, garden with shrine on sightline of door, 4 rooms. One room decorated (style-IV?).

14   Unnamed house, c. 400m². Nonimpluviate atrium, pseudoperistyle with 2-sided colonnade with stairs up, 10 rooms, horticultural plot at rear with kitchen. Style-II decora-

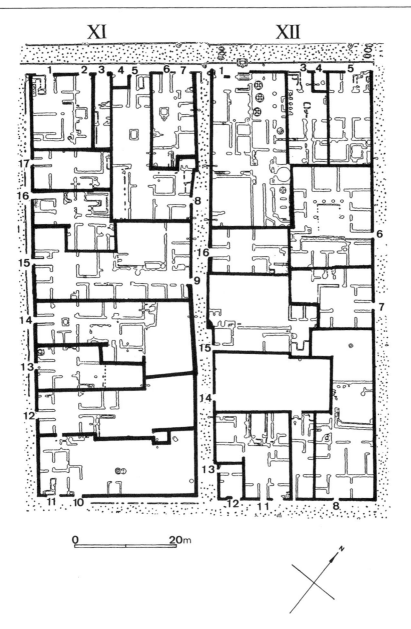

Figure A.3 Pompeii Regio I, Insulae 11 and 12 (after *CTP*).

tion in main room on peristyle, style-II "schematic" in 3 further rooms. Decoration published in de Vos (1975) 48–63.

16   C. di Saturninus, c. 150m². Caupona with bar in central room (bizarrely identified as a *casa* or *domus*, despite local conventions), open triclinium in backyard, 4 rooms, stairs up by entrance and at back. Central area and outdoor triclinium decorated in style IV. Large heap of amphorae piled on triclinium. Illustrated in Jashemski (1979) 73–74. Recently studied by Miele (1989).

17   Unnamed house, c. 140m². Nonimpluviate atrium with stairs up, 4 rooms, and kitchen area. Triclinium opposite entrance decorated in style-IV with architectural details framing view from door.

INSULA 12: unpublished. A neglected block with houses of considerable interest and charm. See Fig. A.3.

1/2   C. del Forno, c. 500m². No. 1 wider entrance, perhaps to retail outlet. No. 2 leads through to extensive bakery structures in previously separate house (approx. 8 rooms/areas) and to private quarters overlooking single-colonnaded peristyle at rear. Rooms and balcony above front, position of stairs unclear. Style-IV decoration in peristyle, triclinium, and cubiculum of private quarters. Discussed in Jashemski (1979) 195; Mayeske (1972) 86–88. See Figs. 2.19–20, 4.4.

3   Caupona (di Sotericus), c. 160m². Shop with counter, style-IV decoration, atrium with storage bins, stairs up, backyard with 2-sided pseudo-peristyle, 3 rooms. House decorated throughout in style III, lararium painting in kitchen. Both reception rooms include style-III mythologicals. See Pl. 6, Fig. 4.14.

4   Officina, c. 15m². Stone mortar in center. Previous link to no. 3 blocked off. No decoration. Possibly for felt making: see Moeller (1976) 51; doubted by Jongman (1988) 165.

5   Caupona (all'Insegna d'Africa), c. 175m². Shop area with counter, nonimpluviate atrium, 3 rooms, backyard with well-constructed masonry stairs up and large lined basin surrounded by low wall. Faded style-III/IV decoration in 3 rooms.

6   Unidentified, c. 175m². Peristyle with 4-sided colonnade surrounded by 11 rooms. No decoration, present state ruinous.

7   Unnamed house, c. 180m². Atrium (with impluvium, though omitted from *CTP* plan), backyard, 5 rooms plus kitchen area. Style-IV decoration with landscapes in one room, otherwise ruinous. Incorrectly mapped by Eschebach and falsely linked to no. 8 (leading to confusion in *Pompei. L'informatica*).

8   Officina del garum degli Umbricii, c. 400m². Peristyle with 2-sided colonnade, 9 rooms, horticultural plot at back. Bins with remains of fish sauce in peristyle, stacks of amphorae in the back plot indicate garum production. Lararium decoration in kitchen, style-III decoration with vignettes in one cubiculum. Eschebach wrongly links this house both to no. 7 and to garden plot at no. 14. Published in Curtis (1979); cf. Jashemski (1979) 195–96.

9/14   House and horticultural plot, c. 385m². Circulation space (with stairs up?), 4 rooms, backyard leading by steps into large horticultural plot with rear entrance at no. 14

(wrongly assigned by Eschebach to no. 8, and wrongly treated as separate by *Pompei. L'informatica*). Faded but elegant white-ground style-III decoration in triclinium (now workmen's shed). Decoration above hearth in kitchen.

10/11 Unnamed house, c. 250m². No. 10 shop/workshop linked to dwelling. No. 11 elegant dwelling, atrium (apparently without impluvium), peristyle with 2-sided colonnade, 8 rooms, stairs up in peristyle. Extensive decoration in styles II and IV (8 areas), incl. Style-IV with mythological painted over earlier style II in triclinium, lararium painting in kitchen, and beast hunt on end wall of garden. This charming house is ignored by tourists and scholars alike, reflecting the extraordinary neglect of the unpublished excavations of this area.

12/13 Shop and back room, c. 40m². No decoration.

15 Horticultural plot with rooms, c. 310m². Surely a vineyard, with attached cellarage, plus outdoor triclinium, food preparation facilities, and 4 rooms. Possibly not for habitation but for temporary usage at time of vintage, etc., as often elsewhere. Lararium above triclinium in direct view from entrance with unusual and striking decoration.

16 Unnamed house, c. 160m². Nonimpluviate(?) atrium, 5 rooms, backyard with garden painting of a fountain on axial view of entrance and outdoor couch in front, illustrated in Jashemski (1979) 60. Atrium decorated in red with decorated lararium niche. Another pretty house that does not deserve its neglect.

SAMPLE 2

HERCULANEUM, INS. III, IV, V, VI

Virtually the only published source is Maiuri (1958), supplemented by Cerulli Irelli (1974). The Bourbon "excavation" records are available in Pannuti (1983). No material corresponding to Eschebach, *Pitture e pavimenti*, *CTP*, or *Pompei. L'informatica* is available. Maiuri was thorough on structures (though see recent study by Ganschow 1989) and decoration, but left finds aside for a subsequent volume, never published. Assignations to styles III and IV are unusually difficult in Herculaneum (see Moorman 1987), and when in doubt I have recorded as III/IV. On the other hand, the site, thanks to its size, is better conserved than Pompeii.

INSULA III

1/2/ Casa dell'Albergo, c. 2450m². No. 1 back entrance. No. 2 shop with back room, 18/19 linked(?). No. 18 a previously separate unit of approx. 6 rooms, linked. Main entrance at no. 19, atrium, 2 full 4-sided peristyles, bath suite, numerous rooms (approx. 30), but neither extent nor number clear because portion over seawall ruinous. Stairs down to lower levels of terracing over seawall. This enormous and evidently very prestigious house was exposed in nineteenth-century excavations and is unreported and ruinous. The virtually complete loss of decoration except some mosaics in the main peristyle and style-II decoration and mosaics in the bath suite creates an obvious statistical anomaly.

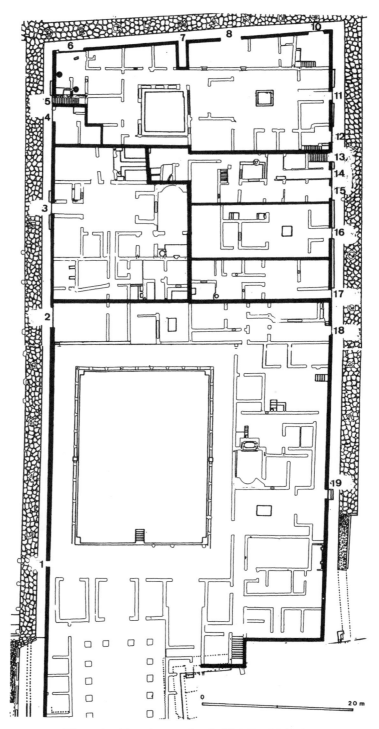

Figure A.4 Herculaneum Insula III (after Maiuri).

3   C. dello Scheletro, c. 410m². Atrium (apparently no impluvium, but this too is early excavation) with fauces/tablinum axial symmetry, leading to 3 main areas each with lightwells, 2 with nymphaea; approx. 18 rooms, 2 narrow spaces for stairs up(?). Extensive decoration (approx. 9 rooms) in style III, several mosaic/opus sectile floors (7 rooms), esp. in large triclinium with apsidal alcove overlooking nymphaeum. See Ganschow (1989) 147–80 for structural history. See Figs. 2.6–7.

4   Workshop with back room, c. 35m². No decoration. Probably belongs to no. 11, but no link.

7   Public latrine, c. 5m².

10   Bottega del Torchio in legno, c. 25m². Single-room shop/workshop with wooden press, undecorated. Stairs up to surviving upper room, decorated in basic white-ground style-IV, with drainage down to no. 9.

11, 8/9,   C. del Tramezzo di legno, c. 520m². No. 11 Classic axial atrium with wooden screen in
6, 5   front of tablinum, peristyle with 2-sided colonnade, 10 rooms associated with atrium/peristyle, mostly decorated in style III. Linked to shops/workshops on all sides: no. 6 shop and 3 back rooms; no. 8/9 3 rooms. Stair from street at no. 5 leads to rooms above back. Very probable that no. 11 controls not only these but shops at no. 4 and no. 12. See Fig. 4.12.

12   Shop, single room, c. 20m². Stairs up. No decoration.

13–15   C. a Graticcio, c. 180m². No. 13 stairs from street to upper flat, kitchen/passage, 4 rooms, lit from balcony. One decorated room has wooden shrine. No. 14 long passage to garden courtyard, approx. 5 rooms, stairs up to 3-room(?) flat, 2 rooms elegantly decorated in style-IV, with beds and wooden shrine incl. collection of statuettes. No. 15 shop and back room, leads to courtyard. No decoration. Window from flat no. 13 opens on atrium of neighboring house no. 16, may imply linked ownership or legal "servitude." See Figs. 5.2, 5.14–15.

16   C. dell'Erma di bronzo, c. 150m². Atrium, stairs up front and back, at back lightwell with garden painting, 4 rooms, and kitchen area. Style-III decoration in atrium and 2 rooms. Bronze bust by tablinum (not original position).

17   C. dell'Ara laterizia, c. 110m². Nonimpluviate atrium, backyard, 6 rooms. Ruinous, but traces of decoration in 1 room.

Insula IV

1/2   C. dell'Atrio a Mosaico, c. 1150m². No. 1 back entrance, no. 2 main door to the atrium, with unusual basilica (*oecus Aegyptius*) in place of tablinum, peristyle with 4-sided colonnades, stairs up at front of atrium and at side and back of peristyle, 14 rooms. Handsome style-IV decoration throughout (except service rooms by front door and at back of peristyle), incl. mythologicals in central exedra of peristyle, mosaics and opus sectile throughout atrium area and in most peristyle rooms. Views over bay. Decoration published in Cerulli Irelli (1971). See Pl. 8, Figs. 2.1–2, 3.23.

3/4   C. dell'Alcova, c. 460m². No. 3 stairs from street to rooms above front. No. 4 entrance to central court (colonnade on 1 side), leading to back with garden court and pseudoperistyle (2-sided colonnade), also stairs down to central court in previously

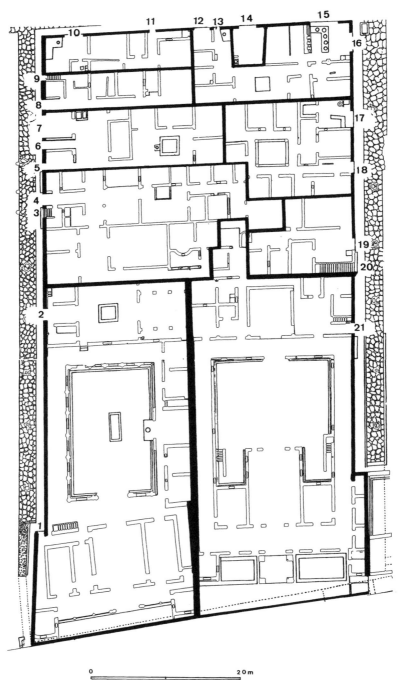

0   20 m

Figure A.5 Herculaneum Insula IV (after Maiuri).

separate house and corridor to lightwell with single-sided colonnade. Architecturally unusual suite here with apsed and vaulted rooms gives house name. Densely packed with rooms (18), style-III/IV decoration in 7, incl. mythologicals in 1, mosaic/opus sectile floors in 2 areas.

5–7 Fullonica, c. 230m². Nos. 5 and 7 shops flanking and linked to no. 6. Circulation space leads to atrium at back, fuller's basin installed in impluvium. Traces of old style-I decoration in several rooms point to smarter early phase before fullery.

8/9 C. del Papirio dipinto, c. 110m². No. 9 stairs up from street. No. 8 long passageway leads to small lightwell and 6 rooms. Style-III/IV decoration in 1 room and courtyard (painting of papyrus).

10/11 Shop and dwelling, c. 110m². No. 10 shop with cereals found in *dolia* (jars), back room, linked to no. 11 dwelling with lararium visible from door, 3 rooms incl. triclinium(?) with quite elaborate style-III/IV decoration.

12/13, 15/16 Taberna and dwelling, c. 215m². No. 15/16 shop with marble-veneered counter, grain and vegetables in containers; food and drinks served to clients in back rooms (decoration predating division for kitchen); linked to no. 13. No. 12 shop. No. 13 private entrance via corridor (stairs up) to atrium at back, 6 rooms; traces of decoration, incl. 1 with mythologicals.

17/18 Taberna and dwelling, c. 240m². No. 17 shop with counter (Priapic decoration, see, Fig. 7.7), back room, linked to no. 18. Finds of pots, pans, and walnuts. No. 18 main entrance down corridor to columned courtyard (*tetrastyle atrium*) surrounded by 10 rooms. Stairs up by door and at back. Possible hospitium. No decoration.

19/20 C. della Stofa, c. 145m². No. 20 stairs from street. No. 19 shop/workshop area, stairs up, passage to small court, 5 rooms. Largest room has black-ground decoration and polychrome marble floor. Traces of decoration in upper rooms.

21 C. dei Cervi, c. 1190m². Side entrance at no. 21 to nonimpluviate atrium with stairs up; leads directly into suite of reception rooms fronting on peristyle with 3-sided colonnade, suite of rooms on fourth side with stairs to upper suites. Kitchen and service area in back extension. Extensive style-IV decoration in reception areas, incl. panel paintings (many removed to Naples) around peristyle, mosaics in 5 rooms. Marble statuary in garden. Views over bay. Studied by Tran Tam Tinh (1988), structural history in Ganschow (1989) 184–217. See Pl. 1, Figs. 2.3, 3.18, 6.6–7.

INSULA V

1/2 C. Sannitica, c. 180m². No. 2 stairs from street. No. 1 handsome atrium with upper colonnade, 5 reception and 4 service rooms, stairs up. Style-I decoration in fauces, elegant style-IV in atrium and all reception rooms, incl. one mythological. House previously led to peristyle now embedded in no. 35; Ganschow (1989) 221–35. Handsome redecoration belongs to present phase without peristyle. See Fig. 2.10.

3/4 C. del Telaio, c. 230m². No. 3 leads to private quarters: peristyle court with 4-sided colonnade, 7 rooms. No. 4 leads to large workshop and 4 further rooms. Activity as weaver's inferred from loom frame and weights in peristyle, though not in workshop area. Rustic condition, no decoration except traces in one room. See Ganschow (1989) 239–57 for structural history.

5   C. del Mobilio carbonnizato, c. 215m². Atrium and garden court with shrine on axis, stairs up by door, 7 reception rooms decorated in III/IV style, incl. mythological and mosaic floor in tablinum, opus sectile in 1 other; 3 service rooms undecorated, incl. kitchen with stairs up. Couch in back reception room gives views through windows of shrine and tablinum decoration. See Ganschow (1989) 261–82 for structures; Moorman (1987) for decoration. See Fig. 3.13.

6/7   C. del Mosaico di Nettuno e Anfitrite, c. 220m². No. 6 wineshop with well-preserved counter and amphora rack, back room separated by wooded partition giving upper storage space. Upper flat with balcony, kitchen, and 2 living rooms, both with style-III/IV decoration, incl. inserted mythological panel, accessible from stairs in back room reached from shop or atrium of main house. No. 7 atrium and back court with outdoor triclinium and notable mosaic on door axis, 5 reception rooms, all decorated in style III/IV, incl. mythological and opus sectile floor in tablinum, mosaic floor in 1 other; 3 service rooms, undecorated. See Figs 4.15, 5.13, 7.3.

8   C. del Bel Cortile, c. 190m². Circulation space leads to unusual courtyard with wide flight of masonry stairs up. Off circulation space, kitchen and 3 small rooms with simple style-IV decoration; off cortile, 2 reception rooms (one exceptionally large) with mosaics and style II/IV decoration; upstairs 4 rooms and balcony, all elegantly decorated (style III/IV). See Fig. 7.11.

9–12   C. anonima, main house flanked by 2 shops, c. 175m². Nos. 9–10 shop with back room, counter with containers, further storage containers at back, no decoration, linked to fauces of no. 11. No. 12 single-room shop with wooden shelving, style-IV decoration on one wall, linked to atrium. No. 11 symmetrically disposed atrium, stairs up at front, tablinum with handsome style-IV decoration with mythologicals, opus sectile floor; 2 further reception rooms, decorated (as atrium) in style-IV, 1 only fragmentary; 2 service rooms. See Figs. 6.3–4, 7.2.

13/14   Shop, c. 25m². No. 13 shop, no decoration, linked to no. 14, private entrance and stairs up. Extensive and elegant apartment above extending over ground-floor rooms of no. 15, with lararium painting at top of stairs (Fig. 5.11); at least 5 rooms nicely decorated in style-IV. Surely same unit of ownership as no. 15, but no linking door.

15/16   C. del Bicentenario, c. 600m². No. 16 shop with stairs up and back room, linking to atrium. Flat above with 2/3 rooms, elegantly decorated incl. mythologicals. Taken by Maiuri as same apartment as above 13/14, but could be divided. No. 15 large symmetrical atrium with alae and tablinum, peristyle with 2-sided colonnade; 7 rooms, but only simple decoration in 3, in triclinium fragmentary; in contrast to good style-IV decoration in atrium, esp. in tablinum with mythologicals and opus sectile floor. Stairs up by tablinum to 3 or more rooms, scarcely decorated, further stairs to second floor. Notable and surprising contrast between poor decoration of no. 15 away from imposing atrium and elegance of upper rooms to associated shops. See Figs. 5.9–11, 6.5.

17/18   Shop, c. 40m². No. 17 shop with back room, both with style-IV decoration. No. 18 stairs from street up to flat with 3 rooms and balcony. Nice style-IV decoration throughout, incl. mythological above; polychrome marble chips in floors; wooden shrine and bed, now in shop back-room, come from upper flat. See Figs. 5.12, 7.8.

19/20   Shops with dwellings, c. 80m². Nos. 19 and 20 shops with back rooms, interconnecting

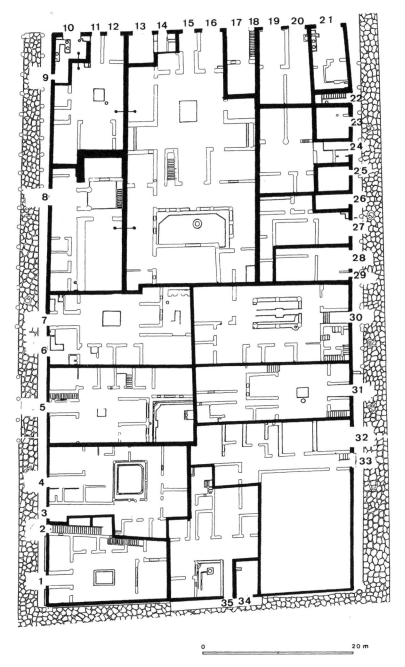

Figure A.6 Herculaneum Insula V (after Maiuri).

at back. Badly damaged, but fragments of style-IV decoration in back room of no. 20. Apartment above accessible by stair from street at no. 22. Parts of 4 rooms survive, incl. 1 with vaulted ceiling, style-IV decoration with panel paintings. Nos. 19/20, 21, and 22 evidently single unit of ownership (apartment above over all 3 below, and window between 20 and 21), but may have operated as 3 units of habitation/work. See Fig. 8.1.

21   Shop with back rooms, c. 55m². Shop with counter, amphorae, containers; back area divided into 2 rooms with latrine. Badly damaged. Belongs with nos. 19/20; see above.

23   Shop, c. 20m². Single room, stair up(?). No decoration. May have belonged to no. 24, but no link.

24   Unnamed house, c. 110m². Fauces with 2 side-rooms, nonimpluviate atrium with 4 rooms. No decoration survives. Position of stairs to upper floor unclear, unless from no. 22. Probably unit with nos. 23, 25.

25   Shop, single room, c. 20m². No decoration.

26   Shop, single room, c. 10m². Bare.

27   Taberna with dwelling, c. 90m². Circulation space and 4 rooms behind, bare.

28/29 Taberna with back room, c. 50m². No. 28 shop, bare. No. 29 stairs up from street. These probably led to united apartment above nos. 26–28, implying single ownership of this block of units.

30   C. dell'Atrio Corinzio, c. 230m². Elegant dwelling built round peristyle with 4-sided colonnade ("Corinthian atrium," but it is dubious whether this is what Vitruvius 6.3.1, mentioning *compluvia*, means by this term), 6 reception rooms, all decorated in style-IV, mosaic floors in 4; 3 service rooms, undecorated, stairs up in kitchen. This handsome and architecturally interesting house has been neglected and badly maintained in recent years. See Fig. 4.13.

31   C. del Sacello di legno, c. 180m². Atrium, stairs up front and back, 6 rooms. Badly damaged and faded, but traces of styles I and III. Finds include wooden shrine, well preserved.

32   Shop, single room, c. 20m². Bare. Room above accessible from no. 33, to which this doubtless belongs.

33   House with horticultural plot, c. 355m². Circulation space with indistinct disposition of 6 rooms. Ruinous, but style-II(?) decoration with Nilotic landscapes in 1 room.

34   Shop, single room, c. 15m². Bare. Surely belongs to no. 33 with which it shares raised pavement.

35   C. del Gran Portale, c. 175m². Circulation space and garden court, 6 reception and 2 service rooms, stairs up in kitchen at back. Fauces axial on triclinium and view of central mythological panel. Elegant style-IV decoration in 5 reception rooms, opus sectile in cubiculum overlooking garden court. Plot previously part of V.1/2; see Ganshow (1989) 285–303. See Fig. 6.1.

INSULA VI: Maiuri's excavations of this block were incomplete at the forum end; for subsequent excavation of nos. 16–18 see Cerulli Irelli (1974).

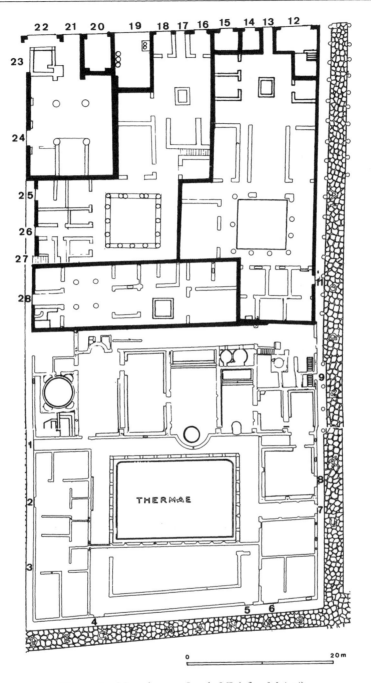

Figure A.7 Herculaneum Insula VI (after Maiuri).

1–10   Public baths, excluded from survey.

12   Shop with back room, stairs up, c. 30m². No decoration.

13/11   C. del Salone Nero, c. 595m². No. 13 main entrance to atrium/tablinum/peristyle with 4-sided colonnade; 10 reception rooms, 3 service rooms at back, with back door at no. 11. Decoration in atrium area perished or poor. Elegant style-IV in tablinum, passage, peristyle, and 4 surrounding rooms. Wooden shrine in large *salone nero*, shrine in small lightwell at end of visual axis of house. See Figs. 8.2–3.

14   Shop, single room, c. 10m². No decoration inside, painting on outside wall advertising drink prices AD SANC(tum), AD CVCVMAS.

15   Shop, single room with stairs up, c. 10m². No decoration.

16–18   C. del Colonnato Tuscanico, c. 385m². No. 16 single-room shop linked to atrium, elegant style-III decoration derives from earlier phase as cubiculum. Currently used to store inscriptions. No. 18 likewise shop linked to atrium, but no decoration. No. 17 entrance to impressive atrium/tablinum/peristyle with 4-sided colonnade (Tuscan columns); 7 reception rooms, finely decorated in styles III and IV, 6 with mosaic floors, 2 with high-quality mythologicals. Wide masonry stairs up behind tablinum. Service quarters at back of peristyle, 3 rooms, no decoration, back door at no. 26. Stairs from street to upper apartment at no. 27. Clear example of multiple occupancy in last phase. Published in Cerulli Irelli (1974); decoration in Manni (1974).

19   Shop, single room, c. 25m². Storage jars. No decoration.

20   Shop, single room, c. 20m². No decoration.

21–24   Sacello degli Augustali, c. 155m². Hall with central shrine and 2 side-rooms. List of members of Collegium of Augustales displayed here found elsewhere. Seen by some, incl. de Vos and de Vos (1982) 300, as the Curia. Structures and identity as *sedes Augustalium* discussed in Guadagno (1983). Rich style-IV decoration in hall and shrine, with grandiose mythologicals in shrine; discussed in Moorman (1983).

25   Shop, with stairs up(?), c. 15m². No decoration.

28/29   C. dei due Atri, c. 250m². No. 28 stairs from street to upper apartment. No. 29 entrance to house with tetrastyle atrium, tablinum, secondary atrium serving as if peristyle; 2 service rooms flank door, 1 with basic white/red decoration; 7 further rooms, 3 finely decorated in style-IV, 2 with basic white/red decoration.

SAMPLE 3

POMPEII REGIO VI, INS. 9–16

This sample has been treated differently from the other two. It does not rely on thorough personal inspection of the houses, except in ins. 12, 15, and 16, but on published lists, especially Eschebach and *Pitture e Pavimenti*. Most of these excavations, from the 1820s onward, date to over a century ago, and outside the grander houses there is all too little to be seen. The data were assembled experimentally on the basis of published sources; and though there clearly is loss of evidence for decoration, in many respects the patterns that emerge from this sample cohere surprisingly well with those from the other two.

INSULA 9

1/14   C. del Duca di Aumale, C. 760m². No. 1 atrium house with yard and cultivated garden, approx. 15 rooms. No. 14 house with nonimpluviate atrium, approx. 7 rooms, stable yard, linked at back to no. 1. Hospitium? Though no decoration survives, mythological of Isis said to have been found here.

2/13   C. di Meleagro, c. 1230m². No. 2 atrium (stairs up at front) and exquisite peristyle with 4-sided colonnade, approx. 13 reception rooms, incl. oecus Corinthius, with fine decoration in style-IV, mythologicals in 11 rooms, mosaics in 8. No. 13 back entrance to yard and service quarters, 6 rooms, 2 stairs up.

3–5   C. del Centauro, c. 1045m². No. 3 atrium with miniperistyle at back, stairs up, service entrance at no. 12; to side full peristyle with 4-sided colonnade, stairs up, further 2-sided pseudoperistyle to side, front entrances at nos. 4 and 5, back entrances at nos. 10 and 11. Approx. 25 rooms and service areas, 17 with some decoration, mainly style III but also styles I and IV, 2 rooms with mythologicals, 3 with mosaics.

6–9   C. dei Dioscuri, c. 1520m². No. 6 atrium with columns (Corinthian atrium?), peristyle at back (2-sided colonnade) and side (4-sided colonnade); service entrances at nos. 10 (with stairs up) and 9. No. 7 secondary house with atrium and service entrance at no. 8, linked at side to no. 6. Approx. 32 rooms, 24 of which are richly decorated, mostly style-IV except 2 in style II; mythologicals in 10, mosaics in 7. Studied in Richardson (1955).

INSULA 10

1/19   Osteria della via di Mercurio, c. 45m². No. 1 bar with counter, 2 back rooms, side entrance at no. 19. Both back rooms decorated, 1 with scenes of drinking, etc., other with mythologicals; style-IV, comparable to VI 14.28. See Fig. 7.9.

2   C. dei Cinque Scheletri, c. 270m². Narrow atrium, pseudoperistyle with 1-sided colonnade, stairs up at back, 9 rooms, 5 with some decoration, styles II and III. Identified as a brothel on basis of obscene painting. Note that *Pompei. L'informatica* distributes the name of this house to a large number of houses in ins. 9 and 10.

3/4   Caupona with dwelling, c. 180m². No. 3 bar with counter. No. 4 dwelling with atrium, stairs up, 4 rooms, back entrance at no. 18. No decoration.

5   Shop with back room, c. 25m². No decoration. Upper rooms accessible from no. 4, probably same unit of ownership.

6/17   C. di Pomponius, c. 475m². No. 6 atrium/tablinum/peristyle with 2-sided colonnade, back entrance at no. 17 with stairs up, approx. 12 rooms. No decoration. Oil-mill has been suggested (*officina olearia*).

7/16   C. dell'Ancora, c. 650m². No. 7 atrium, large sunken peristyle with 4-sided portico, stairs up from peristyle, back entrance at no. 16, approx. 16 rooms, 7 decorated, mostly style-IV, also I and III, mythologicals in 2, mosaics in 3.

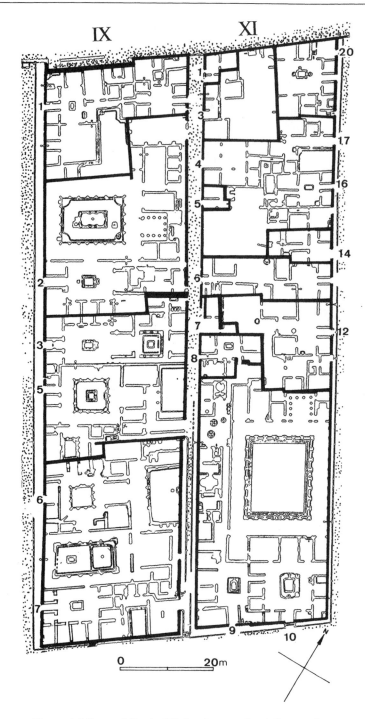

Figure A.8 Pompeii Regio VI, Insulae 9 and 11 (after *CTP*).

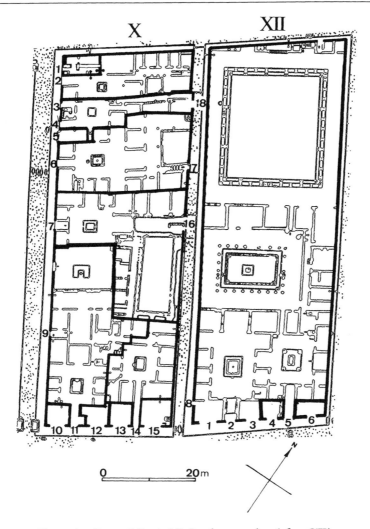

Figure A.9 Pompeii Regio VI, Insulae 10 and 12 (after *CTP*).

8/9/11 C. del Naviglio, c. 650m². No. 11 main entrance to atrium/tablinum/peristyle with
          1-sided colonnade, 10 rooms, style-IV decoration in 6, mythologicals in 1, mosaics
          in 3.

   10   Shop, single room, c. 30m². No decoration.

   12   Shop, single room, c. 35m². No decoration.

   13   Shop, single room, c. 30m². No decoration.

   14   Unnamed house, c. 250m². Atrium, 9 rooms, stairs up at back. No decoration (*casa
          rustica*).

   15   Shop, single room, c. 40m². No decoration.

INSULA 11: see Fig. A.8.

1/2   Dwelling, c. 40m². No. 1 room and back room. No. 2 stairs up(?). No decoration.

3   Unnamed house, c. 350m². Large courtyard, 4 rooms of irregular disposition, stairs up at rear. No decoration.

4/15–17   Irregular cluster of linked units, c. 820m². Main entrance at no. 16 to nonimpluviate atrium with stairs up, 6 rooms, horticultural plot with outdoor triclinium. No. 15 3-room unit with stairs up. No. 14/17 irregular arrangement of 11 rooms around garden court and backyard. No decoration.

5   Workshop, single room, c. 30m². No decoration.

6/13   Dwelling, c. 280m². No. 13 nonimpluviate atrium, backyard, 9 rooms, stairs up at rear, back entrance at no. 6. No decoration.

7   Workshop, c. 60m². Open space and 2 back rooms. No decoration.

8   C. di Eutychus, c. 110m². Atrium and 4 rooms, lararium painting in kitchen. Listed by Eschebach, etc., as separate unit, but in fact linked from early period to C. del Labirinto and presumably functioned as caretaker's apartment, Strocka (1991) 63ff.

9/10   C. del Labirinto, c. 1810m². No. 10 main entrance to tetrastyle atrium, peristyle with 4-sided colonnade, approx. 16 reception rooms incl. oecus Corinthius. No. 9 entrance to secondary atrium, approx. 8 rooms, stairs up, bath suite. Finely decorated in most rooms, esp. in style II in main reception areas, style III in baths, but also all other styles; mosaic floors in 10 rooms, mythologicals in 2. Bakery accessible from entrance 8a installed after A.D. 62, blocking access to baths. See Strocka (1991) for detailed publication. See Fig. 5.17.

11/12   House with workshop, c. 410m². No. 12 nonimpluviate atrium, 5 rooms. No. 11 irregular workshop-area with plant. Decoration (styles I/III/IV) in 4 rooms.

14   Dwelling, c. 110m². Nonimpluviate atrium, 4 rooms, yard. No decoration.

18–20   Unnamed house, c. 285m². No. 19 main entrance to atrium, 7 rooms, yard, and back entrance at no. 18. No. 20 workshop with stairs up. Style-III/IV decoration in 3 rooms.

INSULA 12: see Fig. A.9.

2/5   C. del Fauno, c. 2865m². No. 2 main entrance to atrium, 2 peristyles, each with full 4-sided colonnade. No. 5 secondary entrance to tetrastyle atrium leading to bath suite. Palatial house with outstanding mosaics (12 areas), incl. Alexander mosaic, notable style-I decoration (11 areas), odd examples of styles II/III/IV elsewhere. Four shops open from the facade of this outstanding house; the 2 flanking the main entrance, nos. 1 and 3, connect with the atrium; the 2 flanking the secondary atrium, nos. 4 and 6, do not link. An excellent example of the irrelevance of shops in the facade to the standing of a house.

4   Shop, single room with stairs up, c. 25m². No decoration. Evidently belongs to no. 2/5 (upper rooms cross fauces?).

6   Shop, single room, c. 25m². No decoration. Belongs to no. 2/5.

INSULA 13

1–4   C. del Gruppo dei vasi di vetro, c. 690m². Nos. 1 and 3 single-room shops flanking entry, linked to atrium. No. 4 stairs from street to upper apartment. No. 2 atrium/tablinum/peristyle with 4-sided colonnade, stairs up at back of atrium; 2 back entrances to peristyle at nos. 20 and 21. Seventeen rooms, 4 decorated (styles III/IV), 1 with mythological, 1 with mosaic.

5   Workshop, c. 25m². Identified as *officina textoria* (weaver's shop). No decoration.

6–9   C. di Terentius Eudoxsus, c. 555m². No. 6 entrance to atrium/tablinum/peristyle with 3-sided colonnade, back entrance at no. 9, 13 rooms, 7 decorated in styles III and IV, 1 in style I. No. 7 single-room shop linked to atrium; used as textile production establishment(?) (evidence of graffiti). Moeller (1976) 40.

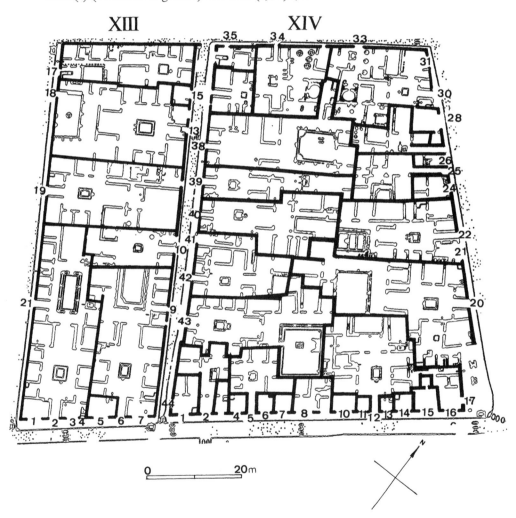

Figure A.10 Pompeii Regio VI, Insulae 13 and 14 (after *CTP*).

10/1   C. di Claudius Eulogus, c. 180m². No. 10 entrance to atrium/tablinum, stairs up in atrium; 5 rooms, 2 with faded style-III decoration. No. 11 shop with access to atrium of no. 10.

12/19   C. di Pompeius Axiochus, c. 460m². No. 19 main entrance to atrium/tablinum/back garden, back entrance at no. 12, 14 rooms, extensive decoration in all 4 styles throughout, incl. mythological in 1.

13–14   Unnamed house, c. 555m². No. 13 entrance to atrium/tablinum/peristyle with 2-sided colonnade, 11 rooms, 5 decorated in styles I/II/IV, 4 with mosaic floors. No. 14 single-room shop, linked to atrium.

15   Shop, single room, c. 25m².

16/17   C. di Gavius Proculus, c. 310m². No. 16 entrance to atrium, stairs up, back passage with stairs up, 11 rooms. No. 17 bar with counter at rear of house. No wall decoration; mosaic and opus sectile in 1 room.

INSULA 14

1/44   Caupona with back room, c. 50m². No decoration.

2   Establishment of irregular plan, c. 90m². Approx. 5 rooms, no decoration. Supposedly belonged to fishmonger.

3   Shop with back room, c. 25m². No decoration.

4   Shop, single room, c. 20m². No decoration.

5   C. di Adelaide d'Inghilterra, c. 155m². Atrium surrounded by 7 rooms, tablinum decorated in style III.

6   Shop, single room, c. 20m². No decoration.

7   Shop, single room, c. 20m². No decoration.

8/9   Double shop with back room and yard, c. 70m². Two rooms decorated in style III, 1 with mythological.

10   Shop, single room, c. 20m². No decoration.

11–13,   C. di Vesonius, c. 470m². This house (and its name) is confused with no. 20, but it is
16–17   surely separate. Nos. 11 and 13 shops flanking entrance at no. 12, linked to atrium. No. 12 atrium, pseudoperistyle with single colonnade, stairs up in atrium and peristyle, 10 reception rooms, extensively decorated in styles I/II, also III/IV. Nos. 16/17 shop with 3 back rooms, linked to atrium of no. 12.

18–20   C. di Orfeo, c. 690m². Nos 18/19 workshop complex, linked to atrium of no. 20, 7 rooms. No. 20 atrium/tablinum/peristyle with 2-sided colonnade, large painting of Orpheus on back wall of peristyle on axis of fauces, 11 rooms, 8 decorated, mostly style III, also I and IV. Supposedly house of M. Vesonius Primus, owner of fullery at no. 22, but whole construction of name and ownership highly conjectural; cf. Castrén (1975) 238; Jongman (1988) 174–75.

21/22   Fullonica, c. 415m². No. 21 single-room shop linked to atrium. No. 22 entrance to atrium/tablinum/peristyle with 2-sided colonnade, stairs up. Peristyle area occupied by vats for fulling; cf. Moeller (1976) 46–49. Twelve rooms, style-II/III/IV decoration in·10, incl. 1 with mythological.

23/24   Shop with dwelling, c. 45m². No. 23 stairs from street to upper apartment. No. 24 shop with 2 back rooms. No decoration.

25   House, c. 170m². Complex of 7 rooms and lightwell at end of passage, identified as *officina tinctoria*. Style-IV decoration in 3 rooms.

26   Workshop with back room, c. 25m². No decoration.

27   C. di Memmius Auctus, c. 135m². Passage to atrium and 5 rooms, wine containers at rear. Seen as establishment of *vinarius* (wine dealer). No decoration.

28   Shop with back room (supposedly *taberna lusoria* [dicing den]), c. 45m². Style-IV decoration with mythological in back room. Linked to no. 30(?). Illustrated by de Vos (1977) 39–40, with pl. 54–55.

29   Shop, single room (*taberna argentaria*), c. 10m². Style-III decoration, previously room in no. 30.

30–33   C. di Laocoonte, c. 350m². No. 30 atrium and garden court. No. 31 shop. Nos. 32 and 33 bakery complex; Mayeske (1972) 104–6. Style-III/IV decoration in 7 rooms, incl. 2 with mythologicals.

34   House with bakery, c. 260m². Atrium/tablinum, decoration in 2 reception rooms (styles I and III). See Mayeske (1972) 106–7.

35/36   Caupona (di Salvius), c. 55m². Bar with counter and back room, style-IV decoration.

37   C. con officina di falegname, c. 100m². Atrium and 6 rooms, style-III decoration in 3. Stairs to upper apartment(?). Supposedly *officina lignaria* (carpenter's workshop).

38   C. di Poppaeus Firmus, c. 420m². Atrium/tablinum/peristyle with 3-sided colonnade, 9 rooms, 7 decorated in styles I, III, IV, 1 with mythologicals.

39   C. con officina di tornitore, c. 210m². Atrium with mosaic impluvium/tablinum/backyard, 7 rooms, 1 shown in old drawing with mythological. Includes workshop of supposed *faber vasarius* (potter).

40   Unnamed house, c. 340m². Atrium/tablinum/pseudoperistyle with single colonnade, 11 rooms, stairs up at back. Seven rooms with decoration in all 4 styles, mosaic in 1.

41/42   C. della Imperatrice di Russia, c. 310m². No. 41 back door with stairs up. No. 43 atrium and backyard, 9 rooms decorated in style III, 1 in IV, 1 with mythological.

43   C. degli Scienziati, c. 500m². Atrium/tablinum/peristyle with 2-sided colonnade, eye-catching mosaic nymphaeum visible from door. Fourteen rooms, extensive decoration in all 4 styles, incl. mythologicals in 2. Supposedly a brothel.

Insula 15

1/27   C. dei Vettii, c. 1100m². No. 1 entrance to atrium and peristyle with 4-sided colonnade, alae, and 12 rooms. Extensive style-IV decoration (13 areas), incl. mythologicals in 5 rooms. Service quarters to side with secondary atrium with lararium, stairs up, 6 rooms, incl. kitchen and supposed *cella meretricia* (prostitute's cell) with pornographic decoration. Back entrance at no. 27. Published in Sogliano (1898), and endlessly discussed and remorselessly visited since then. See Figs. 3.3–4, 3.25.

2/26   C. di Appuleia e Narcissus, c. 325m². Atrium/tablinum/backyard with pseudocolonnade, 6 rooms. Decoration in styles II/III/IV in 4 rooms.

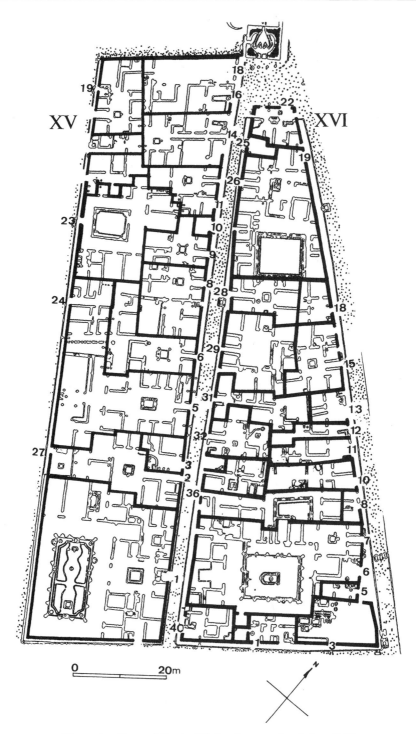

Figure A.11 Pompeii Regio VI, Insulae 15 and 16 (after *CTP*).

3   Fullonica di Mustius (fullery), c. 70m². Workroom and back room with stairs up. No decoration. Vats and treading stalls of fullery; Moeller (1976) 49.

4/5   C. di Pupius Rufus, c. 695m². Atrium/tablinum/peristyle with 2-sided colonnade and nymphaeum. Stairs up from peristyle, back entrances at nos. 26 and 25. Alae and 15 rooms, traces of decoration in all 4 styles (esp. IV) in 13 rooms, mythologicals in 2, mosaics in 3.

6   C. del Focolare di ferro, C. 240m². Atrium/tablinum/back passage, stairs up. Eight rooms, traces of style-IV decoration in 4, mythologicals in 2.

7/8   C. del Principe di Napoli, c. 240m². No. 7 stairs from street to upper apartment. No. 8 entrance to atrium/quasi-tablinum/peristyle with single colonnade, shrine in garden. Stairs up front and back of atrium. Eight rooms, style-IV decoration throughout, incl. mythologicals and opus sectile in triclinium. Published in Strocka (1984a). See Figs. 2.14, 3.14–17.

9   C. del Compluvium, c. 130m². Unusual atrium with upper floor on columns, 6 rooms. No decoration.

10   Shop, single room c. 15m². No decoration.

11/12 C. di Vedius Vestalis, c. 130m². No. 11 shop with back room. No. 12 atrium with 4 rooms. No decoration.

13–15 C. della Matrona ignota, c. 250m². No. 13 side entrance to workshop. No. 14 long passage to atrium, 7 rooms, stairs up. No. 15 caupona with counter and back room. Traces of style-IV decoration in 4 rooms, 2 with mosaic emblemata, incl. fine portrait of lady now in Naples Museum.

16–18 Caupona, dwelling, and stable, c. 325m². No. 16 caupona with bar and back room. Nos. 17/18 stable-yard with rooms/stables, stairs up. No decoration.

19   Shop, single room c. 10m². No decoration.

20   C. di Stlaborius Auctus, c. 215m². Central court with 6 rooms and stables. No decoration.

21   Workshop, c. 65m². Central space and 3 rooms. No decoration.

22   C. di Cinnius Fortunatus, c. 110m². Central space, stairs up, 4/5 rooms. No decoration.

23   Unnamed house, c. 400m². Peristyle with 4-sided colonnade, 11 rooms around, faded decoration in peristyle, style-IV lararium painting in kitchen. Well-built peristyle presumably formerly part of another house, no. 9 or 12.

Insula 16

1/2,   C. degli Amorini dorati, c. 830m². Nos. 1/2 caupona with back rooms, linked (in fact
6/7, 38 dubiously) by Eschebach to peristyle of no. 7. No. 6 caupona, back entrance to peristyle of no. 7. No. 7 main entrance to atrium/tablinum/peristyle with 4-sided colonnade (Rhodian portico), 11 reception rooms, 10 rooms/areas decorated in styles III and IV, incl. mythologicals in 3, mosaics in 4. Service rooms (4) at back with stairs up and back entrance at no. 38. Prime example of elegant and beautifully decorated property with multiple commercial dependencies. See Strocka (1988) 247 for preliminary results of German survey. See Pl. 2.

3/4	Fullonica, c. 150m². Two rooms with vats for fulling (Moeller 1976, 49–50). No decoration. Likely to belong also to no. 7.
5	Shop with back room, stairs up, c. 30m². No decoration.
8/9	Workshop with stairs up to apartment, c. 40m². No decoration.
10	C. di Erastus, c. 125m². Workshop with central yard, indeterminate disposition of rooms. No decoration. Workshop of mosaicist(?).
11	Shop/dwelling, c. 80m². Workshop with back rooms/backyard. No decoration.
12	Shop (caupona?), c. 60m². Shop, back room, yard, end room. No decoration.
13/14	Shop/workshop, c. 70m². No. 13 workshop and back rooms. No. 14 stairs up to apartment. No decoration.
15–17	C. dell'Ara massima, c. 180m². No. 15 atrium and reception rooms, 5 decorated in style-IV, 3 with mythologicals; large lararium painting in atrium. Nos. 16 and 17 secondary entrances to service quarters(?).
18	Workshop with dwelling, c. 100m². Central court and 3 rooms. No decoration.
19/ 26–27	Unnamed house, c. 510m². No. 26 main entrance to atrium (stairs up) and peristyle with 3-sided colonnade. Back entrance to peristyle at no. 27 with stairs up to atrium at no. 19. Approx. 17 rooms, 7 decorated in styles I and IV, incl. 2 with mythologicals.
20–24	Supposed *statio vindemitorum* (grape-gatherers' post), c. 115m². Multiple entrances to central space with indistinct disposition of rooms, 1 with style-IV decoration, 1 with lararium painting.
25	Shop, single room, c. 25m². No decoration.
28	House, c. 145m². Atrium, 6 rooms, stairs up. Style-III and -IV decoration in 4 rooms, incl. mythologicals in 2.
29/30	House and workshop, c. 250m². No. 29 central space with 8 rooms, 3 decorated in style-IV; stairs up. No. 30 workshop.
31	Workshop/dwelling, c. 125m². Passage with rooms off, 2 decorated in styles I and IV, backyard.
32/3	C. di Aurunculeius Secundio, c. 135m². No. 32 atrium, 3 rooms with style-IV decoration, backyard, and stairs up. No. 33 bar with priapic decoration (masturbating figures) in style-IV (*Notizie degli Scari* 1908, 289–95); cf. IV.17 in Herculaneum.
34	Shop, single room, c. 15m². Style-III decoration.
35	House, c. 125m². Atrium, 3 rooms, 1 with style-IV decoration, stairs up, backyard.
36/37	C. di Poppaeus Sabinus, c. 210m². No. 36 passageway to peristyle with 3-sided colonnade, 5 rooms, 2 decorated in styles III and IV, 1 with mosaic floor; stairs up.
39/40	Caupona, c. 95m². No. 40 bar with back rooms. No. 39 side passage (stairs?). No decoration.

NOTES

PREFACE

1. Leach (1988), 75–79.

2. Published as "The social structure of the Roman house," *Papers of the British School at Rome* 56 (1988): 43–97.

3. Published as "Elites and trade in the Roman town" in J. Rich and A. Wallace-Hadrill (eds.), *City and Country in the Ancient World* (London 1991), 241–72.

4. Published as "Houses and households: sampling Pompeii and Herculaneum" in B. Rawson (ed.), *Marriage, Divorce, and Children in Ancient Rome* (Canberra and Oxford 1991), 191–227.

5. Published as "The social spread of Roman luxury: sampling Pompeii and Herculaneum," *Papers of the British School at Rome* 58 (1990): 145–92 [published May 1992].

CHAPTER I
READING THE ROMAN HOUSE

1. Attempts to make sense of the descriptions run into considerable difficulties: see Maiuri (1945) 153–58; Bagnani (1954) 16–39; McKay (1975) 113–14.

2. Cf. Barbet (1985) 214: "C'est là un des charmes de l'étude des maisons pompéiennes, on y decèle parfois la personnalité et les goûts du propriétaire qui a commandé tel ou tel motif."

3. Well discussed by Wiseman (1987). For a good discussion of the role of the patron in dictating styles of decoration, see Leach (1982). Kolb (1977) underestimates the importance of the house as status symbol.

4. Standard treatments, notably Friedländer (1922) 2:330–49 [= 1908, 2:185–202], persist in using these passages as sources of information rather than windows on Roman ideology.

5. So Cato *agr.* 3.1; cf. *ORF* 174, 185; Nepos *Att.* 13.1; Pliny *Pan.* 51.1; and in similar vein Varro *RR* 1.13.6; Columella 1.4.8; Cicero *Pis.* 48; Tacitus *Ann.* 3.37; Juvenal 14.66.

6. Cf. Cato in *ORF* 185; Varro *RR* 1.59.2; cf. 1.2.10 for Lucullus; Pliny *NH* 35.118; cf. Wallace-Hadrill (1983b) 182.

7. Ibid. The same condemnation appears in Varro *RR* 1.13.7, "villis pessimo publico aedificatis."

8. Cicero *de legibus* 3.30. The passage is examined in more detail and its assertions tested below (Chap. 7).

9. Illuminatingly discussed by Zanker (1979).

10. Pliny *NH* 36.110, clearly drawing on Varro, or, more probably, Cornelius Nepos, both of whom were much concerned with the phenomenon of "luxury."

11. Tacitus *Ann.* 3.55: "ut quisque opibus, domo, paratu speciosus per nomen et clientelas inlustrior habebatur."

12. Firmly grasped by Thébert (1987), an excellent discussion of the North African material that reaches similar conclusions to the present study.

13. For the closure of the doors as an exceptional gesture of mourning see Valerius Maximus 5.7.ext. 1; Seneca *Cons. ad. Liv.* 183; *Vit. Beat.* 28.1; *Brev. Vit.* 20.3; *Cons. ad Polyb.* 14.2; Lucan 2.22; Tacitus *Ann.* 2.82; *Hist.* 1.62. (I am grateful to Richard Saller for these references.) On the Gallic sack see Livy 5.41.7: "plebis aedificiis obseratis, patentibus atriis principum."

14. Varro *RR* 2, pref., cf. Vitruvius 6.5.3, with the comments of Carandini (1985) 1* 119, and in Carandini, Ricci, and de Vos (1982) 30, 58f.

15. Columella 1.4.8; cf. Carandini (1985) 1* 107.

16. *Ad Att.* 5.22; see D'Arms (1970) 48ff.

17. See the evidence collected by Friedländer (1922) 1:343ff. [= 1908, 1:287ff.] and D'Arms loc. cit.

18. Veblen (1899). Against Veblen's "conspicuous consumption" see Douglas and Isherwood (1980) 3ff.; Elias (1983) 66ff.

19. The poverty of classical Athenian domestic (as opposed to public) building is striking: see Walker (1983) 82–83; for classical Olynthos, Robinson and Graham (1938). Houses of the Hellenistic period were somewhat more impressive: for those of Delos see the publication of the Îlot de la Maison des Comédiens in Bruneau (1970); for Pergamum see Pinkwart and Stammnitz (1984); for Priene see Wiegand and Shrader (1904) 285–300. Greek houses of the imperial period are another matter: see esp. Strocka (1977) on the Hanghäuser

of Ephesos; Levi (1945) for the rich Antiochene suburb of Daphne. For a fine synthesis on Greek domestic architecture see Hoepfner and Schwandner (1986).

20. There are signs of attempts to "recontextualize" the objects studied, particularly sculpture, notably by Sauron (1980), Dwyer (1982), and Zanker (Zevi 1984) 201–10; and, outside Pompeii, by Neudecker (1988). For mural decoration see the works of Strocka and Barbet cited below.

21. The volume of discussion on the chronology of the styles is immense: see the bibliographical surveys of Ling (1978) and Mielsch (1981), esp. 170–83; and the helpful general books of Barbet (1985) and Ling (1991a).

22. This criticism does not apply to the pioneering work of Mau (1882), which was solidly based on archaeological and structural relationships. For similar criticism, see F. Coarelli's preface to Barbet (1985). The recent study by Ehrhardt (1987) on the transition of second to third style pays more attention to archaeological dating criteria, but such criteria remain all too scarce. See also Strocka (1991) 107–14. For the dramatic discovery of one precise dating criterion, the impression of a coin of Vespasian in the wall plaster, see Descoeudres (1987).

23. The classic modern studies of chronological development are Laidlaw (1985) on the first style; Beyen (1938) and (1960) on the second; and Bastet and de Vos (1979) and Ehrhardt (1987) on the third.

24. See Bastet and de Vos (1979) 100, who observe that a typology of the fourth style can and should be very different, and suggest analysis by room types.

25. Strocka (1984a); cf. my review in (1986a) 433–34.

26. Strocka (1984a) esp. 39–48. The forthcoming study of the C. della Caccia Antica in the same series by P. Allison demonstrates with even greater clarity that the variation in quality of decoration is the result of deliberate differentiation, not of different workshops.

27. Barbet (1985).

28. Esp. pp. 57–77, 123–39, 193–214 on the theme of "adéquation du décor aux locaux" in the successive styles.

29. I have found particular value in studies concerned with the distinctions of public and private space: Bourdieu (1973) is a classic example of an-

thropological method; Girouard (1978) is a justly famous essay on the sociology of the English house; Elias (1983) 41–65 is illuminating on the sociology of early modern French architecture; Daunton (1983a, b) has excellent observations on the redefinition of the boundaries of public and private in the nineteenth century. See also the collection of papers edited by Susan Kent (1990), which includes many stimulating approaches along similar lines.

30. See the excellent discussion by Susan Walker (1983). This and Bourdieu's essay on male and female in the Berber house (1973) provide a model of where to look for gender distinctions of space; in the light of their work, attempts to seek similar distinctions in the Roman house (below) look unconvincing. On the issues of women and space in general see Ardener (1981). For scepticism about Walker's approach see the paper by Michael Jameson in Kent (1990) 92–113, esp. 104f.

31. Nepos *praefatio* 6–8. The context gives the passage peculiar weight: it is at the outset of a series of biographies of Greeks intended to explain to a Roman audience the fundamental differences between Greek and Roman society. See Cicero *Verr.* 2.66 for an incident where Roman insensitivity to Greek segregation at table causes outrage in Sicily.

32. Vitruvius vi.7.2–4. Note that Vitruvius appears to think that segregation serves to protect the men from the women, not vice versa, so strange is segregation to him. His remarks on the transference of the Greek loan-word *andron* are also significant (4–5): in Latin the word applies to a corridor because there are no exclusive "men's rooms."

33. Plautus *Most.* 754–65, 806–9, 822–23. The passage is cited in support of Roman women's quarters by, for example, Carandini (1985) l *p. 120. The only other passage in classical Latin that suggests a gynaeceum in a Roman house is Cicero *Phil.* 2.95, where Cicero decries a corrupt deal fixed between Antony and Deiotarus "in gynaeceo"; that is, through Fulvia. The usage is explained by the desire to defame Antony.

34. Maiuri (1954) identifies various secluded areas as *gynaecea*, but without any cogent argument. The terms *gynaeceum/ -ium/ -onitis* are scarcely used before the fourth century A.D., when they come to refer to an imperial weaving room. Against Lawrence Richardson's attempts to identify separate dining rooms for women, see below, Chap. 3, n. 40.

35. Ariès (1962), esp. 385ff., on the eighteenth-century emergence of the family as a private and

differentiated household unit; Girouard (1978) 286f. on the Victorian novelty of children's rooms.

36. So vividly Tacitus *Dialogus* 28–29; see Bradley (1991), esp. 76ff., on wet nurses.

37. So Virgil *Aeneid* 7.379f., children play with a top in the hall, "quem pueri magno in gyro vacua atria circum / intenti ludo exercent." Also Lucr. 4.401–4: boys spinning themselves around imagine the atrium and columns to spin: "atria vorsari et circumcursare columnae" (a reference owed to Peter Wiseman).

38. For example, Tacitus *Ann.* 15.54. On expressions for *ordines* (official orders), see Cohen (1975).

39. I render *propria/communia* (personal/common) as private/public, conscious that the antitheses are not identical. That we construct the spheres of public and private in a different way from the Romans is precisely the argument of the following pages.

40. "Forensibus et disertis": "Professors of rhetoric" (Granger in the Loeb translation) is surely wrong. Note that the choice of *forensis* (in the forum) underlines the public activity of those concerned.

41. Wiseman (1982).

42. Mau (1902) 248–58; Kroll (1933) 187–90; etc.

43. My account is dependent on Elias (1983) 41–65. On the importance of clientèle in French society, see Kettering (1986).

44. Study of such houses is still inadequate: see Packer (1975); also Packer (1978), noting the lack of regular pattern of inns (e.g., p. 30); Hoffmann (1984); also important is Maiuri (1958) 407ff. for its ranking of houses according to inferred status.

45. Notably Zanker (1979); also note Maiuri (1958), "Case del ceto medio nello schema della *domus*," 243–79.

46. On the importance of social mobility in this respect, compare the remarks of Bezerra de Meneses (1984) 86 on social mobility in Delian society and the use of "classical" motifs in decoration. I pursue this issue further in Part II.

47. Pompeian material shapes the presentation in nineteenth-century handbooks like Marquardt (1886) 213ff. Note also the second edition of Becker's *Gallus* (1880) 213–319, which uses Pompeian material much more confidently than in the first edition (1838) 70–102.

48. Peterse (1984), (1985); Strocka (1991) 71–84.

49. D'Arms (1970).

50. Zanker (1979).

51. Ward-Perkins (1970).

52. Ling (1991a) 3.

53. A difficulty aggravated by the concentration of the publications of these structures on wall painting alone, notably Carettoni (1983).

54. Cf. below, Chap. 6, n. 31.

55. See Millar (1981) for Apuleius as a picture of the Roman world; well used by Thébert (1987).

CHAPTER 2
THE LANGUAGE OF PUBLIC AND PRIVATE

1. Carettoni (1983) 9; cf. Coarelli (1980), 132–33; cf. my criticisms in *JRS* 75 (1985): 247–48.

2. Reception of friends in cubiculo: for example, Tacitus *Dialogus* 3.1. and 14.1, Maternus conducts whole dialogue in his bedroom; Seneca *de ira* 3.8.6, Caelius dines with client; Pliny *ep.* 5.3.11, Pliny recites verse; Suetonius *Vesp.* 21, describing Vespasian's daily routine (see secretaries, then receives amici while putting on shoes), implies reception in cubiculo. Conduct of business in cubiculo: Cicero *Verr.* 3.133, etc., Verres conducts trials; *ad Q.F.* 1.1.25, brother as governor praised for accessibility of cubiculum; Pliny *ep.* 5.1.5, Pliny summons private *consilium*. Imperial trials intra cubiculum: for example, Seneca *de clem.* 1.9 (Augustus), Tacitus *Ann.* 11.2 (Claudius) etc.; abolished by Nero, Tacitus *Ann.* 13.4; Pliny *Pan.* 49.1 and 83.1, contrasting Domitian's "lair" with Trajan's open cubiculum. Cf. Tamm (1963) 113–19; Crook (1955) 106–9.

3. Cf. Coarelli (1983).

4. Maiuri (1958) 286–90, repeating Maiuri (1951). The basilica form and its significance are recognized by Tamm (1963) 145, but the label "dining room" persists; see, for example, McKay (1975) 51.

5. See the good discussion by Tamm (1963) 132–47.

6. Note that there is also a major pediment above the tablinum. Note too the pediment of the "Rhodian" peristyle in the C. degli Amorini Dorati (VI 16.7). Other large rooms with imposing blackground decoration like that in the C. dei Cervi should be compared: the "Salone Nero" in the house of that name at Herculaneum (H VI.13) or the central room of the C. di Fabio Rufo at Pompeii (Ins. Occ).

7. *Thesaurus Linguae Latinae* VII, 320, s.v. "Fastigium"; esp. Vitruvius 5.6.9: "columnis et fastigiis et signis reliquisque regalibus rebus"; see Suetonius *Cal.* 37 for the fastigium of a basilica.

8. On the extraordinary honor of the fastigium and its divine connotations, see Weinstock (1971) 280–81. See Suetonius *Jul.* 81 for the dream. (In Caesar's case, the fastigium was external to the house.) The psychological impact of the fastigiate facade is underlined by comparison with the villas of the slave-plantation owners of the American South, illustrated by Carandini (1985) vol. 1, pls. 177, 179, 181. As Carandini comments, the use of the language of classical forms to legitimate the hierarchies of a slave-owning society is conscious (187f.).

9. Of course Greek houses too may occasionally have had pediments; see, for example, the purely hypothetical reconstruction in Wiegand and Schrader (1904) 286. This, however, has no bearing on the significance the feature had for the Romans.

10. See Vitruvius 5.6.9. (n. 7, above), linking columns with pediments and statues as the apparatus of a regal stage setting. Note too the force of poetic evocations of grandeur: Virgil *Aeneid* 7.170, "tectum augustum, ingens, centum sublime columnis"; Propertius 3.2.9, "non Taenareis domus est mihi fulta columnis"; Ovid *Met.* 2.1, "regia Solis erat sublimibus alta columnis"; Statius *Silv.* 1.2. 147/152, "digna deae sedes . . . innumeris fastigia nixa columnis."

11. Pliny *NH* 17.1.6; cf. Valerius Maximus 9.1.4. Similarly, Pliny *NH* 36.2.5. describes Scaurus dragging marble columns past the terracotta pediments of the gods; see the discussion by Gros (1978) 65f. Pliny exaggerates: there was a marble temple in Rome shortly after 146 B.C. See also *NH* 36.60 on the onyx columns decorating the dining room of Callistus.

12. So Mau (1902) 245ff., vigorously contested by Sulze (1940). Maiuri (1946a) supports the traditional view. Against it, see McKay (1975) 34–35.

13. Well demonstrated by Sulze (1946) 951–54. Columns are attested in Greek houses as early as the fifth century B.C.; see Jones, Sackett, and Graham (1962) 107n.70. For columns as a sign of splendor in a private house, see Aristophanes *Clouds* 815 (reference owed to Peter Wiseman).

14. So Gros (1978) 26, pointing out that the peristyles of the C. del Fauno, in contrast to Greek domestic courts, lack surrounding rooms.

15. Cicero *ad Att.* 1.6, 1.10, etc.; see Varro *RR* 2, pref. "gymnasia urbana"; for other passages, see Sulze (1940) 966.

16. Dwyer (1982) 117, 125 makes too little of this aspect of the use of statuary.

17. Grimal (1943) 76 notes gymnasia and particularly philosophical academies as part of the background for the Roman peristyle; 226f. stress the public nature of the peristyle garden. See Ridgeway (1981) on the lack of evidence for Greek domestic gardens or garden sculpture.

18. Cicero *de leg.* 3.31. On this see Pape (1975).

19. See Hill (1981) for some of the standard pieces of the reproduction trade.

20. See Maiuri (1952a) for the links between Vitruvius and the remains. For Settefinestre see Carandini (1985) 1** 20–23.

21. Described by Callixeinos in Athenaeus 5.196–209; see Studnicza (1914), esp. 32–34, for the Pompeian parallels; see also Ricotti (1989). Fittschen (1976) 544–49 brings out the relevance of these descriptions for the decorative versions of such oeci.

22. Athenaeus 5.207d-e on the gymnasium, promenades, temple of Aphrodite, and library that formed part of the dining complex.

23. Apsed rooms are catalogued and discussed by Tamm (1963) 147–88, bringing out the "sacred" connotations of the apse. For the Auditorium Maecenatis, currently interpreted as a *nymphaeum*/triclinium, see Rizzo and de Vos (1983).

24. See the illuminating discussion of Coarelli (1983).

25. Petr. *Sat.* 77.4: "aedificavi hanc domum. ut scitis, + cusuc + erat; nunc templum est." The sense of the corrupt word *cusuc* is fairly clear.

26. The importance of curtains is nicely captured by Thébert (1987) 388f.

27. For Eastern examples of fabric-style decorations see Rostovzeff, *JHS* 39 (1919): 151–53; Pinkwart and Stammnitz (1984) 86–92. For Italian examples see Barbet (1985) 203, classified, in several cases wrongly, as "zone supérieur"; Barbet and Allag (1972); Carandini (1985) 1** 231–32. The style is increasingly attested in the western provinces: see Drack (1950) 31–34 for Switzerland; Ling (1984) and (1985) 34–36 for Britain; and Ling (1991a) 84–85 in general.

28. See the valuable discussion of Scagliarini (1974/76), generally overlooked in the literature and unknown to me at the time of writing.

29. On the Greek background see Bruno (1969); Barbet (1985) 12–25; Laidlaw (1985) 34–37.

30. Laidlaw (1985) 307ff., 330 for the continued use of first style in public buildings and funerary monuments; 42–46 for preservation of old decoration in private houses.

31. The traditional case, propounded esp. by Beyen (1938) 279ff., was attacked by Engemann (1967) (with further references). Some degree at least of theatrical inspiration must be conceded: see Barbet (1985) 44f.; Ling (1991a) 30.

32. Dependence on Hellenistic palaces is argued by Fittschen (1976); also Schefold (1975). Dependence on Roman villas was proposed by Lehmann (1953) 82–131. Leach (1982) 141–59 rightly sees that both villas and stage settings may be evoked.

33. Carettoni (1961), (1983) 23f.; against Engemann's attack see Allroggen-Bedel (1974) 28–33.

34. Fittschen (1976) 544ff.

35. _Pharsalia_ 10.111–12: "ipse locus templi, quod vix corruptior aetas/ extruat, instar erat . . ."

36. Lucan's observation about marble incrustation is almost correct if Pliny _NH_ 36.48 rightly attributes its introduction to Mamurra, that is, under the dictatorship of Caesar: cf. Fittschen (1976) 555.

37. Notably the fragmentary wall in the C. di Fabio Rufo; see, for example, Barbet (1985) 45, with pl. IIa.

38. Conventionally classed as "megalographiae"; see, for example, Barbet (1985) 52–56. On the Boscoreale paintings see Fittschen in Andreae and Kyrieleis (1975) 93–100.

39. Described by Pausanias _Attika_ 15; cf. Pliny _NH_ 35.59.

40. The Porticus Pompei and Octaviae were notable repositories of paintings and other works of art: see Platner and Ashby (1927) 427–28; Pape (1975) 46ff.

41. The use of telamones in public architecture is illustrated by L. Castiglione in Andreae and Kyrieleis (1975) 211–24.

42. The temporary theater of Aemilius Scaurus of 58 B.C. was notorious: Pliny _NH_ 34.36; 36.50, 113–15; though Pliny regards Curio's theater of 52 B.C. as more extravagant, 36.116–20. On these, see Bieber (1961) 167ff.; Little (1971); Gros (1978) 20f.; and Rawson (1985) 100 for the continued erection of scaenae frontes at Rome. Paoletti in Carandini (1985) 1** 227–28 has good remarks on the social context of scenographic paintings.

43. Fittschen (1976) 543.

44. This analysis follows Barbet (1985) 70, with fig. 27.

45. Strocka (1991) 116–20.

46. Vitruvius 7.5.3: "On the plaster there are monsters rather than definite representations taken from definite things. Instead of columns there rise up fluted reeds; instead of gables, decorative appendages with curled leaves and volutes. Candelabra support shrine-like forms, above the rooves of which grow delicate flowers with volutes containing little figures seated at random. There are also stalks carrying half-figures, some with human, some with animal heads. Such things neither are, nor can be, nor have been" (trans. Ling).

47. See Bastet and de Vos (1979) 8–16 for the dating, now modified by Ehrhardt (1987); cf. Ling (1991a) 36f., 52f. The Casa di Augusto could be of extreme importance for dating the shift, as suggested by Carettoni (1983) 86ff., but inadequate evidence about the structures of the house has been published to confirm Carettoni's hypothesis of building in the period 36–28 B.C. Note also room 12 at Settefinestre with scenographic decoration similar to that of the C. di Augusto, dated to the period of Caesar/Octavian: Carandini (1985) 1** 215–28.

48. Leach (1982) 166: "In the subtle tone of the early third style we may see reflected the changed temper of the Augustan world where the princeps championed the virtues of solid citizens in whose lives quiet prosperity and dutiful service had replaced the republican passions for honour and display."

49. Documented by Eck (1984); see also Wallace-Hadrill (1986b) 79.

50. See Saller (1982), rightly stressing survival of patronage into the empire; see also Wallace-Hadrill (1989).

51. On pinacothecae see Varro _RR_ 1.2.10; Cicero _de leg._ 3.31. See Vitr. 6.5.2 on galleries as an import from the public sector. See also van Buren (1956); Schefold (1972) 50ff.; Leach (1982) 162.

52. Pliny _NH_ 35.118 contrasts the public context of Greek art with the private context of Roman.

53. See Pape (1975) 73–80 on the protests from the elder Cato onward against private possession of masterpieces; Pliny _NH_ 35.26 for Agrippa's proposals. Note too the protest against appropriation of Lysippus's Apoxyomenos by Tiberius: Pliny _NH_ 34.62.

54. Pliny _NH_ 35.24–26 dates public possession of paintings back to the triumph of Mummius, but regards Caesar's dictatorship as the turning point. He omits to mention the importance of the Porticus Pompei.

55. Carettoni (1983) 90–92 thinks Augustus brought an Alexandrian craftsman back in 29 B.C., but Egyptianizing art was a widespread vogue; see de Vos (1980), esp. 75–95.

56. Strabo's description of contemporary high life at Canopus is tantalizing: 7.1.17 (p. 801).

57. For a useful preliminary attempt at classification see Barbet (1985) 193–203.

58. Cf. Barbet (1985) 123–26; Vitruvius 7.7–14 (note the space he devotes to color); Pliny *NH* 35.29–50.

59. Pliny *NH* 35.30, 44–47, 50.

60. On Vestorius, Vitruvius 7.11; D'Arms (1970) 52f. The use of blue is notable at Herculaneum: for example, C. dell'Atrio a mosaico, room 9; C. dei Cervi, room 16; C. dell'Alcova, room 8; C. del Gran Portale, room 6. Blue monochromes are apparently not used in the third style (Barbet [1985] 126), but note the atrium of the C. dei Quadretti Teatrali (I 6.11) and the tablinum of the C. della Caccia Antica (VII 4.48).

61. At Herculaneum, esp. C. del Salone Nero, room G; C. dei Cervi, room 5. At Pompeii, esp. C. di Fabio Rufo, room D (also C); Villa dei Misteri, tablinum 2. At Rome, Villa Farnesina, room C. For others see Barbet (1985) 124.

62. For example, the much illustrated tablinum of the C. di Lucretius Fronto (V 4,a), evidently the climactic point of its surrounding decorative scheme.

63. The C. del Gran Portale (V.34–35) at Herculaneum is an excellent example, where the triclinium lies directly on the axis of the fauces, and the "aedicle" of the decoration continues the vista: see Maiuri (1958) 1:379, fig. 309. At Pompeii I have noted similar arrangements at I 7.18 (a small shop/house, see Fig. 2.17) and I 11.17 (unpublished).

64. On this pattern see Barbet (1985) 130–35. The black triclinium of the C. del Frutteto (I 9.5, room 11) is a good example.

65. Strocka (1975); also see his analysis of the C. del Principe di Napoli (1984).

66. The use of these hierarchies is analyzed in Chapter 7.

67. For example, C. del Principe di Napoli, triclinium k, or, earlier, the white rooms from the Villa Farnesina in Rome and the Villa Imperiale in Pompeii.

68. Of the black rooms cited above, those in the C. del Salone Nero and the C. dei Cervi lack panels and motifs (a style favored in general at Herculaneum), and that in the Villa dei Misteri, of outstanding polish and elegance, has only subordinate motifs.

69. For example, the elegance of the black tab-linum at the Villa dei Misteri gives it suitable grandeur, while its restraint in decorative elaboration allows the more private Sala dei Misteri to come as a climax.

70. See Coarelli (1984) 152–54.

71. Cf. the explosion of *cursus honorum* inscriptions for equites and freedmen in the early empire, originating in a shift in senatorial practice under Augustus: Eck (1984) 149–52.

CHAPTER 3
THE ARTICULATION OF THE HOUSE

1. Cf. Carandini (1985) 1** 111–13 for the seignorial and slave quarters of a villa; 187–206 for valuable comparative material on American slave plantations.

2. Petronius *Sat.* 30. On the various types of household slave, Marquardt (1886) 142–47 is helpful.

3. Dig. 44.15.10.44: "multum interest qualis servis sit, bonae frugi, ordinarius, dispensator an vero vulgaris vel mediastinus vel qualisqualis."

4. For illustrations see A. de Franciscis in Andreae and Kyrieleis (1975) pls. 38–39; Strocka (ibid.) pl. 75 illustrates an example in a passageway in the Praedia Juliae Felicis (II 4.10); see Maiuri (1958) 420 for an example on the exterior of the modest C. dell'Ara Laterizia (III.17) at Herculaneum, comparing (n. 216) the stairway at the Porta Marina at Pompeii; see Eschebach (1979) pl. 67 for the latrine (o) at a public bath. There are traces of similar decoration in the passages of the amphitheater at Pompeii. It is also to be found in the entrance of the C. di Iulius Polybius, and in the atrium and corridors of the interesting but neglected house at I 12.11.

5. Elia (1934) 321–39.

6. Pliny *ep.* 5.6.41, 2.17.9. A. N. Sherwin-White, *The Letters of Pliny* (1966) 188 observes well Pliny's silence.

7. See my comments in Wallace-Hadrill (1986a) 433f. on the C. del Principe di Napoli.

8. The Roman lack of interest in private as opposed to public bathing is visible in the absence of evidence for private bathtubs (as opposed to bath suites) in Vesuvian houses; contrast the frequency of bathtubs at Olynthos: Robinson and Graham (1938) 198ff. On communal latrines as a standard feature of Roman life see F. Drexel, "Das Latrinenwesen," excursus in Friedländer (1922) 6.310–11; and recently Scobie (1986) 429.

9. Carettoni (1983) 92 identifies this "Syracuse" with one upper-floor room discovered in the C. di Augusto. But the language of Suetonius *Aug.* 72, "locus in edito singularis . . . huc transibat," suggests something far more remote than the "retired place at the top of the house" of Rolfe's Loeb translation, let alone a normal upstairs room. It was surely a separate building.

10. See Drerup (1959), esp. 158–59, for the social basis of the phenomenon.

11. This important observation of "optical symmetry" was made by Bek (1980), esp. 17f., 181–89, and documented in more detail by Jung (1984). Symmetrical vistas could also be appreciated from the interior looking outward: see Pliny *ep.* 2.17.5.

12. See Wallace-Hadrill (1989) 63.

13. Examples of painted nature: Pompeii VI 1.10, C. di Sallustio; I 7.19 (at the rear of the C. del Ephebo); VI 8.22, 23, C. della Fontana Grande and Piccola; also VI 14.20, C. di Orfeo, where the figure of Orpheus dominates the scene of nature.

14. Cf. Bek (1980) 186, citing Horace *Epist.* 1.10.23: "laudatur domus longos quae prospicit agros." The C. del Fauno, di Pansa, del Labirinto, etc., at Pompeii give views centered on Vesuvius. The C. del Menandro combines all three types: the vista passes through the peristyle garden to apses painted with scenes of wild nature at the end of the peristyle; while above them from the front doorstep of the entrance is visible, neatly framed, a peak of the Monti Lattari.

15. Cf. Jung (1984) 77. For houses at Delos with some optical symmetry, see *Explorations à Délos* VIII b pl. XIII (Maison du Trident) and XXXVII pl. A (Maison des Tritons, dated to the late second century B.C., ibid.)

16. For example, Pliny *ep.* 3.5.8 on the elder Pliny; 3.1.4–9 on Spurinna; 9.36 on himself; Suetonius *Aug.* 78; *Vesp.* 21; Martial 4.8.

17. For example, the triclinium (8) of the C. degli Amanti (I 10.11) is reached directly from the atrium but is oriented toward the peristyle; the C. di Lucretius Fronto (V 4,a) has a finely decorated triclinium in the atrium, but this supplements one in the garden. The smaller the house, the less likely a clear atrium/peristyle distinction.

18. See above, Chap. 2, n. 12. Cf. Thébert (1987) 357f. on the social significance of the atrium house type.

19. For example, on a very small scale the C. di Fabius Amandio (I 7.23); or, in what is surely a craftsman's house, the C. del Fabbro (I 10.7). See below, Chap. 4.

20. Published by Strocka (1984); see my review, Wallace-Hadrill (1986a).

21. Strocka (1984) 33, 49f.

22. The question of upper bedrooms and who populated them needs further investigation. Note that the interpretation of Petronius *Sat.* 77, which locates the bedrooms of Trimalchio and his wife upstairs (McKay 1975, 113), depends on a questionable reading of the text.

23. Thus in the C. del Menandro the recess in the peristyle apparently containing a shrine of the ancestors has its late republican decoration preserved though the rest of the peristyle has been re-decorated: Maiuri (1933) 98–106; Ling (1983) 45.

24. See Laidlaw (1985) 42–46 for the deliberate preservation of first-style decoration. Maiuri (1954) needlessly identifies the peristyle area as a "gynaeceum." Jashemski (1979) 168–70 sees the house as a hotel; but it shows no affinities with other, more plausible hotels and inns: cf. Packer (1978).

25. For example, at Pompeii the C. dei Quadretti teatrali (I 6.11), or at Herculaneum the C. del Bicentenario (V 15). These might have provoked the barbs of Martial (12.50.7f.): "atria longa patent. sed nec cenantibus usquam/nec somno locus est. quam bene non habitas!"

26. See Meiggs (1960) 253f. for a clear account of the change; also Tamm (1963) 145–46. On the C. di Fortuna Annonaria at Ostia see Becatti (1923) 23–25; Boersma (1985) 47ff., 138ff.

27. See Saller (1982) 7ff.

28. Cf. Jung (1984) 116f.

29. See Thébert (1987) 353–87 for a fine discussion of the public face of the grand houses of Roman Africa in the post-Pompeian period.

30. See Tamm (1963) 189–205 on the varied terminology for dining rooms, rightly suggesting that many such rooms may have served "audience" functions.

31. Girouard (1978) 194f. discusses the use of strings of reception rooms in the eighteenth century; on growing differentiation of function in the nineteenth century, see 239, 300ff. Ariès (1962) 378–81 is excellent on the contrast between the seventeenth century "big house" and the growing privacy and differentiation of the eighteenth and nineteenth century house (see below, Chap. 5). The importance of Roman suites is observed by Scagliarini (1974/76) 24.

32. Plutarch *Luc.* 41.5.

33. Although unpublished, there is a plan and illustration of this suite in Barbet (1985) 241–43.

34. See Maiuri (1958) 306–10 for the suite and its adaptations.

35. Elia (1934) 282ff.

36. Petronius *Sat.* 77; the account of his slaves (*Sat.* 47, 53) implies a servile household larger than twenty bedrooms would accommodate.

37. Suetonius *Aug.* 72.

38. Pliny *ep.* 2.17.6–13 is a giddy succession of cubicula; 20–24, more, including a favorite for the Saturnalia; 5.6.21, 24, 28, 31 (two suites of four and three cubicula), 37.

39. See below, Chap. 5.

40. Richardson (1983) 61–71 identifies the pattern of linked suites, but his assertion that the women ate apart from the men is based on a misreading of passages (Isidorus 20.11.9, Valerius Maximus 2.1.2) contrasting the "ancestral" Roman habits to those of the historical period—women used to sit, but now they lie to eat with the men. The suggestion, repeated in Richardson (1988), is criticized by Ling (1991a), 251–52.

41. Cf. Carandini (1985) 1* 120; also Maiuri (1958) 325 (C. dell'Albergo). Also impressive is the cluster of cubicula around the oecus Corinthius of the C. del Labirinto. Coordinated oecus-cubiculum suites are noted by Scagliarini (1974/76) 23.

42. So too the excavators identify the bedroom (28) of the oecus Corinthius at Settefinestre as that of the dominus (Carandini 1985, 1** 41); doubtless "he" (i.e., over time a succession of domini) used it, but to share with his wife he might also have used rooms 3 and 25.

43. Maiuri (1954) 456–57; cf. de Vos (1982) 171.

44. See Girouard (1978) 144ff. for an illuminating discussion of etiquette and status as the organizing principles of the eighteenth-century "formal" house.

45. This point emerges forcibly from the examination of the historical development of the Menander block (I 10) at Pompeii: Ling (1983).

46. Evidence of this is abundant: note particularly the observations of Maiuri (1958) passim.

CHAPTER 4
HOUSES AND URBAN TEXTURE

1. See, for example, Barker and Lloyd (1991).

2. See Conticello in the exhibition catalogue *Rediscovering Pompeii*, 2ff.

3. Among art historians who *have* shown interest in the social aspect should be singled out Paul Zanker; note also Strocka (1975), (1984a). The works of Karl Schefold, especially (1952) and (1962), are also concerned with the implications of decoration for society, though I find his model of how art reflects society unconvincing (see Wallace-Hadrill 1983b, 182).

4. Minimal use of archaeological evidence is made in the (otherwise illuminating) studies of Andreau (1974), Castrén (1975), and recently Jongman (1988). The main (glowing) exception is Jashemski (1979). Also valuable is the recent dissertation by Gassner (1986).

5. The methodological weaknesses of Della Corte's work are well exposed by Castrén (1975) 31–33, cf. Andreau (1973a), and further by Mouritsen (1988) 13–27, criticizing Castrén in his turn (26).

6. So Maiuri (1958), 247f. Maiuri's views are popularly accessible in his general book on Pompeii (1960), esp. 72ff.; scholarly argument rests on his study of the last building phase of Pompeii (1942), esp. 162ff. For criticisms in detail, see below, Chap. 6.

7. A helpful introduction for nonmathematicians is Rowntree (1981). I am grateful to colleagues in the Department of Applied Statistics at Reading for advice and discussion; despite the possibility of using more sophisticated mathematical procedures to analyze my material, I felt the potential advantages were outweighed by the danger of confusing myself and my readers.

8. Nevertheless, this is the ultimate aim of the Consorzio Neapolis project (see below, n. 19). On the principles of sampling, see the salutary remarks of Hopkins (1983) 130ff.

9. There has been surprisingly little study of smaller houses, despite the example set by Packer (1975); see now Gassner (1986). Note the useful insights of Hoffmann (1984).

10. Note that this term is the invention of modern scholarship. For ancient usage of *insula* as a block of property, see Chap. 6.

11. *Regiones*, like *insulae*, are the product of modern categorization of the site. For the evidence of ancient ways of subdividing the city and providing orientation see Ling (1990). For brief details of the houses sampled see the Appendix.

12. Published by Maiuri (1927), (1929); Elia (1934).

13. See Ling (1983) for an interim report.

14. According to the directorate of Pompeii,

steps are now being taken to repair these much lamented omissions. But while this will provide descriptions of individual houses (esp. de Vos 1976 on I 9.13; 1975 on I 11.12, 14; Jashemski 1967 on I 11.11), it is no substitute for a true excavation report. Note also forthcoming volumes on I 6.15, I 7.1., and I 11.6, 7 in the "Häuser in Pompeji" series (Strocka 1988).

15. Insulae 15 and 16 were particularly well reported in *Notizie degli Scavi* for the years 1897 onward.

16. The finds are now in course of publication, in the series Soprintendenza Archaeologica di Pompei Cataloghi, starting with Scatozza Höricht (1986) and Conticello De' Spagnolis and De Carolis (1988), with a projected volume on jewelry by Scatozza Höricht. Welcome though this is, this form of publication perpetuates the divorce of finds from context.

17. Van der Poel (1987). Eschebach is sharply criticized, for example, on pp. 12, 14.

18. Bragantini et al. (1981–86).

19. On the work of the Consorzio Neapolis, see also Bruschini in the exhibition catalogue *Rediscovering Pompeii*, 106ff.

20. Cicero *de off.* 1.139, cf. *de domo* 116; Sallust *Cat.* 12.3, "villas . . . in urbium modum aedificatas"; Seneca *de ben.* 7.10.5, "aedificia privata laxitatem urbium magnarum vincentia," cf. *ep. mor.* 114.9; Suetonius *Aug.* 72.1; *Cal.* 37.2. Cf. D'Arms (1970) 40.

21. Lex Municipii Tarenti, *CIL* I 22 290 = *ILS* 6089 = *FIRA* 1.18, at lines 26ff.

22. Notable examples of deserted houses include I 6.13 (cf. Maiuri 1929, 430), I 9.8/9/10 (cf. *CTP* IIIA, 16). Evidence of earthquake damage and incomplete recovery in A.D. 79 is widespread (cf. Maiuri 1942, 216f). The importance of deserted houses is brought out in Phythian-Adams (1979) on late-medieval Coventry, a case where a city in steep economic decline had as many as 25 percent of its houses empty.

23. Maiuri (1942), esp. 161ff. Yet even without earthquake damage, constant adaptation of housing stock is to be expected; cf. the substantial changes now revealed in insula I 20 (Nappo 1988).

24. Maiuri (1927) 38–39.

25. The population of this type of accommodation has been much more thoroughly studied: by Packer (1971), Hermansen (1982) 17ff.; also Boersma (1985), questioning the basis of Packer's population estimates (cf. R. Ling, *JRS* 63 (1973): 279–81).

26. See Hoepfner and Schwander (1986), esp. 256ff., for an excellent survey.

27. Ibid., 257.

28. Eschebach (1975) 331 briefly characterizes some of the regional contrasts of Pompeii; cf. the recent and much fuller analysis by La Torre (1988).

29. Most recently discussed by Jongman (1988) 108–12.

30. Petronius *Sat.* 38: Diogenes was now prosperous enough to rent out his garret (*cenaculum*).

31. Gassner (1986) 32, 40.

32. A theme much stressed by Maiuri (1942) 162f.

33. Elia (1934) 320f. On the importance of furniture as a status indicator, see Zeldin (1980) 82: "What the people of this period [1848–1945] liked in their furniture was thus first of all a symbol of status. The poor had virtually no furniture; even the middle classes took a long time to collect more than the bare essentials—a bed, a table and cheap chairs."

34. Della Corte (1965) 251; see also Elia (1934) 317.

35. Jongman (1988) 163.

36. Robinson and Graham (1938) 209: loom weights found "in nearly every room of every house excavated." See also my remarks at (1986a) 434.

37. Maiuri (1958) 1:220, 252, 260, and passim.

38. So Cerulli Irelli (1974) 12–13 on a room in the C. del Colonnato Tuscanico.

39. Thus Michel (1990) 88 reports the C. dei Ceii stripped of finds, but is confident that it was inhabited.

40. See Elia (1934) 292–308 on the finds of I 10.7, a stunning collection meticulously recorded; 336–39 on the disappointing haul of I 10.11, esp. at 336: "The condition of complete confusion in which the material from the eruption presented itself, as far as several metres from the ground, the frequent presence of breaches made in series along each side of the house, in such a way as to render all the rooms intercommunicating, the disappearance of any trace of the furniture commonest in the houses of Pompeii, beds, portable tables and chairs, point clearly to the partial recovery of furniture . . . in a return after the catastrophe."

41. I am greatly indebted in this section to Pim Allison of Sydney University, who has persuaded me of both the importance and the difficulty of closer examination of the finds. Valuable results are to be expected from her own research into these questions.

42. The contrasts are brought out well by Jashemski (1979).

CHAPTER 5
HOUSES AND HOUSEHOLDS

1. E.g., Laslett and Wall (1972).
2. Flandrin (1979) 50ff.
3. Herlihy and Klapisch-Zuber (1985).
4. Phythian-Adams (1979).
5. Saller and Shaw (1984).
6. Flandrin (1979) 11ff.
7. Herlihy (1985) 1ff.
8. Saller (1984).
9. The distinction is that of Hajnal (1983).
10. Laslett and Wall (1972) 130ff.
11. Herlihy and Klapisch-Zuber (1985) 280ff.
12. Laslett (1965) 64.
13. Herlihy and Klapisch-Zuber (1985) 12f., underplaying, so it seems to me, the significance of this point.
14. Phythian-Adams (1979) 238ff.
15. For a conspectus of the literature, see Jongman (1988) 108ff. The lowest estimate is that of Russell (1985) 1ff.
16. Russell (1958) 60ff.
17. cf. Duncan-Jones (1982) 259ff.
18. Fletcher (1981), (1986) criticizing Narroll (1962) and Kolb (1985).
19. Hodder (1982) 193f.
20. Fiorelli (1873) 10ff.
21. Nissen (1877) 374–79.
22. Beloch (1898) 273–74.
23. Eschebach (1970) 60; cf. Jashemski (1979) 24 and n. 56.
24. See above, Chap. 4.
25. Cf. Ling (1983) 50–51.
26. So Andreau (1973b).
27. Kolb (1985).
28. Ibid. 584.
29. Clarke (1972) 32f.
30. Ibid. 34.
31. As by Packer (1975).
32. Frier (1980); cf. Hermansen (1982).
33. See, for example, Boethius (1934).
34. See below, Chap. 6.
35. Dig. 32.91.4–6.
36. Dig. 8.2.26.
37. Dig. 8.4.6.
38. Papinian Dig. 8.2.36.
39. See Dig. 7.8. passim.
40. Dig. 7.1.13.7.
41. See Dig. 7.8.1–4 for the whole dispute.
42. Dig. 7.8.4.1.

43. Dig. 7.8.17.
44. cf. Dig. 18.6.19.
45. Dig. 8.2.41.
46. CIL 4.138: "insula Arriana Polliana [C]n. Al[le]i Nigidi Mai. locantur ex Iulis primis tabernae cum pergulis suis et c[e]nacula equestria et domus. conductor convenito Primum [C]n. Al[le]i Nigidi Mai ser(vum)." On Nigidius Maius see van Buren (1947).
47. Studied by Peterse (1985).
48. CIL 4.1136: "In praediis I[uli]ae Sp. f. Felicis / locantur / balneum venerium et nongentum, tabernae, pergulae,/ cenacula, ex idibus Aug. primis in idus Aug. sextas, anno[s co]ntinuo[s qu]inque. / s.q.d.l.e.n.c." Discussed by Maiuri (1948). *Nongentum* remains hard to explain. The final letters may be extrapolated, as did Fiorelli, as "si quinquennium decucurrit, locatio erit nudo consensu."
49. Della Corte (1965) nos. 80–82, 94.
50. Castrén (1975) 31.
51. Plautus *Amph.* 863.
52. Ennius *Ann.* 30.51 (Skutsch).
53. Livy 39.14.2.
54. Strocka (1984a) 49–50.
55. Maiuri (1958) 417.
56. Boyce (1937); Orr (1978). See also Fröhlich (1991) for an art-historical study.
57. Pliny *ep.* 2.17.21.
58. Tacitus *Dial.* 29; see above, Chap. 3.
59. Suetonius *Tib.* 7.2.
60. *Declamationes minores* 277: *salvo pudore*.
61. Tibullus 1.3.26; Ovid *Fast.* 2.328.
62. Tacitus *Hist.* 5.5: "alienarum concubitu abstinent, inter se nihil inlicitum."
63. Strocka (1991) 135–36.
64. Ibid. 136.
65. The bed alcoves may or may not be considered wide enough for two sleepers (1.14m).
66. Maiuri (1942), (1958).
67. Livy 1.57.
68. Asconius *In Milonem* 43.
69. Cato *Rust.* 12 pr.
70. See above, Chap. 1, n. 37.

CHAPTER 6
HOUSES AND TRADE

1. I owe this apt citation to John Rich.
2. I owe the contrast of door types to Ray Laurence, whose forthcoming study has much light to cast on the question.

3. Weber (1959), esp. 197ff., gives a clear statement of the case, though he does not, as Finley (1981) insists, do justice to the nuances of his position.

4. Frank (1940) 252–66; Rostovzeff (1957), esp. 72f.

5. Moeller (1976), demolished by Jongman (1988) 155ff.

6. See D'Arms (1981).

7. cf. Miskimin, Herlihy, and Udovitch (1977).

8. Clark and Slack (1976) 157; Clark (1984) 22f.

9. Spinazzola (1953) 190–93; cf. Rostovzeff (1957) 100, pl. 16.

10. Schulz-Falkenthal (1971); Franklin (1980) 21f.; Angelone (1986); Jongman (1988) 283ff; see also Mouritsen (1988) 65–68 for caution.

11. Bove (1984).

12. Garnsey (1976).

13. Maiuri's views remain the established orthodoxy: cf. Cerulli Irelli (1974) 74, seeing confirmation of the thesis of commercial invasion and decline in the C. del Colonnato Tuscanico.

14. Castrén (1975).

15. Andreau (1973b).

16. Including most recently Gassner (1986).

17. Ibid. 25.

18. Cf. Ling (1983) 50–51.

19. Well analyzed by Mouritsen (1988) 47ff.

20. See Pagano (1987) for a recent programma opposite the C. del Bicentenario.

21. Tran Tam Tinh (1988) 121ff.

22. Ovid *Met.* 1.173: "plebs habitat diversa locis."

23. See Morel (1987), esp. 133ff.

24. Livy 26.27.2.

25. See Platner and Ashby (1927) 504–5.

26. Livy 39.44.7.

27. As argued by Boethius (1934) 164.

28. Livy 44.16.10: "lanienasque et tabernas coniunctas."

29. Livy 3.48.5.

30. Varro ap. Nonius 532.

31. Pliny *NH* 21.8.

32. See Carandini (1988), 360–73, (1989), and (1990) for preliminary reports.

33. See Plutarch *Gaius Gracchus* 12.1, *Marius* 32.1. I owe these references to John Rich.

34. E.g., Pomponius at Dig. 7.8.16.1, 50.16.166.

35. See above, Chap. 5, n. 46.

36. Discussed above, Chap. 5.

37. Dig. 7.1.27.1.

38. See Harris (1980).

39. Dig. 14.4.14–16.

40. Dig. 33.7.13.

41. Dig. 31.88.3.

42. Dig. 5.3.39.1, 25.1.6, 50.16.79.

43. See below, Chap. 7.

44. Ulpian at Dig. 39.2.40 pr.: "non immoderata cuiusque luxuria subsequenda."

45. Dig. 47.10.26; cf. Hermansen (1982).

46. See Bates (1983) on Silchester; Thébert (1987) on Africa.

47. As Garnsey (1976) 129f. pointed out, cf. Etienne (1960) pl. 3.

48. Eschebach (1975) 331 f.

49. Jashemski (1979) 24 offers a histogram of land use.

50. Raper (1977), cf. (1979).

51. La Torre (1988) 75–102 is a useful discussion, even if the database from which it starts is misleading.

52. Gassner (1986) 1ff. offers good discussion of the usage of the term *taberna*, which is used to describe shops, workshops, 'taverns,' and in general the dwellings of the poor (e.g., Horace *Odes* 1.4.13f.: "pallida Mors aequo pulsat pede pauperum tabernas regumque turris"). Further enquiry into Roman terminology is needed here, particularly into the boundaries between *tabernae/tabernarii* and *officinae/opifices*.

53. Trades that have attracted close study are the most visible: Mayeske (1972) on bakeries; Moeller (1976) on the wool trade; Cerulli Irelli (1977) on lamp manufacture; Curtis (1979) and (1988) on *garum* (fish sauce) production; and the particularly good survey of metal workshops by Gralfs (1988).

54. See Kleberg (1957); Packer (1978); Jashemski (1979) 167f.

55. The crucial role of women in the world of work is brought out in Kampen (1981).

56. See Strocka (1991).

57. Ibid. 69–70.

58. Ibid. 134–35.

CHAPTER 7
LUXURY AND STATUS

1. "cupiditatibus principum et vitiis infici solet tota civitas." Roman luxury as a social phenomenon still awaits proper treatment. There have been several recent accounts of censorial involvement with luxury, including Clemente (1981), Slob (1986), Astin (1988), Baltrusch (1989); see also La Rocca

(1986). Broader and more sociological approaches are adumbrated in Miles (1987) and Edwards (1993).

2. Ovid *Fast.* 6.642. On the incident, cf. Zanker (1988a) 137; for the principle, 129: "The emperor and his family set the standard in every aspect of life, from moral values to hairstyles. And this was true not only for the upper classes, but for the whole of society." The importance of social diffusion of luxury is fully grasped by Zanker, who in a series of works points the way to further research. See esp. (1979) on Pompeian housing, (1983) on municipal bourgeoisie. His recent essay on Pompeii (1988b) is primarily concerned with the public buildings of the city.

3. Tacitus *Ann.* 3.55. For the topic of imperial model-setting see Friedländer (1908) 1:30ff.; Wallace-Hadrill (1983a) 177ff.

4. For Pliny's views on luxury see Wallace-Hadrill (1990).

5. Thus Macmullen (1974) 88ff., stressing the "verticality" of Roman social relationships and minimizing any "middle" class.

6. See Thirsk (1978), esp. 106–32, for social diversity and differentiation; 12ff. for moralizing protest.

7. E.g., Hodder (1982), Bradley (1984), Appadurai (1986).

8. Friedländer (1908) 2:131ff.

9. This account of luxury is indebted to Douglas and Isherwood (1980) and Elias (1983); for a historical sketch see Sekora (1977).

10. The model, with its impact on changing artistic fashions, is lucidly set out by Morris (1987) 16f., drawing on Miller (1985) 184ff.

11. Von Hesberg and Zanker (1987) reveals the potential of this enormous field.

12. D'Arms (1970) remains basic on the social context.

13. Montias (1982).

14. Benedict (1985).

15. Zeldin (1980) 98.

16. Bourdieu (1984). I confess to finding this whole study, closely though it bears on my own, impenetrable.

17. Cato fr. 175. Malcovati = Plutarch *Cat. Mai.* 4.4; cf. fr. 185 for Cato's criticisms of others.

18. Varro *RR* 1.2.10; cf. 1.13.7; against frescoes and mosaic floors in general, 3.1.10, 3.2.4, etc.

19. Papirius Fabianus in Seneca *Controv.* 2.1.13; Pliny *NH* 35.118.

20. Dig. 8.2.13.1.

21. Dig. 39.2.40.

22. Dig. 18.1.34, 6.1.23.3.

23. I see no way of doing this without entering the slippery territory of "connoisseurship." This has not deterred me from registering the occasional personal reaction; but these have no bearing on my statistical analysis.

24. The classic study is still Pernice (1938). de Vos (1984) comments on the rarity of mosaics, which constitute on her figures 2.5 percent of the available floor space (162). On the lithostrota decried by moralists see Dondere (1987), still not wholly clarifying the account of the revolution in fashion dated to Sulla by Pliny *NH* 36.184.

25. See the discussion in Fröhlich (1991).

26. Gassner (1986) 13 rightly suggests that the renting of shops must have been, to judge by literary sources, the normal pattern.

27. Vitruvius 6.5.1–2; see above, Chap. 1.

28. Shop decoration is well discussed by Gassner (1986) 35f. On her reckoning, up to half the shops in Pompeii have some traces of plaster; but this is rarely anything more than simple white, or a high red socle with white above. See the study of lararium paintings by Fröhlich (1991).

29. Maiuri (1958) 238.

30. See Cerulli Irelli (1974) 21–22.

31. Illustrated by de Vos (1977) pls. 54–55. See Gassner (1986) for the tiny handful of other "nicely" decorated shops; see also Fröhlich (1991) 211ff.

32. See above, Chap. 2.

33. For imitations of earlier styles see Schefold (1962) 140ff.; Laidlaw (1985) 42–46; Ehrhardt (1987) 133ff.

34. I am grateful to Jean-Paul Descoeudres who, by pointing out the rarity of early decorative styles in smaller houses, suggested this approach to me.

35. Confirmed by Ganschow (1989) 221ff.

36. Moreover, the distinction between styles III and IV is unusually fluid in Herculaneum; see Moorman (1987).

37. Note however the fragments of first-style decoration emerging in houses of middling size in the blocks near the amphitheater, e.g., I 20.4: Nappo (1988) 189. There is also a fair scatter of first style in the houses in Regio I south of the Via di Castricio that fall outside this survey.

38. Contrast Beard and Crawford (1985) 20: "The explosion of culture did not involve the poor

or the lower classes, as either producers or consumers. It involved, rather, progressively broader bands of the Roman and Italian elite." Even for the Republic, this statement is too uncompromising.

39. On the popularization of wallpaper see Zeldin (1980) 81f.

40. Schefold (1962) 124, characteristic of the tone of the chapter on "Vespasianic" decoration. However, the concept of "kitsch" may be precisely appropriate, insofar as it involves the popularization of aristocratic taste: see the interesting study by Moles (1971). Maiuri took an equally dim view of the vulgarization of imperial art; e.g., (1942) 216: "al mutamento e pervertimento di gusto nel genere e nello stile della decorazione degli ambienti."

41. E.g., Barbet (1981); Strocka (1984a), esp. 37f. on "Filigranborten"; Ehrhardt (1987) passim; and much of the work of M. de Vos.

42. Zanker (1979).

43. See particularly the various contributions to *Pictores per Provincias* (1987). Other material is succinctly assembled in Ling (1991a) 168–74, with bibliography at 230–31.

44. So Barbet (1987), well summarizing the results of much careful work.

CHAPTER 8
EPILOGUE

1. See esp. Andreau (1974); Jongman (1988).

2. See Bove (1984).

3. Described by Maiuri (1946b). I am grateful to my colleague Jane Gardner for invaluable discussion of the legalities of these dossiers.

4. The documents themselves were published by V. Arangio-Ruiz and G. Pugliese Carratelli in six issues of *Parola del Passato*: 1 (1946) 379–85; 3 (1948) 165–84; 8 (1953) 455–63; 9 (1954) 54–74; 10 (1955) 448–77; 16 (1961) 66–73.

5. E.g., Tabulae Herculanenses (TH) 4, a contract between Q Iunius Theophilus and Tetteius Severus. Did it or did it not come from V.22, where a signet ring of Q Iunius Philadespotes was found? There is another apparent muddle: TH 2 should be part of the Cominius Primus dossier from V.22, but is said to come from the C. del Bicentenario.

6. Maiuri (1946b) 375 in fact reports further finds in H IV.17–18, the C. del Larario di legno (V.31), C. dell'Alcova (IV.3–4), and C. dei due Atri (VI.28–29). These have apparently never been published.

7. See *Parola del Passato* 3 (1948): 165–84 for the text, revised by Arangio-Ruiz (1974) 552–70; cf. 327–44, 375–81, 431–39. Most recently see Weaver (1991), with previous discussion.

8. Suetonius *gram.* 21. On alumni see Rawson (1956); Sigismund Nielsen (1987).

9. TH 16.

10. TH 19, 20.

11. Gardner (1986b) well stresses the imporance of the oral element of oath-taking.

12. TH 2, 33, 66, 68.

13. TH 2, 53.

14. TH 2: "testatus est et oste[n]dit ianuas sibi lapidatas quod tran[s]paruit," which Arangio-Ruiz (1974) 304 understands as "stoned the doors to the point that one could establish that the light passed through," perhaps straining the Latin. Arangio-Ruiz initially assumed (ibid.), with Maiuri, that Cominius was the owner of the Casa del Bicentenario and that these were the doors that were stoned, but he later retracted this view when it became clear that Cominius belonged in V.22 (ibid. 553).

15. TH 7, 8, 52, 54, 90 (all Venustus); 43 (Felix).

16. Maiuri (1958) 472n. 51.

17. See Weaver (1990), (1991).

18. So Arangio-Ruiz (1974) 535–51.

19. See, e.g., D'Arms (1981) 121ff.

20. On the identity of the building see Guadagno (1983).

21. Published by Guadagno (1977).

22. Guadagno (1978) 137.

23. Elegantly studied by Mack Smith (1977); on the use of archaeology see Manacorda and Tamassia (1985).

24. Pliny *NH* 33.134; 36.60.

25. Zanker (1976) 14; cf. Zanker (1988a) 5–9 on the Hellenization of Oscan Pompeii.

GLOSSARY

Aedificatio: Construction of private residence (*aedes*).

Alae: "Wing" rooms flanking *tablinum*.

Atrium: Central hall of Roman house.

Caupona: Tavern; inn.

Cenaculum: Upper room/apartment.

Clientela: Clientele; group of dependents.

Cubiculum: Bedroom.

Diaeta: Dayroom; living room.

Dignitas: Dignity; social respect/standing.

Dominus: Master/owner, especially of house (*domus*).

Domus: House; household.

Eques (pl. *Equites*): Member of equestrian order; "knight."

Familia: Family. Technically the Roman *familia* covers all persons, including slaves, under the legal control of the paterfamilias.

Fastigium: Peak or pinnacle, especially top of pediment.

Habitatio: Legal right of habitation in a house.

Horreum: Storeroom, especially granary.

Hospitium: Guest house.

Impluvium: Rainwater basin in center of *atrium*.

Ingenuus/Ingenua: Freeborn citizen (male/female).

Insula: Block of apartments under single ownership; literally, "island."

Insularius: Caretaker of *insula*.

Libertinus: Freedman; freed slave; person of servile extraction.

Libertus/Liberta: Freed slave (male/female).

Negotium: Business; opposite of *otium*, leisure.

Oecus: Reception room (see also *oikos*).

Officina ferraria: Ironmonger's shop/workshop.

Officina lignaria: Carpenter's shop/workshop.

Officina olearia: Oil mill.

Officina sutoria: Cobbler's shop/workshop.

Officina textoria: Weaver's shop/workshop.

Officina tinctoria: Dyer's shop/workshop.

Officina vasaria: Potter's shop/workshop.

Oikos: House (Greek); used also to refer to reception room.

Patrimonium: Inheritance; paternal estate.

Pinacothecae: Picture galleries.

Popina: Bar; drinking house.

Princeps: Leading member of society, including emperor.

Taberna: Shop/workshop; tavern.

Tablinum: Record room; dominant reception area of *atrium*.

Thermopolium: Dubious term applied by archaeologists to refer to a bar or drinking house, properly *popina*.

Triclinium: Dining room: literally, "three-couch room."

Vestibulum: Entrance lobby.

BIBLIOGRAPHY

Allroggen-Bedel, A. 1974. *Maskendarstellungen in der römisch-kampanischen Wandmalerei*. Munich.

Andreae, B., and H. Kyrieleis (eds.). 1975. *Neue Forschungen in Pompeji*. Recklinghausen.

Andreau, J. 1973a. "Remarques sur la société pompéienne," *Dialoghi di Archeologia* 7:213–54.

———. 1973b. "Histoire des séismes et histoire économique: le tremblement de terre de Pompei (62 ap. J.-C.)." *Annales E.S.C.* 28: 369–95.

———. 1974. *Les affaires de Monsieur Jucundus*. Coll. Ec. Fr. Rome. Rome.

Angelone, R. 1986. *L'officina coactiliaria di M. Vecilio Verecondo a Pompei*. Naples.

Appadurai, A. (ed.). 1986. *The Social Life of Things: Commodities in Cultural Perspective*. Cambridge.

Arangio-Ruiz, V. 1974. *Studi epigrafici e papirologici*, ed. L. Bove. Naples.

Ardener, S. (ed.). 1981. *Women and Space. Ground Rules and Social Maps*. Oxford University Women's Studies Committee, vol. 5. London.

Ariès, P. 1973. *Centuries of Childhood*. 2d ed. Trans. R. Baldick. Harmondsworth.

Astin, A. 1988. "Regimen morum." *Journal of Roman Studies* 78:14–34.

Bagnani, G. 1954. "The house of Trimalchio." *American Journal of Philology* 75:16–39.

Baltrusch, E. 1989. *Regimen Morum. Die Regelmentierung des Privatlebens der Senatoren und Ritter in der römischen Republik und frühen Kaiserzeit*. Munich.

Barbet, A. 1981. "Les bordures ajourées dans le IVe style de Pompéi." *Mélanges École Française Rome* 93:917–98.

———. 1985. *La Peinture murale romaine: les styles décoratifs pompéiens*. Paris.

———. 1987. "La diffusion des Ier, IIe et IIIe styles pompéiens en Gaule." in *Pictores per Provincias*, 7–28.

Barbet, A., and C. Allag. 1972. "Techniques de préparation des parois dans la peinture murale romaine." *Mélanges École Française Rome* 84:992–1006.

Barker, G., and J. A. Lloyd (eds.). 1991. *Roman Landscapes: Archaeological Survey in the Mediterranean Region*. Rome.

Bastet, F. L., and M. de Vos. 1979. *Proposta per una classificazione del terzo stile pompeiano*. Arch. Stud. Nederlands Instituut te Rome, IV. The Hague.

Bates, W. 1983. "A spatial analysis of Roman Silchester," *Scottish Archaeological Review* 2 (2): 134–43.

Beard, M., and M. Crawford. 1985. *Rome in the Late Republic*. London.

Becatti, G. 1948. *Case ostiensi del Tardo Impero*. Rome.

Becker, W. 1838. *Gallus oder römischen Scenen aus der Zeit des Augustus*. 2d ed. rev. H. Göll. Berlin, 1880.

Bek, L. 1980. *Towards Paradise on Earth*. Analecta Romana IX. Rome.

Beloch, J. 1898. "Le città dell'Italia antica." *Atene e Roma* 1:257–78.

Benedict, P. 1985. "Towards the comparative study of the popular market for art: the ownership of paintings in seventeenth-century Metz." *Past and Present* 109:100–117.

Beyen, H. G. 1938, 1960. *Die pompejanische Wanddekoration vom zweiten bis zum vierten Stil*. Vol. I (1938); vol. II.1 (1960). The Hague.

Bezerra de Meneses, U. T. 1984. "Essai de lecture sociologique de la décoration murale des maisons d'habitation hellénistiques à Delos." *Dialoghi di Archeologia*, 3d ser. 2:77–88.

Bieber, M. 1961. *A History of the Greek and Roman Theatre*. Princeton.

Boersma, J. S. 1985. *Amoenissima Civitas: Block V. ii at Ostia: description and analysis of its visible remains*. Assen.

Boethius, A. 1934. "Remarks on the development of domestic architecture in Rome." *American Journal of Archaeology* 24:158–70.

Bourdieu, P. 1973. "The Berber house." In M. Douglas (ed.), *Rules and Meanings: The Anthropology of Everyday Knowledge*, 98–110. Harmondsworth.

———. 1984. *Distinction. A Social Critique of the Judgement of Taste*. Trans. R. Nice. Cambridge, Mass.

Bove, L. 1984. *Documenti di operazioni finanziarie dall'archivio dei Sulpici*. Naples.

Boyce, G. K. 1937. *Corpus of the Lararia of Pompeii*. MAAR, vol. 14. Rome.

Bradley, K. R. 1991. *Discovering the Roman Family*. Oxford.

Bradley, R. 1984. *The Social Foundations of Prehistoric Britain: themes and variations in the archaeology of power.* London.

Bragantini, I., M. de Vos, F. Parise Badoni, and V. Sampaolo (eds.). 1981–86. *Pitture e Pavimenti di Pompei.* Repertorio delle fotografie del Gabinetto Fotografico Nazionale. Parte I: Regioni I, II, III (1981); II: Regioni V, VI (1983); III: Regioni VII, VIII, IX (1986). Rome.

Braund, S. H. 1989. "City and country in Roman satire." In S. H. Braund (ed.), *Satire and Society in Ancient Rome,* 23–47. Exeter.

Bruneau, P. et al., 1970. *L'Ilot de la Maison des Comédiens.* Explorations archéologiques de Délos, XXVIII. Paris.

Bruno, V. J. 1969. "Antecedents of the Pompeian first style." *American Journal of Archaeology* 73:305–17.

Carandini, A. 1985. *Settefinestre: una villa schiavistica nell'Etruria romana.* 3 vols. Modena.

———. 1988. *Schiavi in Italia. Gli strumenti pensanti dei Romani fra tarda Repubblica e medio Impero.* Rome.

———. 1989. "Le origini di Roma." *Archeo. Attualità del Passato* 48 (February): 48–59.

———. 1990. "Il palatino e le aree residenziali." In *La Grande Roma dei Tarquinii.* Catalogo della mostra, Roma, 12 giugno–30 settembre 1990) 97–99. Rome.

Carandini, A., A. Ricci, M. de Vos. 1982. *Filosofiana. The villa of Piazza Armerina.* Palermo.

Carettoni, G. 1961. "Due nuovi ambienti dipinti sul Palatino." *Bolletino d'Arte* 46:188–99.

———. 1983. *Das Haus des Augustus auf dem Palatin.* Mainz.

Castiglione Morelli del Franco, V., and R. Vitale. 1989. "L'*insula* 8 della *Regio* I: un campione d'indagine socio-economica." *Rivista di studi pompeiani* 3:185–221.

Castrén, P. 1975. *Ordo Populusque Pompeianus. Polity and Society in Roman Pompeii.* Rome.

Cerulli Irelli, G. 1971. *Le Pitture della Casa dell'Atrio a Mosaico.* Mon. Pit. Ant. It. III Ercolano I. Rome.

———. 1974. *La Casa "del Colonnato Tuscanico" ad Ercolano.* Mem. Att. Arch. Lett. Bell. Art. Napoli, vol. 7. Naples.

———. 1977. "Officina di lucerne fittili a Pompei." In M. Annecchino et al. (eds.), *L'instrumentum domesticum di Ercolano e Pompei nella prima età imperiale,* 53–72. Rome.

Clark, P. (ed.). 1984. *The Transformation of English Provincial Towns.* London.

Clark, P., and P. Slack (eds.). 1976. *English Towns in Transition 1500–1700.* Oxford.

Clarke, J. I. 1972. *Population Geography.* 2d ed. Oxford.

Clemente, G. 1981. "Le leggi sul lusso e la società romana." In A. Giardina and A. Schiavone (eds.), *Società romana e produzione schiavistica,* 3:1–14. Rome.

Coarelli, F. 1980. *Roma.* Guide archeologiche Laterza. Bari.

———. 1983. "Architettura sacra e architettura privata nella tarda repubblica." In *Architecture et Société.* Coll. Ec. Fr. Rome, vol. 66, 191–217. Rome.

———. 1984. "Discussione." *Dialoghi di Archaeologia* n.s. 2:152–54.

Cohen, B. 1975. "La notion d'ordo dans la Rome antique." *Bulletin Association Budé,* ser. 4 2:259ff.

Crook, J. A. 1955. *Consilium Principis.* Cambridge.

Curtis, R. I. 1979. "The garum shop of Pompeii." *Cronache Pompeiane* 5:5–23.

———. 1984. "A personalised floor-mosaic from Pompeii." *AJA* 88:557–66.

———. 1988. "A. Umbricius Scaurus of Pompeii." In R. I. Curtis (ed.), *Studia Pompeiana et Classica in honor of W. I. Jashemski,* 1:19–49. New Rochelle.

D'Arms, J. H. 1970. *Romans on the Bay of Naples: a social and cultural study of the villas and their owners from 150 B.C. to A.D. 400.* Cambridge, Mass.

———. 1981. *Commerce and Social Standing in Ancient Rome.* Cambridge, Mass.

D'Arms, J. H., and E. C. Kopff (eds.). 1980. *Roman Seaborne Commerce: Studies in Archaeology and History.* MAAR 36. Rome.

Daunton, M. J. 1983a. "Public space and private space. The Victorian city and the working-class household." In D. Fraser and A. Sutcliffe (eds.), *The Pursuit of Urban History,* 212–33.

———. 1983b. *House and Home in the Victorian City: Working-class Housing 1850–1914.* London.

De' Spagnolis, M. Conticello, and E. De Carolis. 1988. *Le lucerne di bronzo di Ercolano e Pompei.* Vatican.

de Vos, A., and M. de Vos. 1982. *Pompei, Ercolano, Stabia.* Guide archeologiche Laterza. Bari.

de Vos, M. 1975. "Scavi Nuovi sconosciuti (I 11,14; I 11,12): pitture memorande di Pompei." *Mededelingen Nederlands Instituut Rome* 37:47–85.

———. 1976. "Scavi Nuovi sconosciuti (I 9,13): pitture e pavimenti della Casa di Cerere a Pompei." *Mededelingen Nederlands Instituut Rome* 38:37–75.

————. 1977. "Primo stile figurato e maturo quarto stile negli scarichi." *Mededelingen Nederlands Instituut Rome* 39:29–47.

————. 1980. *L'Egittomania in pitture e mosaici Romani-Campani della prima età imperiale.* Et. Prel. Rel. Or. Emp. Rom., vol. 84. Leiden.

————. 1981. "La bottega di pittori di via di Castricio." In *Pompei 1748–1980: i tempi della documentazione,* 119–30. Rome and Pompei.

————. 1984. "Pavimenti e mosaici." In Zevi (1984), 161–76.

de Vries, J. 1984. *European Urbanization 1500–1800.* London.

Della Corte, M. 1965. *Case ed abitanti di Pompei.* 3d ed. Naples.

Descoeudres, J.-P. 1987. "The Australian expedition to Pompeii: contributions to the chronology of the fourth Pompeian style." In *Pictores per Provincias,* 135–47.

Dondere, M. 1987. "Die antiken Pavimenttypen und ihre Benennung." *Jahrbuch des deutschen archäologischen Instituts* 102:365–77.

Douglas, M., and B. Isherwood. 1980. *The World of Goods. Towards an anthropology of consumption.* Harmondsworth.

Drack, W. 1950. *Die römische Wandmalerie der Schweiz.* Monog. zur Ur- und Frühgesch. der Schweiz VIII. Basel.

Drerup, H. 1959. "Bildraum und Realraum in der römischen Architektur." *Römische Mitteilungen* 66:147–74.

Duncan-Jones, R. 1982. *The Economy of the Roman Empire.* 2d ed. Cambridge.

Dwyer, E. J. 1982. *Pompeian Domestic Sculpture. A study of five Pompeian houses and their contents.* Rome.

Eck, W. 1984. "Senatorial self-representation: developments in the Augustan period." In F. Millar and E. Segal (eds.), *Caesar Augustus: Seven Aspects,* 129–67. Oxford.

Edwards, C. 1993. *The Politics of Immorality in Ancient Rome.* Cambridge.

Ehrhardt, W. 1987. *Stilgeschichtliche Untersuchungen an römischen Wandmalereien von der späten Republik bis zur Zeit Neros.* Mainz.

Elia, O. 1934. "Relazione sullo scavo dell'Insula X della Regio I (1)." *Notizie degli Scavi* 1934:264–344.

Elias, N. 1983. *The Court Society.* Oxford. Translation of *Die höfische Gesellschaft,* 1969. Darmstadt.

Engemann, J. 1967. *Architekturdarstellungen des frühen zweiten Stils.* xii. Heidelberg.

Eschebach, H. 1970. *Die städtebauliche Entwicklung des antiken Pompeji* Röm. Mitt. Suppl. 17. Heidelberg.

————. 1975. "Erläuterungen zum Plan Pompejis." In Andreae and Kyrieleis (1975), 331–38.

————. 1979. *Die Stabianer Thermen in Pompeji.* Berlin.

Etienne, R. 1960. *Le quartier nord-est de Volubilis.* Paris.

Finley, M. I. 1981. "The ancient city: from Fustel de Coulanges to Max Weber and beyond." In *Economy and Society in Ancient Greece,* 3–23. London.

————. 1985. *The Ancient Economy,* 2d ed. London.

Fiorelli, G. 1873. *Relazione sugli Scavi di Pompei dal 1861 al 1872.* Naples.

Fittschen, K. 1976. "Zur Herkunft und Entstehung des 2. Stils," In P. Zanker (ed.), *Hellenismus in Mittelitalien,* 2:539–63. Göttingen.

Flandrin, J. L. 1979. *Families in Former Times. Kinship, Household and Sexuality.* Cambridge.

Fletcher, R. 1981. "People and space: a case study on material behaviour." In I. Hodder, G. Isaac, and N. Hammond (eds.), *The Pattern of the Past,* 97–128. Cambridge.

————. 1986. "Settlement archaeology: worldwide comparisons." *World Archaeology* 18:59–83.

Frank, T. 1940. *Economic Survey of Ancient Rome.* Vol. 5. Baltimore.

Franklin, J. L. 1980. *Pompeii: the Electoral Programmata, Campaigns and Politics, A.D. 71–79.* MAAR, vol. 28. Rome.

Friedländer, L. 1908, 1913. *Roman Life and Manners under the Early Empire.* 4 vols. Trans. L. A. Magnus and J. H. Freese. London.

————. 1922. *Darstellungen aus der Sittengeschichte Roms in der Zeit von August bis zum Ausgang der Antonine.* 10th ed. Leipzig.

Frier, B. W. 1980. *Landlords and Tenants in Imperial Rome.* Princeton.

Fröhlich, T. 1991. *Lararien- und Fassadenbilder in den Vesuvstädten. Untersuchungen zur "volkstümlichen" pompejanischen Malerei.* Röm. Mitt. Suppl. 32. Mainz.

Ganschow, T. 1989. *Untersuchungen zur Baugeschichte in Herculaneum.* Bonn.

Gardner, J. F. 1986a. *Women in Roman Law and Society.* London.

————. 1986b. "Proofs of status in the Roman world." *Bulletin of the Institute of Classical Studies* 33:1–14.

Garnsey, P.D.A. 1976. "Urban property investment." in M. I. Finley (ed.), *Studies in Roman Property,* 123–36. Cambridge.

Garnsey, P.D.A., and R. Saller. 1987. *The Roman Empire. Economy, Society and Culture*. London.

Gassner, V. 1986. *Die Kaufläden in Pompeii*. Ph.D. diss., Vienna, no. 178.

Girouard, M. 1978. *Life in the English Country House. A Social and Architectural History*. New Haven and London.

Gralfs, B. 1988. *Metallverarbeitende Produktionsstätten in Pompeji*. BAR Int. Ser. 433. Oxford.

Grimal, P. 1943. *Les Jardins Romains à la fin de la république et aux deux premiers siècles de l'empire*. Paris.

Gros, P. 1978. *Architecture et société à Rome et en Italie centro-méridionale aux deux derniers siècles de la République*. Brussels.

Guadagno, G. 1977. "Frammenti inediti di albi degli Augustali." *Cronache Ercolanesi* 7:114–23.

———. 1978. "Supplemento epigrafico ercolanese." *Cronache Ercolanesi* 8:132–55.

———. 1983. "Herculanensium Augustalium sedes." *Cronache Ercolanese* 13:159–73.

Hajnal, J. 1983. "Two kinds of pre-industrial household formation system." In R. Wall, J. Robin, and P. Laslett (eds.), *Family Forms in Historic Europe*, 65–104. Cambridge.

Harris, W. V. 1980. "Roman terracotta lamps: the organisation of an industry." *Journal of Roman Studies* 70:126–45.

Heers, J. 1977. *Family Clans in the Middle Ages*. Amsterdam, New York, Oxford.

Herlihy, D. 1977. "Family and property in Renaissance Florence." In Miskimin, Herlihy, and Udovitch (1977), 3–24.

———. 1985. *Medieval Households*. Cambridge, Mass.

Herlihy, D., and C. Klapisch-Zuber. 1985. *Tuscans and their Families. A Study of the Florentine Catasto of 1427*. New Haven and London.

Hermansen, G. 1982. *Ostia. Aspects of Roman City Life*. Alberta.

Hill, D. K. 1981. "Roman domestic garden sculpture." In E. B. MacDougall and W. F. Jashemski (eds.), *Ancient Roman Gardens*. Dumbarton Oaks Colloquium on the History of Landscape Architecture VII, 83–94. Washington.

Hingley, R. 1989. *Rural Settlement in Roman Britain*. London.

Hodder, I. 1982. *Symbols in Action. Ethnoarchaeological Studies of Material Culture*. Cambridge.

Hoepfner, W., and E.-L. Schwandner, 1986. *Haus und Stadt im klassischen Griechenland*. Munich.

Hoffmann, A. 1984. "L'architettura privata." In Zevi (1984), 105–18.

Hopkins, K. 1978. "Economic growth and towns in classical antiquity." In P. Abrams and E. A. Wrigley (eds.), *Towns in Societies: Essays in Economic History and Historical Sociology*, 35–77. Cambridge.

———. 1983. *Death and Renewal*. Cambridge.

Jashemski, W. 1967. "The Caupona of Euxinus at Pompeii." *Archaeology* 20:37–44.

———. 1979. *The Gardens of Pompeii, Herculaneum and the Villas destroyed by Vesuvius*. New York.

Jones, J. E., L. H. Sackett, and A. J. Graham. 1962. "The Dema house in Attica." *Annual British School Athens* 57:75–114.

Jongman, W. 1988. *The Economy and Society of Pompeii*. Amsterdam.

Jung, F. 1984. "Gebaute Bilder." *Antike Kunst* 27:71–122.

Kampen, N. 1981. *Image and Status: Roman Working Women in Ostia*. Berlin.

Kent, S. (ed.). 1990. *Domestic architecture and the use of space: an interdisciplinary cross-cultural study*. Cambridge.

Kettering, S. 1986. *Patrons, Brokers, and Clients in Seventeenth Century France*. Oxford.

Kleberg, T. 1957. *Hôtels, restaurants et cabarets dans l'antiquité romaine: études historiques et philologiques*. Uppsala.

Kolb, C. C. 1985. "Demographic estimates in archaeology: contributions from ethnoarchaeology on Mesoamerican peasants." *Current Anthropology* 26:581–99.

Kolb, F. 1977. "Zur Statussymbolik im antiken Rom." *Chiron* 7:239–57.

Kroll, W. 1933. *Die Kultur der ciceronischen Zeit*. 2 vols. Stuttgart.

La Rocca, E. 1986. "Il lusso come espressione di potere. Significato e valore economico degli 'horti.'" In *Le tranquille dimore degli Dei*. Catalogo della mostra romana sulla residenza imperiale degli Horti Lamiani, 2–35. Rome.

La Torre, G. F. 1988. "Gli impianti commerciali ed artigiani nel tessato urbano di Pompei." In *Pompei, L'informatica al servizio di una città antica*, 75–102. Rome.

Laidlaw, A. 1985. *The First Style in Pompeii: Painting and Architecture*. Rome.

Laslett, P. 1965. *The World We Have Lost*. London.

Laslett, P., and R. Wall (eds.). 1972. *Household and Family in Past Time*. Cambridge.

Leach, E. W. 1982. "Patrons, painters and patterns: the anonymity of Romano-Campanian painting and the transition from the second to the third style." In B. K. Gold (ed.), *Literary and Artistic Patronage in Ancient Rome*, 135–73. Austin.

———. 1988. *The Rhetoric of Space: Literary and Artistic Representations of Landscape in Republican Augustan Rome*. Princeton.

Lehmann, P. W. 1953. *Roman Wall Paintings from Boscoreale in the Metropolitan Museum of Art*. Cambridge, Mass.

Lepore, E. 1950. "Orientamenti per la storia sociale di Pompei." In A. Maiuri (ed.), *Pompeiana. Raccolta di studi per il secondo centenario degli scavi di Pompei*, 144–66. Naples.

———. 1955. "Sul carattere economico-sociale di Ercolano." *Parola del Passato* 10:423–39.

Levi, D. 1945. *Antioch Mosaic Pavements*. 2 vols. Princeton.

Ling, R. 1978. "Pompeii and Herculaneum: recent research and future prospects." In *Papers in Italian Archaeology I*, pt. 2, 153–74.

———. 1983. "The insula of the Menander at Pompeii: interim report." *Antiquaries Journal* 63:34–57.

———. 1984. "Two Silchester wall-decorations recovered." *Antiquaries Journal* 64:280–97.

———. 1985. *Romano-British Wall Painting*. Shire Archaeology, 42. Princes Risborough.

———. 1990. "A stranger in town: finding the way in an ancient city." *Greece and Rome* 37:204–14.

———. 1991a. *Roman Painting*. Cambridge.

———. 1991b. "The architecture of Pompeii." *Journal of Roman Archaeology* 4:248–56.

Little, A.G.M. 1971. *Roman Perspective Painting and the Ancient Stage*. Kennebunk.

Mack Smith, D. 1977. *Mussolini's Roman Empire*. Harmondsworth.

McKay, A. G. 1975. *Houses, Villas and Palaces in the Roman World*. London.

MacMullen, R. 1974. *Roman Social Relations 50 B.C. to A.D. 284*. New Haven.

Maiuri, A. 1927. "Pompei. Relazioni sui lavori di scavo dal marzo 1924 al marzo 1926." *Notizie degli Scavi* 1927:3–83.

———. 1929. "Pompei. Relazioni sui lavori di scavo dall'aprile 1926 al dicembre 1927." *Notizie degli Scavi* 1929:354–438.

———. 1933. *La Casa del Menandro e il suo tesoro di argenteria*. Rome.

———. 1938. *Le pitture delle case di "M. Fabius Amandio." del "Sacerdos Amandus" e di "P. Cornelius Teges."* Mon. Pitt. Ant. It. III, Pompei II. Rome.

———. 1942. *L'ultima fase edilizia di Pompei*. Italia Romana: Campania Romana II. Rome.

———. 1945. *La Cena di Trimalchione di Petronio Arbitro*. Naples.

———. 1946a. "Portico e peristilio." *Parola del Passato* 1:306–22.

———. 1946b. "Tabulae ceratae Herculanenses." *Parola del Passato* 1:373–79.

———. 1948. "Note d'epigrafia Pompeiana." *Parola del Passato* 3:152–64.

———. 1951. "Oecus aegyptius." In G. E. Mylonas (ed.), *Studies presented to D. M. Robinson*, 423–29. Saint Louis.

———. 1952a. "Gli *oeci* vitruviani in Palladio e nella casa pompeiana ed ercolanese." *Palladio*, n.s., 2:1–8.

———. 1952b. "Nuove pitture di giardino a Pompei." *Bolletino d'Arte* 37 (1952): 5–12.

———. 1953/54. "Due singolari dipinti Pompeiani." *Römische Mitteilungen* 60/61:88–99.

———. 1954. "Gineco e 'hospitium' nella casa pompeiana." *Memorie Accademia Lincei*, 8th ser., 5:451–61.

———. 1958. *Ercolano. I nuovi scavi (1927–1958)*. 2 vols. Rome.

———. 1960. *Pompeii*. Novara.

Manacorda, D., and R. Tamassia. 1985. *Il piccone del regime*. Rome.

Manni, M. 1974. *Le Pitture della Casa del Colonnato Tuscanico* Mon. Pit. Ant. It. III Ercolano II. Rome.

Marquardt, J. 1886. *Das Privatleben der Römer*. Handbuch der römischen Altertümer, vol. xvii. 2d ed. Leipzig.

Mau, A. 1902. *Pompeii. Its Life and Art*. Trans. F. W. Kelsey.

———. 1882. *Geschichte der decorativen Wandmalerei in Pompeji*. Berlin.

Mayeske, B. 1972. "Bakeries, Bakers and Bread at Pompeii." Ph.D. diss., University of Maryland.

Meiggs, R. 1960. *Roman Ostia*. 2d ed. Oxford.

Michel, D. 1990. *Casa dei Cei (I 6,15)*. Häuser in Pompeji, Band 3. Munich.

Miele, F. 1989. "La casa a schiera I, 11, 16, un ensempio di edilizia privata a Pompei." *Rivista di studi pompeiani* 3:165–84.

Mielsch, H. 1981. "Funde und Forschungen zur Wandmalerei der Prinzipatszeit von 1945 bis 1957, mit einem Nachtrag 1980." In *Aufstieg und Niedergang der römischen Welt*, pt. II, vol. 12, pt. 2, 157–264.

Miles, D. P. 1987. "Forbidden Pleasures: sumptuary laws and the ideology of morality in decline in ancient Rome." Ph.D. diss., University College London.

Millar, F.G.B. 1981. "The world of the *Golden Ass*." *Journal of Roman Studies* 71:63–75.

Miller, D. 1985. *Artefacts as Categories: a study of ceramic variability in central India*. Cambridge.

Millett, M. 1990. *The Romanization of Britain*. Cambridge.

Miskimin, H. A., D. Herlihy, and A. L. Udovitch (eds.). 1977. *The Medieval City*. New Haven.

Moeller, W. O. 1976. *The Wool Trade of Ancient Pompeii*. Leiden.

Moles, A. 1971. *Die Psychologie des Kitsches*. Munich.

Montias, J. M. 1982. *Artists and Artisans in Delft: A Socioeconomic Study of the Seventeenth Century*. Princeton.

Moorman, E. M. 1983. "Sulle pitture della Herculanensium Augustalium sedes." *Cronache Ercolanesi* 13:175–77.

———. 1987. "Die Wandmalereien der Casa del Mobilio Carbonizzato in Herculaneum." In *Pictores per Provincias*, 127–34.

Morel, J.-P. 1987. "La Topographie de l'artisanat et du commerce dans la Rome antique." In *L'Urbs. Espace urbain et histoire*. Coll. Ec. Fr. Rome 98, 127–55.

Morris, I. 1987. *Burial and Ancient Society. The Rise of the Greek City-state*. Cambridge.

Mouritsen, H. 1988. *Elections, Magistrates and Municipal Elite: Studies in Pompeian Epigraphy*. Analecta Romana, Suppl. 15. Rome.

Nappo, S. C. 1988. "Regio I, insula 20." *Rivista di Studi Pompeiani* 2:186–92.

Narroll, R. 1962. "Floor area and settlement population," *American Antiquity* 27:587ff.

Neudecker, R. 1988. *Die Skulpturenausstattung römischer Villen in Italien*. Mainz.

Nissen, H. 1877. *Pompeianische Studien zur Städtekunde des Altertums*. Leipzig.

Orr, D. G. 1978. "Roman domestic religion: the evidence of the household shrines." *Aufstieg und Niedergang der römischen Welt* pt. II, vol. 16, pt. 2, 1557–91.

Packer, J. 1971. *The Insulae of Imperial Ostia*. MAAR 31. Rome.

———. 1975. "Middle and lower class housing in Pompeii and Herculaneum: a preliminary survey." In Andreae and Kyrieleis (1975), 133–46.

———. 1978. "Inns at Pompeii: a short survey." *Cronache Pompeiane* 4:5–53.

Pagano, M. 1987. "Una iscrizione elettorale da Ercolano." *Cronache Ercolanesi* 17:151–2.

Pannuti, U. 1983. *Il "Giornale degli Scavi" di Ercolano (1738–1756)*. Att. Acc. Lincei ser. 8, vol. 26, no. 3. Rome.

Pape, M. 1975. "Griechische Kunstwerke aus Kriegsbeute und ihre öffentliche Aufstellung in Rom." Ph.D. diss., Hamburg.

Patten, J. 1978. *English Towns 1500–1700*. Folkstone.

Pernice, E. 1938. *Pavimente und figürliche Mosaiken (Die hellenistische Kunst in Pompeji VI)*. Berlin.

Peterse, C.L.J. 1984. "Der oskische Fuß in pompejanischen Atrien." *Bulletin Antieke Beschaving* 59:9–30.

———. 1985. "Notes on the design of the House of Pansa (VI,6,1) in Pompeii." *Mededelingen Nederlands Instituut Rome* 46:35–55.

Phythian-Adams, C. 1979. *The Desolation of a City. Coventry and the Urban Crisis of the late Middle Ages*. Leicester.

Pictores per Provincias. 1987. Cahiers d'archéologie romande 43. Avenches.

Pinkwart, D., and W. Stammnitz. 1984. *Altertümer von Pergamon XIV. Peristylhäuser westlich der unteren Agora*. Berlin.

Platner, S. B., and T. Ashby. 1927. *A Topographical Dictionary of Ancient Rome*. London.

Pugliese Carratelli, G. (ed.). 1990. *Pompei. Pitture e mosaici*. 2 vols. Rome.

Purcell, N. 1987. "Town in country and country in town." In E. G. MacDougall (ed.), *Ancient Roman Villa Gardens*, 187–203. Dumbarton Oaks.

Ramage, E. S. 1973. *Urbanitas: Ancient Sophistication and Refinement*. Norman.

Raper, R. A. 1977. "The analysis of the urban structure of Pompeii: a sociological examination of land use (semi-micro)." In D. L. Clarke (ed.), *Spatial Archaeology*, 189–221. London and New York.

———. 1979. "Pompeii: planning and social implications." In B. C. Burnham and J. Kingsbury (eds.), *Space, Hierarchy and Society: Interdisciplinary Studies in Social Area Analysis*, 137–48. BAR International Series, vol. 59. Oxford.

Rawson, E. 1985. "Theatrical life in republican Rome and Italy." *Papers of the British School at Rome* 53: 97–113. Reprinted in *Roman Culture and Society. Collected Papers*, 468–87. Oxford, 1991.

Richardson, L., Jr. 1955. *Pompeii: The Casa dei Dioscuri and Painters*. MAAR 23. Rome.

————. 1983. "A contribution to the study of Pompeian dining-rooms." *Pompeii Herculaneum Stabiae. Bolletino dell'associazione internazionale Amici di Pompei* 1:61–71.

————. 1988. *Pompeii: An Architectural History.* Baltimore and London.

Ricotti, E.S.P. 1989. "Le tende conviviali e la tenda di Tolomeo Filadelfo." In R. I. Curtis (ed.), *Studia Pompeiana et Classica in honor of W. I. Jashemski,* 2:199–239. New Rochelle.

Ridgeway, B. S. 1981. "Greek antecedents of garden sculpture." In E. B. MacDougall and W. F. Jashemski (eds.), *Ancient Roman Gardens.* Dumbarton Oaks Colloquium on the History of Landscape Architecture 7, 9–28.

Rizzo, S., and M. De Vos. 1983. In *L'archeologia in Roma capitale tra sterro e scavo.* Roma Capitale 1870–1911 exhibition catalogue, 225–47.

Robinson, D. M., and J. W. Graham. 1938. *Excavations at Olynthos VIII. The Hellenic House.* Baltimore.

Rostovzeff, M. 1957. *Social and Economic History of the Roman Empire.* 2d ed. Oxford.

Rowntree, D. 1981. *Statistics without Tears.* Harmondsworth.

Russell, J. C. 1958. *Late Ancient and Medieval Population.* TAPS vol. 48, no. 3.

————. 1985. *The Control of Late Ancient and Medieval Population.* Philadelphia.

Saller, R. P. 1982. *Personal Patronage in the Early Empire.* Cambridge.

————. 1984. "Familia, domus and the Roman concept of family." *Phoenix* 38:336–55.

Saller, R. P., and B. D. Shaw. 1984. "Tombstones and Roman family relations in the Principate: civilians, soldiers and slaves." *Journal of Roman Studies* 74:124–56.

Sauron, G. 1980. "*Templa serena.* A propos de la 'Villa dei Papiri' d'Herculaneum: contribution à l'étude des comportements aristocratiques à la fin de la république." *Mélanges École Française Rome* 92:277–301.

Scagliarini, D. C. 1974/76. "Spazio e decorazione nella pittura pompeiana." *Palladio* 23–25:3–44.

Scatozza Höricht, L. A. 1986. *I vetri romani di Ercolano.* Rome.

Schefold, K. 1952. *Pompejanische Malerei. Sinn und Ideengeschichte.* Basel. Translated as *La Peinture pompéienne. Essai sur l'évolution de sa signification.* Brussels, 1972.

————. 1957. *Die Wände Pompejis.* Berlin.

————. 1962. *Vergessenes Pompeji: unveröffentlichte Bilder römischer Wanddekoration in geschichtliche Folge herausgegeben.* Bern.

————. 1975. "Der zweite Stil als Zeugnis alexandrinischer Architektur." In Andreae and Kyrieleis (1975), 53–60.

Schulz-Falkenthal, H. 1971. "Die Magistratenwahlen in Pompeiji und die Kollegien." *Das Altertum* 17:24–32.

Scobie, A. 1986. "Slums, sanitation and mortality." *Klio* 68:429.

Sekora, E. 1977. *Luxury: the concept in western thought from Eden to Smollett.* Baltimore.

Sherwin-White, A. N. 1966. *The Letters of Pliny.* Oxford.

Sigismund Nielsen, H. 1987. "Alumnus, a term of relation denoting quasiadoption." *Classica et Medievalia* 38, 141–88.

Slob, E. 1986. *Luxuria: Regelgeving en maatregelen van censoren ten tijde van de Romeinse Republiek.* Zutphen.

Smith, J. T. 1978. "Villas as a key to social structure." In M. Todd (ed.), *Studies in the Romano-British Villa,* 149–85.

Sogliano, A. 1898. *La Casa dei Vettii in Pompei.* Mon. Ant. Acc. Lincei 8. Rome.

Spinazzola, V. 1953. *Pompei alla luce degli scavi nuovi di via dell'Abbondanza (anni 1910–23).* 3 vols. Rome.

Strocka, V. M. 1975. "Pompejanische Nebenzimmer." In Andreae and Kyrieleis (1975), 101–14.

————. 1977. *Forschungen in Ephesos VIII.1.2. Die Wandmalerei der Hanghäuser in Ephesos.* Vienna.

————. (ed.). 1984a. *Casa del Principe di Napoli (VI 15,7.8).* Häuser in Pompeji, Band I. Tübingen.

————. 1984b. "Ein mißverstandener Terminus des vierten Stils: die Casa del Sacello Iliaco in Pompeji (I 6,4)." *Römische Mitteilungen* 91:125–40.

————. 1988. "Internationales Forschungsprojekt 'Häuser in Pompeji.' Berichte über die Kampagne 1987." *Rivista di Studi Pompeiani* 2:246–47.

————. 1991. *Casa del Labirinto.* Häuser in Pompeji, Band 4. Munich.

Studnicza, F. 1914. *Das Symposion Ptolemaios II nach der Beschreibung des Kallixeinos wiederhergestellt.* Leipzig.

Sulze, H. 1940. *Real-Encyclopädie.* Suppl. VII, 950–71, s.v. "Peristylium." Stuttgart.

Tamm, B. 1963. *Auditorium und Palatium: a study on assembly-rooms in Roman palaces.* Stockholm.

Thébert, Y. 1987. "Private life and domestic architecture in Roman Africa." In P. Veyne (ed.),

A. Goldhammer (trans.), *A History of Private Life. I From pagan Rome to Byzantium*, 319–409. Cambridge, Mass., and London.

Thirsk, J. 1978. *Economic Policy and Projects: the Development of a Consumer Society in early modern England.* Oxford.

Tran Tam Tinh, V. 1988. *La Casa dei Cervi a Herculaneum.* Rome.

Treggiari, S. M. 1980. "Urban labour in Rome: mercennarii and tabernarii." In P. Garnsey (ed.), *Non-slave Labour in the Greco-Roman World*, 48–64. Cambridge.

van Buren, A. W. 1947. "Gnaeus Alleius Nigidius Maius of Pompeii." *American Journal of Philology* 68:382–91.

————. 1956. *Real-Encyclopädie* Suppl. VIII, 500–502, s.v. "Pinacotheca." Stuttgart.

Van der Poel H. B. (ed.). 1981, 1987. *Corpus Topographicum Pompeianum. Pars 3A The Insulae of Regions I–V* (1981). *Pars 5. Cartography* (1987). Rome.

Veblen, T. 1899. *The Theory of the Leisure Class.* New York.

von Hesberg, H., and P. Zanker (eds.). 1987. *Römischer Gräberstrasse. Selbstdarstllung-Status-Standard.* Munich.

Walker, S. 1983. "Women and housing in classical Greece: the archaeological evidence." In A. Cameron and A. Kuhrt (eds.), *Images of Women in Antiquity*, 81–91.

Wallace-Hadrill, A. 1983a. *Suetonius: the Scholar and his Caesars.* London and New Haven.

————. 1983b. "Ut pictura poesis?" *Journal of Roman Studies* 73 (1983): 180–83.

————. 1986a. Review of Strocka (1984), *Antiquaries Journal* 66, no. 2:433–34.

————. 1986b. "Image and authority in the coinage of Augustus." *Journal of Roman Studies* 76:66–87.

————. (ed.). 1989. *Patronage in Ancient Society.* London.

————. 1990. "Pliny the Elder and Man's Unnatural History." *Greece & Rome* 37:80–96.

Ward-Perkins, J. B. 1970. "From Republic to Empire: reflections on the early provincial architecture of the Roman west." *Journal of Roman Studies* 60:1–19.

Weaver, P.R.C. 1990. "Where have all the Junian Latins gone? Nomenclature and status in the early Empire." *Chiron* 20:275–305.

————. 1991. "Children of freedmen (and freedwomen)." In B. Rawson (ed.), *Marriage, Divorce and Children in Ancient Rome*, 166–90. Canberra and Oxford.

Weber, M. 1959. *The City.* Trans. and ed. D. Martindale and G. Neuwirth. New York.

Weinstock, S. 1971. *Divus Julius.* Oxford.

Wiegand, T., and H. Shrader. 1904. *Priene. Ergebnisse der Ausgrabungen und Untersuchungen in den Jahren 1895–1898.* Berlin.

Wiseman, T. P. 1982. "*Pete nobiles amicos*: poets and patrons in late republican Rome." In B. K. Gold (ed.), *Literary and Artistic Patronage in Ancient Rome*, 28–49. Austin.

————. 1987. "*Conspicui postes tectaque digna deo*; the public image of aristocratic and imperial houses in the late Republic and early Empire." In *L'Urbs. Espace urbain et histoire.* (Coll. Ec. Fr. Rome, vol. 98, 393–413.

Zanker, P. (ed.). 1976. *Hellenismus in Mittelitalien.* 2 vols. Göttingen.

————. 1979. "Die Villa als Vorbild des späten pompejanischen Wohngeschmacks." *Jahrbuch des deutschen archäologischen Instituts* 94:460–523.

————. 1983. "Zur Bildnisrepräsentation führender Männer in mittelitalischen und campanischen Stadten . . . ." In *Les bourgeoisies municipales Italiennes aux IIe et Ier siecles av. J.-C.*, 251–66. Paris.

————. 1988a. *The Power of Images in the Age of Augustus.* Ann Arbor.

————. 1988b. *Pompeji. Stadtbilder als Speigel von Gesellschaft und Herrschaftsform.* Mainz.

Zeldin, T. 1980. *France 1848–1945. Taste and Corruption.* Oxford.

Zevi, F. (ed.). 1984. *Pompei 79. Raccolta di studi per il decimonono centenario dell'eruzione vesuviana* (1979, reissued 1984). Naples.

INDEX